NECESSARY
WOMEN

NECESSARY
WOMEN

THE UNTOLD STORY
OF PARLIAMENT'S
WORKING WOMEN

MARI TAKAYANAGI AND ELIZABETH HALLAM SMITH

First published 2023

The History Press
97 St George's Place, Cheltenham,
Gloucestershire, GL50 3QB
www.thehistorypress.co.uk

British Library Cataloguing in Publication Data.
A catalogue record for this book is available from the British Library.

ISBN 978 1 80399 015 6

Typesetting and origination by The History Press
Printed and bound in Great Britain by TJ Books Limited, Padstow, Cornwall.

Trees for LYfe

CONTENTS

LIST OF ILLUSTRATIONS

INTEGRATED ILLUSTRATIONS

PLATE SECTION

PROLOGUE

On 2 April 1911, the suffragette Emily Wilding Davison hid overnight in the crypt chapel in the Houses of Parliament. This dramatic protest was to record her presence there on census night, as a woman in the male bastion of Parliament, and to make a claim to equal political rights with men.

What Davison may not have known was that there were sixty-seven other women resident in Parliament that night, by right – housekeepers, kitchen maids, domestic servants, and wives and daughters living in households. Their homes ranged from the extremely grand – the Speaker's House, a palatial dwelling within the Palace of Westminster with a distinguished family and multiple servants – to humble single-person rooms, such as the one occupied by the House of Lords Housekeeper. And while Davison hid in the crypt, other women were also hard at work in Parliament. Although not resident, they were performing necessary roles, as they had done for many centuries.

This is their story.

IN OUR OWN WORDS

In 2017, we realised by chance that we were both researching women working in Parliament – not as MPs, not as Members of the House of Lords, but behind the scenes. The women we found so compelling were largely invisible yet essential: out of sight, keeping the show on the road, making the engine run. They were cleaning the corridors of power, feeding parliamentarians through long night sittings, typing up the debates, ensuring that fees and wages were paid. Mari was filling out twentieth-century wartime innovations, pioneering Girl Porters and female clerks, painstakingly teasing their stories of prejudice and unequal pay from obscure office files. Liz was excavating tales of women enduring the hugely unpleasant working conditions in the Palace of Westminster a century earlier, prising them out of the cracks of the building, finding them selling oranges, working in cramped, smoky kitchens and – conversely – named as high office holders despite never coming anywhere near their place of work. We were both fascinated by the parliamentary families we came across – wives, sisters and daughters popping up in the lofty accounts of their menfolk; the births, marriages, deaths and toxic relationships which cruelly ended some lives and careers while giving opportunities to others; the great and hidden underbelly of women living on site exposed in census returns for the Palace.

We clinked glasses over lunch, nearby in Westminster Abbey Cellarium, and agreed that we would put all these women into a book, reconstructing their lives and work – some extraordinary, some mundane, and many deeply poignant – and showcasing their achievements. A couple of years later, having celebrated a suffrage centenary in 2018 and a century of women in the legal profession in 2019, and completed research projects on lost buildings of the Palace of Westminster, we returned to our plan mid-global pandemic. A couple more years later, informed by a huge amount of new research, especially drawing on freshly released online historical newspaper sources and the 1921 census, we are proud to present our cast of Parliament's 'Necessary Women'.

THE NECESSARY WOMEN

Women have always been part of the history of Parliament at Westminster. As workers, they emerge obliquely and occasionally from historical sources from the Middle Ages onwards, but by the late Georgian era, they begin to appear more strongly and visibly as real people whose stories can be told. We pick these stories up from around 1800, drawing on hitherto untapped parliamentary archives, government records, works of art and family history sources. These provide striking new evidence, enabling us to trace and understand the lives of some of these unheralded women. We explore their duties, lives and families, and recognise their often unknown yet essential support for Britain's evolving political world.

A 'necessary woman' was a woman employed to 'do the necessary', such as emptying chamber pots. Parliament employed necessary women both literally – the first known Necessary Woman was Margery Hatrum, appointed in the Lords in the late seventeenth century – and also figuratively, as women worked for the House of Commons and House of Lords in necessary roles as cleaners, fire-lighters and cooks. Such women could be prominent and important in parliamentary life, such as Jane Julia Bennett, keeper of the keys of the House of Lords for more than fifty years; and Elizabeth Burton, the famous 'Jane' who dispensed beer, pies and chops in Bellamy's legendary refreshment rooms. Others had much shorter and less-successful working lives. Our most tragic story is probably that of Eliza Arscot who, as we discovered late in our research, went from reigning as Principal Housemaid at the House of Lords to being consigned to a lunatic asylum for thirty years.

Some women served parliamentarians in local hostelries and coffee houses or ran fruit stalls in the very heart of the Palace of Westminster. Other women provided essential support as the wives, daughters and servants of the male occupants of official grace-and-favour residences. This might entail being the supreme political hostess and leading the parliamentary community, as did Elizabeth Abbot, Ellen Manners Sutton and Elizabeth Gully, wives of Speakers of the House of Commons; acting as unpaid secretary to a senior Commons official, as did Anne Rickman for her father John, the Clerk Assistant; or playing a leadership role during the fire that burned down the Palace of Westminster in 1834, as did Anne's resourceful sister Frances.

By the time that Emily Davison hid in the crypt in 1911, women had entered office work in the wider world. In Parliament, this move was spearheaded by the redoubtable and ever-youthful May Ashworth, who provided typewriting services to Parliament for decades, unaffected by marriage, war and divorce. Ashworth's manager in the House of Commons was Ethel Marie Anderson, and as we put the finishing touches to this book, we made the thrilling discovery of a hitherto unknown suffragette – her American mother, Mary Jane Anderson, who scrawled 'Votes for Women' across their census form. Like a schoolteacher correcting a wayward student, the census enumerator struck it out in harsh red ink.

Meanwhile, Amelia de Laney stubbornly refused to give up her on-site residence as House of Lords Housekeeper and demanded furniture for it. During the First World War, as men were called up in increasing numbers and women entered many new areas of work in society, the House of Commons found itself compelled to employ Girl Porters. This radical change was very successful – although not successful enough to survive the war, alas. However, as Parliament granted the vote for the first set of women in 1918, the House of Lords employed its first woman Clerical Assistant, May Court.

She kept her job and rose to become Accountant, with a career spanning the decades through to another world war before her retirement in 1942.

The Second World War brought Blitz bombing to the heart of Westminster, where Commandant Edythe Mary Thomson ran the First Aid Post, Elsie Hoath served meals to the House of Lords and other women staff and volunteers watched for fires, drilled with the Palace of Westminster Home Guard, and toiled underneath Central Lobby in the Westminster Munitions Unit. The war also necessitated radical, if temporary, changes in the House of Commons, with the appointment of pioneering female clerks, who ran committees and provided expert specialist advice to MPs. A huge milestone was reached when Jean Winder was appointed as the first permanent Hansard reporter in 1944 – only to spend the next ten years fighting the Treasury for equal pay with male colleagues, in common with so many other working women. Winder's retirement in 1960 brought with it something of a lull in the appointment of pioneering female parliamentary staff and brings this book to a natural close.

Overall, women were present in large numbers, working in the centre of British political life, with significant responsibilities, and making a far greater contribution at both the political and domestic levels than has hitherto been recognised. Their stories are of great interest individually, and collectively they uncover many new perspectives on the political and social cultures of the changing life of the 'Westminster Village'. Parliament had much in common with other workplaces in many ways yet was unique in aspects such as its timekeeping and seasonal work, linked to the sittings of the House of Commons and House of Lords. And being there gave some of these women access to, and even some influence over, the people – almost invariably men – who shaped laws and policies for the country at large.

In Her Own Words

'Poor Mamma was much overcome at first, but that made me stronger, as I felt I must look to everything. I chained the door so as to prevent any dangerous visitors. Henry Taylor and Edward Villiers insisted on being active chief managers under me.'

Frances Rickman, daughter of the Clerk Assistant,
House of Commons, on her part in rescuing
the family's possessions from the 1834 fire

1

THE CHAOTIC WORLD OF THE OLD PALACE OF WESTMINSTER: MEET THE WOMEN

In 1792, during the long reign of King George III, the Lobby just outside the House of Commons chamber bustled with Members of Parliament, officials and journalists going about their business. None of these were women – and yet, a woman was also present. A young female orange seller called Mullins was plying her trade in the heart of Parliament, in the very place where Prime Minister Spencer Perceval would be assassinated some twenty years later. Oranges would have been a welcome snack for politicians working long into the evening, but Mullins's trade had long been linked with prostitution – and it was with this scandalous implication that she was described by a satirist:

> A young, plump, rosy-looking wench, with clean white silk stockings, Turkey leather shoes, [and a] pink silk short petticoat, to show her ankle and calf to the young bulls and old goats of the House. With her black cloak thrown aside a little, her black eyes, and black hair, covered by a slight curtained bonnet, did that young slut kill members with her eyes.

The scurrilous author was Joseph Pearson, a celebrated Commons Doorkeeper. From his box in the Lobby, Pearson directed Members to their parliamentary business in his famously stentorian tones – and would have had ample opportunities to observe Mullins's charms with repelled fascination while excoriating what he saw as the undue influence that she exercised over besotted MPs. Alongside young Mullins was, he tells us, her employer, another woman of a rather different nature: 'Old Mother Dry', with, sneers Pearson, her baskets of hard biscuits and sour fruit. Characterised – inevitably – as the orange seller's pimp, 'she knows more of members' private affairs than all the old bawds in Christendom put together'.[1]

'Mother Dry' was in reality that rare thing, a successful female entrepreneur in her own right. Born in 1761 as Jane Caroline Drybutter into a wealthy, unconventional and litigious family, she had been apprenticed in 1773 to a draper and milliner in Chelmsford, Essex; such roles were a prestigious way for girls to enter the world of business. Possessed of a strong entrepreneurial streak, by the 1790s Jane had become a wealthy confectioner and fruiterer in the Westminster area. Although by now she was known also as Gibbs, there is no evidence that she ever married.

Jane Drybutter achieved her success without any help from her male relatives. Her colourful uncle Samuel, a prosperous jeweller and bookseller who ran an upmarket souvenir stall in Westminster Hall, had gained spectacular notoriety and experienced several arrests for his openly homosexual lifestyle and fled to Paris around 1778 after being attacked by a violent mob. He had 'always had a great dislike and disregard' for Jane and disinherited her. Meanwhile, her estranged father, James, described her in his will as his 'very wicked and undutiful daughter' and cut her out of his substantial estate with a shilling – far more, he said, than she deserved.[2] Jane died in 1803, a prosperous businesswoman, having made her own way in life.

Selling oranges might seem a rather trivial occupation, but the sale of fresh fruit – a luxury item which was the snack of choice for MPs during sittings – was a profitable operation in the late eighteenth century. Behind his sneers and innuendos, Pearson suggests that her trade gave Jane Drybutter and her young employee Mullins privileged access to – and perhaps even some influence in – the corridors of power. And they were only the least invisible of Parliament's necessary women.

THE CHAOTIC WORLD

Many features of the political world that Joseph Pearson and Jane Drybutter inhabited look familiar today: the periodic parliamentary elections; the sitting periods known as sessions; the ceremonies of State Openings and Prorogations; and even the striking visual signifiers of the green benches in the Commons and the red in the Lords. And there were clerks, just as today, who supervised and recorded the business and proceedings of Parliament, with Black Rod in the Lords and the Serjeant at Arms in the Commons there to maintain order and oversee ceremonial occasions.

But much of this world is deeply unfamiliar too, for the parliamentary reformers had yet to begin the process of widening the franchise and laying down the standards under which elections must be conducted. MPs were sent to Westminster on the say-so of a very limited number of constituency electors who were often open to bribery – or, in the case of rotten boroughs such as Old Sarum, were chosen by individual grandees. 'Old Corruption' – of which much more below – was rife across many parts of the public service. From the 1780s, the clamour for political and administrative reforms grew ever louder, but vested interests and political considerations always got in the way of progress. Not until 1832 did this begin to change, with the hotly contested passage of the first Reform Act.

Portrayed by the reformers as a metaphor for political corruption, the old Palace of Westminster was also a world away from the new Palace, the Victorian gothic behemoth which today occupies much the same site. Unlike the well-ordered Palace of today, framed by Big Ben at one end and the Victoria Tower at the other, the fabric and layout of the old Palace was chaotic: travel-writer Thomas Allen dismissed the effect from the river as 'a confused and ill-formed assemblage of towers, turrets and pinnacles, jumbled together without taste or judgment'.[3] Its component parts were an eclectic mix of medieval and later structures, tightly interwoven. It was contested space too, as the old Palace housed not just Parliament but also the Law Courts and several government offices, including the Exchequer, all of whose officers were constantly vying for extra accommodation. At its core was the vibrant, and at times lawless, public meeting place of Westminster Hall, dating back to 1098 and easily the oldest and most historic part of Parliament; and New Palace Yard to the north of the Hall, which had also long been a famous location for riots and disturbances. The old Palace also encompassed several official residences, private offices and numerous and often ill-managed record stores along with coffee houses and taverns. Many of its buildings and their contents were highly flammable.

As is still the case today, the House of Lords was located at the southern end of the Palace, sitting in the compact medieval White Hall until 1801 and then in the great Romanesque Lesser Hall. The House of Commons had been housed in medieval St Stephen's Chapel nearby since 1548. Despite numerous modifications, by the early nineteenth century this small space, once a sublime expression of royal piety and power, was recognised as being grotesquely inadequate for its vital parliamentary functions. But for more than a century, all attempts to improve Parliament's accommodation had foundered.

In 1834, a major fire would reduce both chambers and much of the rest of the old Palace to a smouldering shell, as graphically revealed in a sketch plan by Clerk Assistant John Rickman (Plate 1). That momentous event would tear apart the lives of many of its inhabitants – men and women alike.

AN INVISIBLE ARMY OF WORKING WOMEN

Almost all the senior posts in the old Palace were filled exclusively by men. An exception was the role of Housekeeper, characteristically also a female preserve in the world outside. The House of Lords Housekeepers – mainly women, during the eighteenth century – were rather grand. With a substantial suite of rooms next to the chamber, they were tasked with overseeing security and cleaning for the House. Their equivalents in the Commons, the Deputy Housekeepers, also mainly female, had more mundane but still well-paid duties – including managing the ventilation system for the chamber and organising the flushing out and cleansing of the infamous Commons stool room. Unappealing as it might sound, this was a sought-after post: back in 1758 no fewer than three rival claimants were vying for it, two of them women.

In 1773, John Bellamy was appointed as Deputy Housekeeper to the Commons and branched out by setting up an official dining room close to the Lobby, known to posterity as Bellamy's. Its fame rests on the parliamentary legend that, on his deathbed in 1806, Prime Minister William Pitt the Younger asked for one of Bellamy's meat pies. This might be assumed to refer to John, but in fact it was 'Mother Bellamy', John's wife Elizabeth, who presided in the dining room, also selling copious quantities of the wine in which they traded as a lucrative sideline. The satirist Joseph Pearson remarked, 'Here the Members, who cannot say more than *Yes* or *No* below, can speechify for hours to Mother Bellamy about beef steaks and pork chops.' Enduringly popular with the customers, the cooks and waitresses who dished up delicious meals to hungry MPs were soon to attain a legendary status in their own right.

Clinging to the old Palace of Westminster like barnacles, there was an ever-changing array of other, unofficial, catering outlets such as bars and coffee houses which relied heavily on female labour. Pearson mentions Alice's, good for soups, which were not on Mother Bellamy's menu, and Jacob's, 'kept by a Black fellow of that name in Old Palace Yard', where MPs' servants awaited their masters' whims. Meanwhile, serving the House of Lords was the ever-popular Waghorn's coffee shop, which during State

Trials extended its opening hours to accommodate all comers. The death of its famed proprietor, Sarah Butler, in 1789 at the age of 70 was even noted officially in the *Gentleman's Magazine*.[4]

By the 1830s, most of the coffee houses had been cleared away, but one, Howard's, successor to Alice's, survived next to the House of Lords and was a magnet for MPs, peers and the many barristers working at the Law Courts. All of the women working in these establishments would have had significant interactions with parliamentarians and with other staff from both Houses, as would those serving in the many local pubs, including the Star and Garter in Old Palace Yard.

Away from the dining rooms and bars, an invisible army of workers, many of them women, was needed to keep the chambers and committee rooms running to the high standards demanded by parliamentarians. The great majority of these – including almost all of the housemaids and cleaners – lived offsite, mostly in the warren of streets around the old Palace. Some, such as Martha Harrison who in the 1770s was paid about £3 a year for night work and for emptying the privies of both Houses, and Elizabeth Mills, Hall-keeper, who opened and shut the doors for the workmen, start to be named in the records. So too do the Necessary Women. They were tradition-ally domestic servants tasked with 'doing the necessary', emptying chamber pots and cleaning. But the Lords' Necessary Woman post was so valuable that in 1726 it was awarded to a man as a sinecure – before being wrested back by a woman, Mary Phillips, in 1761.[5]

There was space for a few resident staff on the premises of the two Houses; at the time of the 1834 fire, six were to be found in the Commons, all of them waiting staff and four of them female – including a legendary waitress known as Jane, of whom more anon. The Lords had room for about twenty, again more than half of them women. They included Jane Julia Wright, the young Deputy Housekeeper (also of whom more anon), and her servants, as well as a few housemaids.[6] Other servants, male and female, lived in the old Palace too – in the Law Courts and in the grace-and-favour residences of the Speaker and other parliamentary and government officials. Irrespective of station or rank, many of these women would have an important part to play on the night of the cataclysmic fire.

THE RICKMAN FAMILY

Within a stone's throw from the House of Commons but separated from the waitresses, cleaners and orange sellers by a huge social chasm, lived well-to-do

John Rickman, a senior Commons official, and his wife Susannah. Their invaluable archive gives us rare insights into family life in the old Palace. In line with the social norms of the day, the role of Susannah – and of the couple's two clever daughters, Anne and Frances – was to support John Rickman's professional and personal life to the full. Yet, although behind his austere and formal manner Rickman was clearly devoted to his womenfolk, he was also an unusually controlling and exacting taskmaster.

By 1805, Rickman, prodigiously active secretary to the Commons Speaker, had grown tired of living in his small official residence near Westminster Hall with no more than his housekeeper and a maid to look after his needs. He decided to marry, and picked Susannah Postlethwaite, a long-standing and valued acquaintance whose views he claimed to have moulded and shaped over the previous decade.[7] Driven by the conviction that statistics offered a cure for social ills, John packed his days with his many official duties: setting up and managing Britain's censuses; organising important Royal Commissions; and discharging with distinction a succession of responsible roles in the House of Commons. Any spare time he filled to the brim with an array of literary and scientific pursuits. But Susannah had been waiting for Rickman and knew what to expect. Dutiful and subservient, she was also efficient, good-natured and sociable – qualities which well fitted her for the role of his wife.

As well as running his household, Susannah was required to entertain her husband's friends from among the literary, political and scientific elite of London and to engage in high-powered discussions with them. After an uncertain start, her kind and hospitable nature won them over and, as John became increasingly busy with duties in the House in the evenings, she mixed freely and frequently with them in her own right. She proved herself a most suitable spouse for Rickman.

Susannah and John produced three children who survived into adulthood: Anne, born in 1807; Frances who followed in 1810 – and who was named after a close family friend, satirical novelist and bluestocking Fanny Burney; and William, who arrived in 1812. Their earliest years were spent under the care of their kindly mother and the housemaids in their small official residence near to Westminster Hall. Susannah encouraged the children to play in the beautiful gardens, with lawns fringed by cherries, jasmines and vines that stretched behind their house to the banks of the Thames, often with the family of their neighbour and friend Samuel Wilde, Teller of the Exchequer.

From a young age, the Rickman children received instruction from their father – who demanded much of them. For his time, John had a relatively progressive approach to educating his daughters and drummed into them a wide range of subjects, including mathematics, science, Latin and history – as well as expecting them to mix and converse with his high-powered friends. This was not least to train Anne and Frances to share the role of his secretary, amanuensis and companion. Intelligent, diligent, self-effacing and compliant like her mother, 'little Anne' could readily be shaped for these tasks. Having visited all of England's cathedrals by the time she was 8, at the age of 12 she was put to work to index the 700 illustrations in *Camden's Britannia*, a gargantuan task. But while she was at least as clever, Frances, who was sent away to school in Brighton to benefit her health, would prove considerably less compliant than her sister.

In 1820, Rickman was promoted from Second Clerk Assistant to Clerk Assistant in the Commons, with pay of £2,500 (equivalent to some £143,000 today), a larger house and a continuing remit to improve the way in which the procedures of the House were recorded. He also continued to lead Royal Commissions on roads, bridges and churches in Scotland, working with leading engineer Thomas Telford. Anne was required to act as her father's assistant, for much of her time being 'occupied seated square before a sheet of paper, copying out some official papers, circulars or otherwise, or drawing papers from beneath Papa's hand just so exactly that he could go on signing paper after paper to the number of 500 or more perhaps!' 'Now you see,' she adds in her memoirs, 'why I never could stitch but always could write.'[8] So fine did her script become that she was frequently tasked with making multiple copies of papers for her father's many meetings on Highlands roads and bridges.

Eventually, in 1823, even the gentle Anne rebelled – to her father's cold fury – declining to 'acquire the preliminary knowledge to make [her] useful as a scribe and assistant' in etymology, which Rickman was pursuing as a new interest.[9] But equilibrium was soon restored, and she always maintained a special bond with John. His expectations of her were extremely high and – despite some setbacks – she was a thoroughly satisfactory secretary to him. This was a part she would continue to play until his death in 1840, a few months before his fifth population census was taken.

MEMORIES OF OLD WESTMINSTER

Insofar as her duties allowed, Rickman encouraged Anne to observe and record events in the old Palace. Her memoirs have a particular interest, as 'her girlhood was lived through stirring times'.[10] She was fascinated by the travails of Caroline, estranged wife of King George IV and a great crowd-pleaser. In 1820, the queen was facing a Bill of Pains and Penalties in the Lords – in effect a trial – on a charge of adultery. Anne describes how, while this was happening, she and her father sat behind the barricades protecting their house, avidly watching Her Majesty travel past by carriage each day to face her accusers. After chaotic proceedings and scenes of violence from her supporters in New Palace Yard, from which the Rickmans emerged unscathed, the queen was acquitted for lack of evidence – but the king remained unreconciled with her.

The next stage of Caroline's battle with George IV took place during his coronation, in 1821, an event again enthusiastically recorded by Anne. From outside their new house in New Palace Yard, the Rickman family witnessed the first of Caroline's doomed attempts to join the vast royal procession and her ignominious departure. They all enjoyed the day enormously: the pageantry and spectacle of the colourful procession, the immense and glittering royal banquet in Westminster Hall which they observed in turn from the gallery, and the illumination of the streets all around with coloured oil lamps.[11] Anne also made many sketches and watercolours of the Palace and its surroundings, including one of their house in New Palace Yard (centre), with her father walking out of the front door (Plate 2). Alongside her memoirs, these artworks provide a unique insight into this lost world.

ELIZABETH ABBOT, HEAD OF THE PARLIAMENTARY COMMUNITY

John Rickman owed his career at Westminster to Charles Abbot, Speaker of the House of Commons from 1802 to 1817. Upwardly mobile, combative, reforming and brilliantly clever, Abbot's role placed him firmly at the top of the social tree among the residents of the Palace of Westminster. And Abbot's wife Elizabeth, who was Anne Rickman's godmother, was the very model of a competent and respectable Speaker's consort. Although hers could only ever be a supporting role, it still had value and significance to her husband and his office.

Charles had married Elizabeth in 1796 when a backbench MP, her higher social status and ample fortune giving him considerable satisfaction. Their union was evidently a success and would produce two sons. Born in 1760, Elizabeth had been raised by her mother in England, at Hilton Park Hall, Staffordshire. Her father was the wealthy Sir Philip Gibbes who farmed Springhead Plantation, Barbados, where as many as 300 enslaved African people produced sugar for the British market. Gibbes was an 'ameliorationist' –

one of those men who advocated that for both moral and economic reasons enslaved people should be treated with 'humanity' – but the extremely cruel system over which he presided was founded upon forced labour.[12] Abbot, who counted leading abolitionist William Wilberforce as a close friend, had been sympathetic to his cause before he married Elizabeth. Thereafter, he no longer supported it openly, although the Abolition of the Slave Trade Act was passed in 1807 on his watch as Speaker. But it was not until 1833 that slavery was made illegal in the British Empire, and the repercussions of this unconscionable practice remain unresolved to this day.

Abbot's election as Speaker in 1802 thrust Elizabeth into the limelight. Whenever the Commons was sitting, she was expected to reside with him at the Speaker's House and to act as his consort and hostess. Simply being there posed a considerable challenge: the Speaker's large and crumbling mansion, recently acquired by the Commons from the Exchequer, was undergoing a major and much-needed restoration and remodelling. While the project included the provision of new private accommodation with ample space for the Speaker's family and servants, the layout and styling of the house was the domain of fashionable official architect James Wyatt, for whom Abbot was now the client. Only occasionally was Elizabeth permitted to make decisions, and these were on relatively small matters such as the final choice of wallpaper.

Worse still, the project was so complex and ill-managed that it took almost a decade to complete, and at an embarrassingly large cost to the public purse. The Abbots had, meanwhile, to reside in the middle of a building site when at Westminster, at considerable inconvenience and discomfort, and often took refuge at their private estate at Kidbrooke Park, Sussex. But eventually, in 1809, the Speaker's House emerged as a glittering and opulent gothic revival palace. Confected as a manifestation of the antiquity and prestige of Abbot's office, it formed an ostentatious showcase for his political discussions and entertainments. Although it was criticised by some contemporaries as a riot of bad taste and shoddy workmanship, for Abbot's friend William Wilberforce it was 'much the handsomest thing of its size I ever saw'. He was 'intoxicated with the glitter and parade' of dining there.[13]

While Abbot's regular round of lavish official banquets were for male guests only, it fell to Elizabeth to preside over their grand private dinners and receptions, which wives and daughters could also attend. The palatial Speaker's House was also a magnet for visiting dignitaries, both national and international, and, as Abbot was required in the House during sitting hours, Elizabeth was required to host them as his representative. Among these many distinguished visitors were three royal princesses, daughters of

King George III, in 1812, and two years later Tsar Alexander I of Russia and his sister the Grand Duchess Catherine. In 1815, Anne Rickman excitedly observed a party of grandees passing by to a luncheon given by Elizabeth: 'It was Queen Charlotte and the Duke and Duchess of Wellington after the Battle of Waterloo, when the Duke came to the House of Commons to receive public thanks.'[14]

Elizabeth also took on a leadership role within the little community living around the House of Commons, signified by the regular Sunday processions for the residents of the Palace to attend church services in St Margaret's, Westminster. Stepping out in front with her husband, she evidently looked the part. On one occasion, Anne tells us, she sported a 'bright emerald silk pelisse, trimmed with deep ermine, a muff as large as a pillow, deep cuffs and a long tippet, the footman behind her with her prayer book'.[15]

For fifteen years, Elizabeth Abbot did everything that could have been expected of a Speaker's wife, setting high standards as his consort and hostess and acting as the doyenne of the Palace community. Then in 1817 Charles Abbot stepped down as Speaker for reasons of ill health. Ennobled as Baron Colchester, he died in 1829, but Elizabeth, now Lady Colchester, did not pass away until 1847. Respectably domiciled in London with family members, she would outlive by two years her colourful and dramatic successor at the Speaker's House, Ellen Manners Sutton.

POLITICS AND INFLUENCING: ELITE WOMEN IN THE VENTILATOR

The departure of Speaker Abbot led to a change for female visitors to the House of Commons. Many women from the social and political elite of the land – the great and the good of their age – were keen to visit Parliament to observe the proceedings and to promote their menfolk's interests. For them, the spaces from where the ladies could watch the proceedings of both Houses were vital political spaces: places to see and be seen, to observe and seek to influence politicians and events, and to form political alliances. In the House of Lords, an area was reserved for the ladies, and especially the wives of peers, to listen from behind the royal throne. Here they were often concealed behind a curtain – but by the early 1830s attendance levels were so high that female observers often spilled out into the body of the House, to the annoyance of their Lordships.[16]

The Commons was an infinitely more hostile environment for these women spectators. Since 1778, they had been banned by the Speaker altogether, a prohibition generally upheld until the arrival of Abbot's successor, Charles Manners Sutton, in 1817. In 1818, Manners Sutton quietly permitted a few select women – the first probably the eminent prison reformer Elizabeth Fry – to access the attic storey above the House of Commons on an occasional basis, under the supervision of the Serjeant at Arms. There they could view the proceedings by peering down through a ceiling void known as the Ventilator, designed to void hot and foul air from the chamber below, in cramped, dirty and unpleasant conditions.

The area soon developed into a semi-official viewing gallery for the ladies, with Manners Sutton – a man known to have a strong liking for the 'fair sex'[17] – turning a blind eye. After some major works in the roof space, by 1822 an expanded Ventilator had been surrounded by a large octagonal wooden structure known as the Lantern. Through its sixteen apertures, the women could peer down on the proceedings below; the view was restricted, but the acoustics were better than in many parts of the chamber itself, enabling them to hear more of the debates than most of the men in the House and its galleries. Despite the discomforts, the Ventilator became a popular attraction, and to control access, twenty-five tickets were issued each day by the Serjeant at Arms. The successful applicants were ushered into the roof by the younger John Bellamy, Deputy Housekeeper, who in 1811 had succeeded his father of the same name. He and his staff ensured that MPs who ascended to converse with the ladies did not linger to listen, taking up spaces reserved for women. Bellamy also supplied them with food and drink, and at times a festive atmosphere prevailed, to the fury of MPs below when their speeches were drowned out by the noise of female chatter.

The draw for many elite women was the opportunity to hear serious political debates on issues such as slavery and parliamentary reform, and the Ventilator was a significant political and social meeting place for them. Here were to be found influential female political commentators and the wives of MPs, generally seated on party lines, along with society ladies, often with their servants in attendance. These ladies could listen to the proceedings and consult with and advise Members who were their husbands or friends and who were speaking in debates. Political and social alliances were forged, and information harvested for sharing. Some of the regular attendees penned descriptive letters which were circulated among their friends, and in the early 1830s one, possibly Caroline Sheridan, published in-depth reports from the Ventilator in the *Court Magazine*.[18]

When an important debate was scheduled to take place in the Commons, John Rickman often acquired tickets to the Ventilator for Anne and Frances. Here, the sisters could mix with the ladies and hear some of the greatest orations of the day. The most informative image of the Ventilator to survive is a pencil sketch by Frances, drawn on 25 June 1834, a quiet day when the main business in the House was the committee stage of the Highways Bill (Plate 3).

'SHE IS OF FIRM MIND': FRANCES RICKMAN AND THE 1834 FIRE

Later that same year, on the night of 16–17 October 1834, much of the old Palace was burned down in a fire which began in the heating furnaces of the House of Lords. Anne Rickman was away, staying with an uncle, but fortunately, Frances was at home. The letter she sent to Anne the next day, one of the most vivid accounts to survive of this cataclysmic event, reveals the vital part she had played in saving her family's worldly goods. Frances describes how fear gripped the residents of the Palace as flames 'burst from the House of Commons windows' and ripped through the surrounding areas. Firefighting equipment was in short supply and all the efforts of the firemen, soldiers and passers-by were directed towards saving the precious Westminster Hall. That left the neighbouring houses of the Speaker, the Wildes and the Rickmans in serious danger.

As the flames advanced towards their residence, John Rickman, having returned from a good dinner at the Athenaeum Club, was provokingly disengaged – perhaps in disbelief. And Susannah was at first in a state of panic, so, Frances told Anne, 'I felt I must look to everything'. In great contrast to the terror and confusion which prevailed elsewhere, Frances competently devised and oversaw an orderly operation to evacuate her family's possessions. In this she was assisted by their servants and friends, and by two of Rickman's recent dining companions, man-of-letters Henry Taylor and aristocratic lawyer Edward Villiers, who were 'active chief managers under me'.[19] As an appreciative Rickman reported, 'Miss Fr did not quail in the least', for she 'is of firm mind'.[20] Frances also found time to comfort their frightened maids, Hannah and Jane, and to ensure that their friends the Wildes were safe.

In the event, the flames did not reach the Rickmans' house, and although they were very shocked by the dramas of the night, once the fire had died down their belongings were soon put back in place. When John Rickman and Frances toured the ruins during the next few days – including a visit with the king when Frances was the only lady present – they realised just how fortunate they had been.[21] In this, they were in a minority. While the Rickman sisters would go on to marry clergymen, to produce eleven daughters between them and to live out their days in placid respectability, the conflagration would completely reshape the Palace and the lives of many of its other inhabitants – including several of the women whose stories we tell below.

About Ellen Manners Sutton

'Her history is no secret in the higher circles.'

Press criticism of Ellen, wife of Commons Speaker
Charles Manners Sutton, February 1835

2

ELLEN MANNERS SUTTON: SCANDAL AT THE SPEAKER'S HOUSE

On 6 December 1828 the Rt Hon. Charles Manners Sutton, great-grandson of the third Duke of Rutland, son of the Archbishop of Canterbury and Speaker of the House of Commons, married beautiful and vivacious Irish widow Mrs Ellen Home Purves at St George's Church, Hanover Square:

> In vain his daughters … threw themselves at their parent's feet and implored him not to disgrace himself; tears and supplications were in vain. The Speaker would have his way, would give his casting vote and Mrs Purves is at length nestled within the precincts of St Stephen's Chapel.

Or so speculated William Beckford, embittered social outcast, expressing horror that Manners Sutton, 'the *ex-officio* as it were of public morals', was now bound to 'that errant lady'.[1] The contrast with Ellen's predecessor, respectable Elizabeth Abbot, could not have been greater.

Other contemporaries agreed. Although Ellen Manners Sutton was soon established in high society, her past – reputedly as a kept woman and the mother of several illegitimate children – was always to be held against her by those professing more traditional values. So too was the fact that she was the younger sister of Lady Blessington, a high-profile author and literary hostess, much reviled for her own racy life.

But the Speaker's new spouse soon became one of the 'fashionables', a prominent society hostess and a powerful, dominating and dramatic presence in the Palace of Westminster. The press reported her activities with relish, and she evoked a mixture of repulsion, envy and admiration. The story of her rise reveals the extent to which an attractive, unconventional, determined and ruthless woman was able to carve out political and social influence at Westminster, while at the same time enjoying the benefits of her lifestyle to the full. However, her later decline into financial hardship and ill health shows how fragile and transitory such a gilded existence could be.

ELLEN'S FORMATIVE YEARS

Born in 1791, at Knockbrit near Clonmel, County Tipperary, Ellen hailed from an old Irish Catholic gentry family. Her father, Edmund Power, a magistrate and businessman, was unstable, violent and periodically insolvent. Ellen first comes into public view in her early teens, attending society assemblies in Clonmel. Here, she and her older sister Margaret, both well educated, were said to have impressed the people of the town with their precocious cultivation and charm, although Ellen, already very comely, 'seemed conscious of being entitled to admiration'.[2] At this time, there was nothing to suggest that these two sisters would go on to lead lives which – even discounting jealous gossip and vitriol – would enthral any modern soap-opera audience and which would take them to the heart of the British establishment.

In 1804, as soon as she reached 15, the legal minimum age for marriage, Margaret was forced by her parents into wedlock with an apparently prosperous army captain, Maurice St Leger Farmer. Farmer soon proved violent and abusive towards Margaret and was disgraced after making a brutal attack on his commanding officer. He was rapidly banished to serve in India, but Margaret's refusal to accompany him there left her a social outcast. Ellen's name was, meanwhile, linked with polished and cultured William Stewart of Killymoon, later a lieutenant colonel and Westminster MP, and a pillar of Irish society. One of her many detractors later alleged that she produced three daughters with him out of wedlock, who would subsequently be brought up by her first husband.[3] This oft-repeated canard is not supported by any other evidence.

In about 1809, Captain Thomas Jenkins, a family friend, became Margaret's protector. He spirited her away to England, installing her in his house in Hampshire with his mother and sisters. This liaison would change Ellen's life as well. For when in 1810 – beautiful, vivacious and penniless – she went to stay with Margaret and the Jenkins family, she met John Home (soon styled as Home Purves), of Purves Hall, Berwickshire. A gentleman of independent means, he was a good marriage prospect. In September 1810, Ellen, aged 19, duly wed John at the Anglican parish church of St George, Hanover Square, London, with her sister Margaret Farmer as a witness. The couple settled down into a respectable union, producing a son and heir, John, born in 1815, and four daughters who survived into adulthood. The eldest was Louisa, born in 1811 – well after the end of any liaison that Ellen might have had with William Stewart – and the youngest was Ellen, born between 1820 and 1823. By that time, though, the relationship between Mr and Mrs Home Purves was coming to an end.

In 1816, Ellen's sister Margaret had found a new protector in the person of a very wealthy and hedonistic Irish peer, Charles John Gardiner, Viscount Mountjoy, who installed her in style in his house in Manchester Square, London. The fortuitous death of Margaret's husband in 1817 – from injuries sustained during a drinking spree at the King's Bench prison – enabled her to marry Mountjoy, by now Earl of Blessington, in 1818. To be known henceforth as Marguerite, Lady Blessington, and an exquisite and accomplished woman, she reinvented herself as a society hostess and author, residing mainly on the Continent, in France and Italy.

A 'KEPT WOMAN'

On 30 September 1823, on one of his journeys across the Alps, Lord Blessington was both delighted and very surprised to encounter Ellen Home Purves, his sister-in-law, in the company of Charles Manners Sutton, Speaker of the House of Commons. They were staying together at a fashionable inn just outside Geneva, along with all their respective children, nannies and governesses. After travelling convivially with them for a month, Lord Blessington offered Ellen the use of his grand house in St James's Square, Piccadilly, on her return to London. This became Ellen's official residence for the next few years, where she entertained the Speaker in private. She was also to be seen in company with Manners Sutton at dinners and events, and in 1824 travelled with him to Paris to see the sights.[4] But she was a social outcast in much of polite society, which regarded her as a kept woman.

What had become of John Home Purves, the husband whom Ellen had left for the Speaker? As a contemporary euphemistically put it, 'circumstances led to him separating himself from his country and his family'.[5] In April 1824, having obtained a posting as the British Consul for Florida, he set off for Pensacola, a strategically significant and far-flung port recently acquired by the United States from Spain. But this appointment, although dutifully discharged, did not bring him contentment. Pensacola was an expensive place to live and his consular salary of £500 (approximately £28,000 today) was 'barely sufficient to live on with any degree of respectability, or importance, that the situation otherwise authorises me to keep up'.[6] In September 1826, Purves died aged 43, one of the many victims of Pensacola's notoriously unhealthy climate. Ellen was now free to marry her paramour.

As already noted, Charles Manners Sutton had been Speaker since 1817. Tall and gentlemanly in demeanour, with a sonorous voice and a commanding presence, he soon gained the respect of the House despite retaining his strong Tory views in private. Charming, witty and congenial, although not a heavyweight intellectual, he was noted for his facility in managing debates. Moving with him into the Speaker's House were the servants needed to sustain his daily life and the pomp of his office, along with his much-cherished two young sons and one daughter from his marriage to Lucy Denison, who had died in 1815, leaving him a widower.

Manners Sutton continued his predecessor's custom of holding grand political banquets and receptions, and in July 1821 he hosted the new king, George IV, at the Speaker's House on the eve of his coronation. But behind its glittering gothic revival surfaces all was not well with the structure. In 1824, some substantial and costly alterations were suddenly set in train and in 1826 the Speaker's kitchens were cleared out of the central cloister court and relocated as the smoke from their chimneys was annoying the residents.[7] It is tempting to see Ellen's hand in all this, not least as some contemporaries were of the view that she was living there.

THE SPEAKER'S WIFE

When Ellen married Charles Manners Sutton in December 1828 at St George's, Hanover Square, he was 48 years old and she was 39, and 'still very beautiful' according to an admiring guest (Figure 1).[8] She was now at last officially resident at the Speaker's House, and an old friend, the Irish poet Thomas Moore, visiting her in February 1829, was 'not a little amused to see her enshrined in her magnificent establishment'. On a further visit in May, he was beguiled by the beauty of the house and garden and again 'amused to see her, in all her state, the same hearty, lively Irish-woman still'.[9]

A crucial part of the duties of the Speaker's wife was acting as her husband's hostess for his frequent soirées and private dinners at his Westminster

Figure 1: Ellen Manners Sutton in about 1833, engraving after a portrait by Sir Thomas Lawrence.

residence and accompanying him on official engagements. Ellen shone in this role, famously enlivening her husband's entertainments both formal and informal with vivacity and wit. She also ensured that the extensive private entertaining space in the house was fitted out to the height of fashionable opulence, purchasing costly furniture and fittings to supplement those provided at public expense. The couple's spending spree was made possible by the Speaker's generous allowance of £6,000 a year (with a further £500 for coals and candles) on top of his personal wealth. By 1834, with these possessions supplemented by more furniture from his former country seat at Mistley Hall, Essex, the Manners Suttons had amassed enough for two or three residences.

Although she was soon presented to King George IV at Court in April 1829, Ellen's colourful past continued to be held against her by many contemporaries. The influential Mrs Harriet Arbuthnot, snobbish Tory political obsessive – and close confidante of Prime Minister Arthur Wellesley, Lord Wellington – squarely blamed the king for letting down the royal dignity by receiving her.[10] Mrs Arbuthnot and her cousin, the famous political hostess Sarah Villiers, Lady Jersey, were leading lights at Almack's Club, the prestigious assembly rooms in London's West End. Membership was highly prized and while the Speaker was clearly welcome at the glittering receptions and balls held there, Ellen's recorded appearances at Almack's events were infrequent and must have been on sufferance.

The arrival of children prompted further unkind comment. In December 1829, Ellen gave birth to a daughter, Frances Diana Manners Sutton, and a son followed in 1831, but died at birth. Having been born after her marriage, these children were, sarcastically carped the Whig diarist Charles Greville, 'triumphant witness of her immaculate virtue'.[11] Novelist Mary Shelley was, it seems, so enraged by Ellen's treatment by her critics that in 1830 she befriended her, although this may not have helped Ellen's advance in society.

But Ellen could be ruthless too. In 1831, she insisted that her eldest daughter, Louisa, married the underwhelming John Fairlie, land agent to the Duke of Rutland, apparently against Louisa's own wishes. Ellen's sister Marguerite, Lady Blessington, returned to London in 1830 after the sudden death of her husband in Paris, and notoriously set up a home and literary salon with her own stepdaughter's estranged husband, the handsome French dandy Alfred, Count d'Orsay. Marguerite's many detractors criticised this setup as vulgar as well as scandalous, and by July 1831 the newly respectable Manners Suttons had, lamented one of Marguerite's more loyal friends, 'thrown my Blessington overboard'.[12]

All this was set against the background of the social whirl in which Ellen was now caught up and which she had clearly craved for so long. Despite being ostracised by parts of respectable society, she cultivated a wide circle of friends and the press portrayed her as one of the 'fashionables'. Her comings and goings, splendid parties and attendances at society events and performances, both with and without the Speaker, were widely reported. She was spotted dining with King William IV in Brighton and presiding over lavish dinners and entertainments at Mistley Hall, her husband's seat.

Noted too were her appearances in London, at the Vauxhall Pleasure Gardens, at the circus, at the ballet and at the opera where, 'strikingly conspicuous', her presence was said even to have outshone the singers.[13] At the State Opening of Parliament in 1830, she completely upstaged all the other ladies attending the Lords chamber. They were clad in sombre mourning for the recently deceased George IV, but Ellen dramatically and elegantly subverted the rules of etiquette by wearing 'a few brilliants intermixed with jet in her hair and ears'.[14] At Court in February 1833, Mrs Manners Sutton was gloriously attired in a 'magnificent dress of white figured satin [with] a train of cherry coloured velvet. Head dress, diamonds and feathers.'[15] And when, in August 1833, the Speaker was awarded the signal honour of a knighthood grand cross of the Order of the Bath, Ellen could now style herself as Lady Manners Sutton.

Well connected and well informed, behind the scenes Ellen was tireless in seeking to further her husband's standing and position, and her penchant for political gossip and machination, not expected of a Speaker's wife, was widely noticed. Doubtless with the encouragement of her husband, she rapidly laid ostentatious claim to a privileged status in the Commons Ventilator. For example, she attended twice in May 1829 to hear the House discuss Catholic Emancipation, an issue of personal interest to her. Her dramatic entrances through the Lobby of the House accompanied by the Speaker's trainbearer and two of her daughters were duly noted by the press. So too were her invariable and loyal appearances at key political moments for her husband. At times, Ellen also attended the House of Lords to hear debates, sitting in the area behind the throne which was reserved for the ladies. Her female critics were often there too – but at Westminster, Ellen's social position was for now secure.

Charles Manners Sutton remains the only Speaker to be elected to lead his fellow MPs seven times. Conciliatory and courteous, in the early 1830s he was still respected by most Members for his ability to guide the House on a light snaffle and for his relative impartiality when in the chair. But his lustre was beginning to fade. Having emerged as an unlikely candidate for Tory prime minister in 1832, he deterred his supporters by a pompous, interminable and incomprehensible speech and was dismissed by those present as 'nothing but a verbose ninny'.[16] Soon after that, exhausted by many gruelling and fractious months of debate in the stifling chamber to pass the 1832 Reform Act, Manners Sutton attempted to stand down, only to be coaxed back into office by the new Whig government to deal with the boisterous new crop of MPs. But by 1834 his health was breaking down, and in October he and Ellen were staying in fashionable Brighton, where he was taking the waters.

A YEAR OF CRISIS

The Speaker's House came close to total obliteration from the flames that raged through the old Palace of Westminster on the night of 16–17 October 1834. As with adjoining Westminster Hall, it was only through the extreme exertions of the firemen and the army that just over half of its fabric survived relatively unscathed (Plate 1). Its contents, hastily removed by the servants, a posse of soldiers and assorted bystanders under the limp direction of Charles, the Speaker's eldest son, fared far less well. After being thrown out of the windows or dragged out on to the front lawn next to the Thames, the Speaker's fabled possessions lay in huge, jumbled and chaotic heaps. The Speaker's son judged that there had been as least as much damage from removals and theft as from the flames themselves,[17] a view endorsed by the Manners Suttons on their hasty return to town.

The fate of the opulent Speaker's House and the plight of its occupants was a source of great fascination to the press. One story featured brave Charlotte Howse, housemaid to her Ladyship, who, as the fire raged, discovered some soldiers in the kitchens. Drunk on the Speaker's cherry brandy, they were raucously munching their way through his cakes and jam, but Charlotte heroically prevented them from breaking into his wine cellar. Another tale told of how a second housemaid did her utmost to rescue all of Ellen's clothes and jewellery, ironically left behind for safe-keeping, as she knew how much store her mistress set by these costly items. Many of Ellen's favourite jewels had, however, disappeared.[18]

When Ellen, accompanied by her eldest daughter, Louisa Fairlie, made a well-publicised visit, she warmly thanked both housemaids in person, but so great was the effect of seeing the devastation for herself that she 'gave vent to her feelings by a flood of tears'.[19] Her neighbour Frances Rickman felt sorry for 'poor Lady Sutton, she has been crying' and kept her correspondence for her at their house.[20] Soon after this, the Speaker ordered the damaged areas of his residence to be secured, repairs to be done and its contents to be put back in as soon as possible. As it was meanwhile uninhabitable, when in London he and Ellen stayed with James Baillie MP at Seymour Place.

Among the ruins, essential parliamentary processes continued, and Ellen was in attendance. On 23 October 1834, she appeared with a group of her political friends to witness the low-key Prorogation, held in the House of

Lords Library, as its chamber was still a smouldering shell. Manners Sutton was embroiled with the king, who made a private visit to Westminster and, almost dumbstruck by the devastation, made an embarrassing offer of the future Buckingham Palace as Parliament's new home. Parliamentarians were having none of it, resolving to get the two Houses back on site as soon as possible after repairs had been done. Temporary chambers were needed, and the necessary work would take until February 1835 to complete. But well before that, on 12 November 1834, Ellen and the Speaker had moved back into their official residence at St Stephen's,[21] although twenty-three of its rooms – almost half of the total – were uninhabitable. So overcome was Ellen by all this that she ostentatiously took to her bed, citing anguish and fatigue.

To the Speaker's many woes was added, in November 1834, a full-blown political and constitutional crisis. King William IV dismissed Lord Melbourne's Whig government and put Sir Robert Peel in as prime minister leading a minority – and short-lived – Tory administration. Manners Sutton was accused by his growing band of critics of political collusion – unfairly, but it stuck. And although he indicated his intention of standing again when the House reconvened in February 1835, it was clear that his bid for re-election would this time be strongly contested by the Whigs. Ellen, now reunited with her sister Marguerite, Lady Blessington, actively politicked on his behalf, and she too was roundly criticised for her efforts. The charge that 'her history is no secret in the higher circles' once more appeared in the press.[22]

When the fateful day of the vote, 19 February 1835, arrived, Ellen and her political friends provided her husband with the strongest possible show of support. Displaced from their lost Ventilator – and flouting the convention that women must never be seen in the House of Commons – the ladies publicly made their way to the area directly behind the Speaker's chair. This was the same spot from where they had been able to witness House of Lords debates in the years before October 1834, since the House of Commons was now meeting in a large temporary structure within the shell of the former Upper House. So many of the ladies turned up to support Sir Charles that some had to wait outside in their carriages. But all the politicking was in vain: Manners Sutton's Whig opponent James Abercromby emerged victorious by 316 to 306 votes. The ladies were now banished from the temporary House of Commons altogether for several years – thereafter being allocated no more than a tiny hidden closet. And when, on 24 February 1835, Ellen attempted to attend State Opening in the temporary Lords chamber, she was rudely turned away.

In March, a grateful Peel rapidly elevated Manners Sutton to the peerage as Viscount Canterbury, with a pension of £5,000 a year, and lined him up for the prestigious role of High Commissioner to Canada. But, whether out of concern for her husband or herself, the new Lady Canterbury soon put paid to these plans. Her health suddenly deteriorated dramatically, and she did not recover from what the press dubbed her 'Canada Influenza' until her husband's new posting had been cancelled.[23] By April 1835, she was so much better that she was able to accompany her husband on visits in his carriage, and in May to appear at Court with her debutante daughter Margaret.

Still residing in the damaged Speaker's House – which they had been due to leave back in February – Lord and Lady Canterbury had by now shamelessly and ostentatiously reinstated their daily political soirées there, while attempting without success to sell some of their high-end furniture items to the Treasury for £500. This was an early sign of their mounting money troubles. Speaker Abercromby, who would soon be found an alternative official residence, had indicated that he did not wish to live in the old Palace. But the Speaker's House was urgently needed by the House of Commons for committee rooms; instead, space had to be rented at considerable public expense. Ellen was blamed for Lord Canterbury's refusal to leave,[24] and it took his public shaming by the press and in the House of Commons, along with a formal notice to quit, to prise her out. In early August 1835, an auction of all their possessions at the Speaker's House was suddenly announced, on the grounds – not universally believed – that the Canterburys were planning to relocate to the Continent for several years.

First to go, on 13 August 1835, was the former Speaker's well-chosen wine cellar. This was followed, from 29 August, by the rest of the contents, which were so extensive that, in all, nine days were needed for the auction. It caused a sensation, with the 'quality' rushing in to view the lavish array of treasures on offer and to snap them up. Enthused the *Morning Post*:

> We never witnessed a more superb collection of drawing room and levée furniture, all in the style of Louis Quatorze ... richly gilt, superb chased chandeliers, candelabra, and clocks, tables of all descriptions, besides five Speaker's chairs, magnificent cabinets, noble pier glasses in splendid massive carved frames ... beautiful Dresden and Sèvres china.[25]

Competition was fierce, even for the items from the kitchens, the sale raising almost £4,700.

DECLINE AND FALL

By October 1835, Lord and Lady Canterbury had relocated to a hotel in Paris, and the next year took a house in the Place de Montblanc. Here, their social whirl continued: in 1837, her Ladyship's two younger daughters, Margaret and Ellen Home Purves, were belles of the ball at the Tuileries. But fast forward to 1841, and Margaret and Ellen were staying with their older sister Louisa Fairlie at Cheveley Park near Newmarket while the Canterburys, back in London, were facing financial ruin. Despite his very generous pension of £5,000 a year and the proceeds of the furniture sale, Charles seemed unable to pay off even the smallest of debts. In 1842, in distressed and muddled replies to demands for sums as small as £40, he pleaded with one creditor: 'I have sent *all* I have at this moment', and 'it is impossible for me to effect impossibilities'.[26] His claim of £5,000 for the uninsured possessions that he had lost in the 1834 fire was rejected by the House of Commons in 1837 and now failed in the Court of Chancery as well. And when in 1843 Lord and Lady Canterbury hastily relocated to Rockbeare House in faraway Devon, their creditors followed, sending in the Exeter bailiffs to seize and sell their goods and chattels against a debt of more than £1,600.

Ellen loyally adapted to her straitened circumstances with good grace, giving up all the luxuries to which she had become accustomed, including her carriage and her ornaments of value. After Lord Canterbury's sudden death from an apoplexy in July 1845, his will was found to have made generous provision for his wife and family, but his estate would soon be swallowed up by his many outstanding debts. It was left to Marguerite, Countess of Blessington, to look after Ellen and her children, despite her own money troubles. Living at Gore House in Kensington, Lady Blessington was by now a very successful and prolific author – but the income from her royalties was unreliable and her annual jointure of £2,000 was gradually eroding in value.[27] Yet she may well have bailed out the Canterburys on occasions and was certainly a devoted aunt to Louisa Fairlie and her beautiful and deaf daughter, both of whom spent much time with her before they both died in 1843.

Marguerite also, it seems, gave a home to Louisa's sisters, Margaret and Ellen Home Purves, until in 1846–47 she found them suitable husbands. For her nephew, the able Colonel John Home Purves of the Grenadier Guards, Lady Blessington arranged a prestigious appointment as Comptroller of the Household to Princess Augusta, Duchess of Cambridge. Ellen's youngest daughter, the Hon. Frances Diana Manners Sutton, would go on to marry the Hon. and Rev. Delaval Loftus Astley, later Lord Hastings, in 1848.

But by that time, in November 1845, scarcely four months since her husband's demise, Ellen had herself died at the age of 54 from liver disease. Her last painful weeks were spent in lodgings at Rodney Place, Clifton, near Bristol, a fashionable area famed for its healing waters, and where she would be buried. Her will was generous to her family and included bequests to her three surviving daughters totalling £6,000, but it is most unlikely that the funds were there to pay for them. Lady Blessington – who in 1849 would herself die penniless in Paris after her own sudden reversal in fortune – had tenderly nursed her sister through her last illness. She wrote of Ellen to a friend, the poet Walter Savage Landor, that 'the ties of blood may sometimes be severed but how easily, how quickly are they reunited again when the youthful days are recalled. All that affection has sprung up afresh in my heart since my poor sister has known affliction.'[28] During her dramatic years at the Speaker's House, Ellen Manners Sutton had alienated as many people as she had mesmerised, entertained and impressed. Yet it was the sister who she had cast aside at her height of fame and fortune who would bring her comfort in her final days.

In Her Own Words

'It has devolved upon me to have the entire care of the House of Lords, which I venture to hope I have diligently and vigilantly manifested, to the satisfaction of your Lordship with the performance of my really responsible if not incessant duties.'

Jane Julia Bennett, Deputy Housekeeper, House of Lords,
writing to the Lord Great Chamberlain, 1847

3

WOMAN IN CHARGE: JANE JULIA BENNETT, HOUSE OF LORDS HOUSEKEEPER

In April 1847, the new House of Lords, one of the greatest glories of the new Palace of Westminster, was ready for the sittings of Queen Victoria's loyal peers. To signify its transfer to the House authorities, a set of keys was handed over to one of its senior staff, a woman: Mrs Jane Julia Bennett, the Housekeeper. During the previous decade, throughout one of the most challenging periods in its history, Jane had acted as the House's respected custodian during all its non-sitting times. The temporary House of Lords had been marooned in the cramped medieval Painted Chamber – once King Henry III's bedroom – at the heart of one of the largest building sites in western Europe. So Jane had needed all her resilience and skills to ensure that its business and fabric were properly guarded and maintained to meet the exacting standards of the peers and of her superior officer, Sir Augustus Clifford, Black Rod. The moment she received the keys to the new House marked an end to a particularly difficult era for Members and staff alike and crowned all her efforts.

Yet when Jane Julia Bennett retired in 1877, having served the Lords with distinction for half a century, she would be replaced by a man in a blatant act of patronage by the Deputy Lord Great Chamberlain, the Crown's representative within the Palace. This was an uncanny reversal of the unlikely circumstances of her appointment by an earlier Black Rod, Sir Thomas Tyrwhitt, in 1822 – when she was Miss Jane Julia Wright, a child of 11. That arrangement had enabled her father, William Wright, to draw the lucrative perquisites of her role, then Deputy Housekeeper. Despite this most improbable of starts, Jane Julia would go on to take up her job in person when she reached the age of majority and to exercise it triumphantly as a married woman. This is the story of her rise and of how she survived – and even thrived – in this most masculine of worlds, only through no discernible fault of her own to see her role and reputation decline in her final years.

'OLD CORRUPTION' AND PARLIAMENT

To understand how a girl of 11 could possibly be appointed to a senior role in the House of Lords administration requires an unedifying dip into 'Old Corruption', a term coined by radical critic William Cobbett MP. In the early nineteenth century, some parts of the public service were characterised by efficiency and frugality, while in others, greed, torpor and waste prevailed. The Exchequer, neighbour to the Commons, was notorious for pointless bureaucracy, the charging of excessive fees, and the prevalence of sinecures: positions which demanded little or no effort but provided their holders with often substantial financial benefits and status. To their opponents, these practices were immoral and parasitic. But to those who benefited, they were a well-tested way for patronage to be dispensed, which enabled power and wealth to be amassed as a reward for services to the nation.

In the House of Lords, Lord Eldon – Lord Chancellor and Speaker from 1801 to 1827 – was infamous for creaming off at least £18,000 a year from fees and the sale of offices.[1] Notorious too for their own lucrative portfolios and minimal involvement with their official duties were the sinecurist Clerks of the Parliaments, George Rose MP and his son, self-styled Sir George Henry Rose MP, successively in office between 1788 and 1855. The older George Rose was much ridiculed when in 1797 he purchased a reversion – a guarantee of appointment when his post was next vacant – for his adult son, on the grounds of securing talent. And although in 1824 the Lords ruled that its next incumbent must do this job in person, the younger George Rose lived on to enjoy its perquisites for three more decades. Meanwhile, the duties were actually carried out by the Clerk Assistant, and at least four of the clerks on his payroll were either drawing two salaries for one job or occupying phantom roles. Over in the Commons, five of the clerks' posts were also held as sinecures.[2]

To the ire of the radical reformers, women and minors had their part to play in 'Old Corruption' too, to reward their male relatives. In 1807, William Cobbett excoriated reversions as they were awarded 'frequently, if not generally, to children, or for persons in trust for children, or for women'.[3] In 1832, another prominent critic, John Wade, fulminated about the 'ludicrous incongruities' thrown up when 'offices of Clerks, Tide-Waiters, Harbour-Masters, Protonotharies and other degrading situations' were occupied by the dependants of powerful men.[4]

One of these was the feckless Charles, son of Commons Speaker Charles Manners Sutton, who on the night of the 1834 fire had proved unequal to saving his father's most precious possessions. In 1832, Manners Sutton had secured for this son, then a minor, the reversion of the 'perfect' sinecure of Principal Registrar to the Prerogative Court of Canterbury, bringing in a whopping £16,000 a year (equivalent to more than £1 million today) for doing nothing.[5] There were also several dependant appointees, this time women, on the House of Lords' books. In 1830, Frances Brandish, Housekeeper, was a sinecurist, as were also Elizabeth Oldrini, Necessary Woman, Sarah Gurr, Deputy Necessary Woman – and our heroine, the young Jane Julia Wright, Deputy Housekeeper. Yet the minors for whom sinecures and reversions were secured were generally boys; as a girl who was drawn into this system and who then went on to exercise her duties in person, Jane was probably extremely rare.

By the time Jane retired from her long and illustrious career in 1877, much of the public service had undergone a transformation. A government-led programme to reform 'Old Corruption', which had started back in the 1780s, had reached its peak in the 1830s. Sinecures had fallen like dominos, the House of Commons quashing its own in 1834. This was followed by a gradual shift towards making public appointments on merit. Yet, as Jane would later discover to her cost, some of the old ways continued right up to the 1870s and beyond.

THE ABSENT MRS BRANDISH

Jane's future career was made possible only because in 1812 the post of Lords Housekeeper was awarded to Mrs Frances Brandish as a sinecure. That grant exemplifies the machinery of patronage at its most capricious and disruptive. It was made by the Lord Chamberlain, the most senior officer of the Royal Household, in whose gift it lay, on the Crown's behalf; and it came 'with all rights, profits, privileges and advantages': about £130 a year together with the right to occupy a suite of rooms which could be profitably sublet.[6] Frances's predecessor, Mrs Margaret Quarme, had both lived on site and performed the significant duties that the post required. Mrs Brandish did neither.

When handed this plum, Frances was seemingly in attendance at Court with her husband, Dr Samuel Brandish, a famed medical practitioner of his day and a leading citizen of the town of Alcester, Warwickshire. The previous year, Samuel had joined the household of Augustus Frederick, Duke of Sussex, the wayward sixth son of King George III, whose many health problems included long-standing and chronic asthma. But the grant of the sinecure to his wife was not, it seems, a reward for Samuel's services to the prince, for there is nothing to suggest that he had any more success in curing him than any of the other surgeons in his medical team.

The award of the sinecure to Mrs Brandish was, rather, a by-product of some lucrative property deals made between her husband and the Lord Chamberlain, the powerful Francis Seymour Ingram Conway, 2nd Marquess of Hertford. Conway was notorious for amassing offices and dispensing patronage on an epic scale. Over the preceding decade he had purchased from Dr Brandish two highly prized pieces of land in Alcester, immediately adjacent to his estate at Ragley Hall, for almost £13,000. But all this had necessitated quashing Mrs Brandish's legal rights to some of the property, which would have applied after her husband's death. Conway's grant of the income from the Lords sinecure was evidently made as some compensation for that.[7]

Undisturbed by any duties – and known to posterity only for not being at Westminster on the night of the 1834 fire – Mrs Brandish would continue to enjoy the emoluments long after her husband passed away in 1822. She remained as the notional Lords Housekeeper right up until her own demise in 1843, at the age of 88.

THE WRIGHT FAMILY TO THE RESCUE

The Lords Housekeeper was responsible for security and access in the House of Lords during all non-sitting times, signified by her control of the keys. She had also to organise accredited workmen, supervise furniture and fittings, receive respectable visitors and oversee the housemaids who kept the building clean. Since 1690 this post, a Crown appointment, had almost always been passed down through the female line, its holders being married to other senior officials in Black Rod's department.[8]

In Mrs Brandish's absence, the Housekeeper's duties still needed to be performed, and it is likely that at first the Doorkeepers stepped into the breach. But in 1818, Black Rod, Sir Thomas Tyrwhitt, created a new role of Deputy Housekeeper. It was to be funded from the right to charge visitors to Parliament for access to and tours of the Lords, at the rate of a 'donation' of 1 shilling per person. According to the official listings, he awarded it to 'Mrs W. Wright' – in accordance with the House of Lords convention that the

Housekeeper role should normally be held by a woman. The appointee was Mary Wright, the wife of one of his senior and most trusted Doorkeepers, William Wright. After Mary's untimely death in 1821 she was replaced in the listings by the couple's elder daughter, 'Miss Jane Wright', baptised in 1811 as Jane Julia Wright – and at that time a child of 11.[9]

In reality, the job was being carried out by William Wright, whose large and confident signature – 'Wm Wright, Deputy Housekeeper' – adorns official records from 1818 onwards alongside that of his equivalent in the Commons, the younger John Bellamy. It was William who held the keys, organised access and supervised repairs and maintenance throughout his domain and drew the substantial fees attached to this role. In 1821, allocated an apartment in the 'top gallery' of a building above Peers' Entrance, he was vociferous in complaining about its inconvenience.[10]

But Jane held the reversion and in 1827, when she was 16, Black Rod issued her with a formal warrant of appointment as Deputy Housekeeper. William had meanwhile remarried and his new wife, Elizabeth Wright, now Jane's stepmother, was awarded a well-paid housemaid post at the same time. The takings from Jane's remit were extremely lucrative and by the early 1830s the Wrights had collectively developed their visitor services into a flourishing enterprise, realising as much as £900 a year. That enabled them to employ three resident servants to greet visitors and conduct the tours. Assertive like her father before her, Jane was later to claim all these achievements as her own.

In 1832, when Sir Thomas Tyrwhitt retired from the service of the House, with him went William Wright. This coincided with Jane reaching her age of majority and she could now legally exercise all her duties in person. Her deputy, who stayed on in employment at the House of Lords, was Elizabeth Wright – described in the official report on the 1834 fire as her mother-in-law, not incorrectly as this term could at that time equally denote the stepmother she actually was.[11] Jane remained in the capacious seven rooms above Peers' Entrance that her father had so disdained. Her immediate neighbours included Doorkeeper Herman Mullencamp and his wife, Resident Housemaid Mary Anne Mullencamp, while nearby lived William Moyes, Senior Doorkeeper, and his wife Elizabeth. These stalwarts survived the fire and would all continue to work together in the service of the House for decades to come.

DISASTER!

The House of Lords chamber was the highlight of the Wrights' tours. Here, their visitors could admire the royal throne and the famous Armada tapestries, a focus of patriotic pride. But all was not well with the poorly maintained heating system beneath the raised floor, which often debouched heat and smoke into the chamber. On 16 October 1834, Elizabeth Wright, deputising for her stepdaughter Jane, became increasingly worried about the unusually high levels of smoke and heat in the chamber. She was concerned to discover that this was because old wooden tallies from the recently abolished Exchequer were being burned in the stoves, rather than the usual coal. But Elizabeth accepted the reassurances given by Office of Works employees that everything was under control – even when late in the afternoon the chamber became so smoky that her visitors were unable to see the tapestries and so hot that parts of the floor coverings were melting. She locked the chamber up at 5 p.m. and went off duty.

At 6 p.m., the Wrights' neighbour, Mary Anne Mullencamp, returning from an errand, rushed to find her and cried out, 'Oh, good God, the House of Lords is on fire!' Elizabeth found Black Rod's box ablaze and the flames taking hold beyond it – and raised the alarm. As the fire ripped through the old Palace, she and her maid rushed outside, with the lead from the melting roofs falling on their shoulders.[12]

A graphic lithograph (Plate 4) depicts the scene at Old Palace Yard when the blaze was at its peak, with a multitude of keen sightseers impeding the firefighters. At centre right is the tall gothic building where the Wrights and the Mullencamps lived, with flames leaping out of its turrets. Behind it is the Stone Building housing Bellamy's kitchen, where his waiting staff resided, also on fire. Much of the central and southern part of the old Palace was soon burnt to a shell, including the House of Lords and its surrounds and the Commons Library. Parts of the Speaker's House were also badly damaged (Plate 1). Irreplaceable treasures such as the Armada tapestries and most of the Commons records were lost.

On 20 October, only four days later, Elizabeth Wright was hauled up in front of the parliamentary inquiry into the causes of the fire, a daunting prospect. She was the only female Lords employee to give evidence. Her testimony is rich and shows an understanding of what her duties entailed, but it is also in places halting and muddled. Elizabeth's interrogators were singularly unimpressed with her account of her actions. It was, the inquiry reported, 'unaccountable that Mrs Wright, when she felt alarmed, as she states herself to have been, was not led by such manifest indications of danger to make immediate representations in the proper quarter'. Its Members were more critical still of the men who had fed the tallies into the boilers, who had confused and exceeded their instructions from the Office of Works. They were acquitted of all 'guilty design' but were found to have behaved with 'gross neglect, disobedience of orders and utter disregard of all warnings'. The fire was 'wholly attributable to carelessness and negligence'.[13]

Many radicals rejoiced to see Parliament, to them a symbol of corruption, reduced to ashes by the tally sticks from the hated Exchequer. But, for those whose livelihoods depended on the old Palace, the fire was a disaster. Efficient John Bellamy, Deputy Housekeeper in the Commons, swung immediately into action and requisitioned new quarters for his kitchen at the southern end of the still intact Law Courts, including residential space for his six waiting staff. The Lords had more undamaged buildings at its disposal than the Commons, but Jane and her servants seem to have fared far less well, apparently having been left to fend for themselves for six months. Their jobs at least were safe, and after Parliament resumed proceedings in its temporary accommodation in February 1835, Jane and the Mullencamps were soon found new dwellings on site.

Sir Augustus Clifford, Tyrwhitt's successor as Black Rod, submitted claims to the Treasury on behalf of his subordinates to compensate them for the possessions they had lost in the blaze: £218 18s for the Mullencamps and £135 10s for Jane Wright. John Bellamy did likewise, asking for £136 16s 6d for his kitchen servants' uniforms. But the Treasury was not persuaded. Although numerous small sums were paid out to people who had assisted with the rescue efforts, none of the claims for the losses sustained by the residents of the old Palace were successful.[14]

JANE JULIA TAKES CONTROL

Jane then took matters into her own hands, increasing and resubmitting her case for compensation to a Select Committee investigating the losses by fire of former Speaker Lord Canterbury:

> Your Memorialist lost property to the amount of £400 ... all that she possessed. Others suffered at the time, but to no-one has the visitation been so severe or lasting as to your Petitioner. Entirely dependent on the fees received for showing the House, her income totally ceased at the time it was most needed.[15]

Not least because they were out of scope for the Committee, her efforts were in vain, but like her father William Wright before her, she was clearly ready and able to stand up for herself.

In 1840, Jane decided to marry, choosing Edwin Bennett, a man of independent means who took up residence with her in the House of Lords. Perhaps Edwin himself, and certainly the compilers of the official listings, assumed that the role of Deputy Housekeeper was now his, and he is listed as such in 1841–42. But Mrs Jane Julia Bennett, as she now styled herself, was evidently having none of it and by 1843 she was firmly back in the saddle, Edwin making an appearance in 1845 as a supernumerary Doorkeeper. And looking ahead to the 1851 census where Edwin – inevitably – appears as the head of their household, his occupation would there be described as his wife's deputy.

By the time of the Bennetts' marriage, the new Palace of Westminster, designed by Charles Barry, was rising rapidly around the ever-diminishing remains of its predecessor. The Lords and Commons were meeting in their temporary chambers – the Commons in the spacious Lesser Hall and the Lords in the compact Painted Chamber – at the epicentre of a vast building site. Parliament's facilities were shoehorned into all the available and often unsuitable old buildings in the immediate vicinity that were not yet demolished.

Although separated from the almost incessant operations by hoardings, parliamentarians and staff alike would have found their working conditions noisy, dirty, unhealthy – and at times dangerous. From the construction works emanated dust, toxic chemicals and sewage. Within the enclave where the two Houses were operating, hazardous live trials of cutting-edge ventilation systems for the two temporary chambers were taking place. These required thumping steam engines and an enormous chimney looming over the site, belching smoke. For the little band of Lords employees and their families who lived on site – in 1841, twenty-one people, of whom thirteen were women and four were children – there was no escape from this turmoil. Most of them, like Jane herself, Mary Anne and Herman Mullencamp, and Elizabeth and William Moyes, had come through the perils of the fire together and they must have formed a close-knit and supportive community.

Under these exceptional circumstances, Jane Julia Bennett needed all the resilience and determination she could muster to carry out her job. As she wrote to the Lord Great Chamberlain, Lord Willoughby de Eresby, in May 1847, she felt that 'the entire care of the House of Lords' was resting upon her. Her role as Deputy Housekeeper involved her in 'really responsible if not incessant duties … which I venture to hope I have diligently and vigilantly manifested'.[16] Symbolic of her authority in the Lords was the delivery to her of the keys to Barry's magnificent new chamber, in the same year.

JANE JULIA'S REWARD

As Lord Great Chamberlain, the monarch's representative, Lord Willoughby had overall charge of the Palace of Westminster. Jane had written to him because in April 1847 the other – and even more senior – officer controlling the Palace, the Lord Chamberlain, had suddenly announced that visits to the new Lords chamber would be by ticket only. Expected to be hugely popular, as indeed they were, these would be issued by his office to applicants in person and without charge.[17] But this unexpected decision would, in practice, end the access fees of 1 shilling per visitor on which Jane's livelihood still depended. She pointed out to Willoughby that since 1834 her income had plunged to about £200 a year because of the sharp decline in the numbers of visitors allowed on site. This she had accepted in the hope that her remuneration would recover when the new House was completed. But now her funding would cease altogether, making her position untenable.

The speed and vigour with which he pursued this matter shows just how much Lord Willoughby valued the work Jane had done. Ensuring the future of her role was no simple matter: he had to go all the way up to the prime minister and then to the Select Committee on the Parliament Office. But in July 1847 he emerged with a warrant appointing Jane Julia Bennett as Housekeeper to the House of Lords on a salary of £150 along with £50 for servants to assist her. This promotion Jane acknowledged with 'sincere thanks for your Lordship's kindness'.[18] But Jane had been up against a strong challenge from two external candidates for her elite and desirable role. Nineteen peers, led by William, Duke of St Albans, lobbied Willoughby on behalf of Mrs Elizabeth Browne of the George IV Hotel, Nottingham, known probably to this peer from his sojourns at Bestwood Lodge nearby; and Mrs Browne forcefully put herself forward for the post. Willoughby also considered an expression of interest from the well-connected Hon. Mrs George Massey. But as the capable incumbent, Jane clearly had an overwhelming advantage.

All the irregularities of Jane's original appointment now lay behind her. But notionally attached to her team were three other women still holding sinecures by warrant from Black Rod, and over whom she had no direct control. In 1849–50, the Select Committee on the Parliament Office and the Office of Black Rod turned its attention to these posts. Members castigated the 'complete sinecure' held by Elizabeth Oldrini, Necessary Woman, along with Sarah Gurr's long-lasting and equally fruitless role as her notional deputy. Both posts, which benefited their Doorkeeper husbands, were lined up for abolition, as was yet another bogus job of 'Firelighter', held by Mrs Theresa Poisnel.

But such sinecures could take a long time to disappear: Elizabeth Oldrini's payments, established back in 1830, continued up to 1870. And the Select Committee failed altogether to spot that several of the most long-serving of Jane's ten housemaids, again holding warrants of appointment, were also drawing £50 a year each for doing nothing. No longer attending to their duties in person, they deputed the real work of cleaning to underpaid – and largely unsupervised – women 'Dusters'. As a result, for Jane it was an increasing struggle to keep the House and its surroundings clean.

Nor was the new Palace yet complete. Although new facilities for Members gradually came on stream, including in 1852 the Peers' Refreshment Rooms, major and disruptive works continued unabated until 1860. But after a temporary relocation to Royal Court at the southern end of the new River Front, in 1857 Jane Julia Bennett finally moved into her substantial Victorian gothic apartment on the west front, not far from where her pre-fire accommodation had been and similarly controlling what was then the main public entrance to the House of Lords. On three floors, with its drawing and dining rooms, bedroom, servants' quarters and kitchens, and furnished at public expense, this would be her residence for the next two decades – although without her husband Edwin, who died in 1858.

It made good sense for Jane to take on the role of Housekeeper to the Parliament Office when its long-serving incumbent Mary Truscott retired in 1857. But at the same time, while grander in title and notionally wider in its scope, Jane's own post was in reality becoming narrower and more domestic in its powers. Although she was still keeper of the keys, responsible for the Lords when the House was not sitting, she had lost most of her former security duties, including organising and supervising visitors, which were now the preserve of the Doorkeepers and the on-site police. Meanwhile, her authority to supervise repairs and furnishings had passed to Office of Works staff and to other more senior colleagues in the Lords hierarchy. Her new remit in the Parliament Office included ordering candles, soap, brooms and pails for official use – but even such mundane requisitions as these had to be signed off by the Clerk of the Parliaments.[19]

THE HOUNDING OF ELIZABETH MOYES

In 1866, William Moyes, long-standing Resident Doorkeeper, died in office. His apartment was needed by his successor and so his wife Elizabeth, a working housemaid and, since 1856, Housekeeper to the Crown Office, moved into the lower storey of the Clerk of the Crown's apartments. The Office of Works unkindly insisted that she hand back her late husband's pre-fire furniture, which she cherished, issuing her with standard replacements.[20] So her supportive colleagues covertly liberated some choice additions from that office's overflowing store. But in December 1872, Elizabeth Moyes suffered a cataclysmic personal reverse when she was suddenly and very publicly declared bankrupt, having neglected to 'pay, secure or compound' her debts – perhaps inherited from her late husband – owed to a moneylender.[21] A stigma of blame, shame, sinfulness and dishonesty attached to bankruptcy in the mid-Victorian era. This was magnified in Elizabeth's case by the public office she held and by the fact that she was a woman: at that time only about one in twenty bankrupts were female.

Elizabeth Moyes's fall from grace prompted a frenzied official reaction. The new Deputy Lord Great Chamberlain, Gilbert Heathcote-Drummond-Willoughby, Lord Aveland – exercising his office in the name of two female relatives, its hereditary incumbents – demanded her immediate resignation and her departure from her quarters. In this, Aveland was aided and abetted by Elizabeth's successor-to-be, Ellen Lovegrove, and her sanctimonious and controlling husband, James. James Lovegrove was fast-tracked into the clerkship in Aveland's office, the award to his wife in the Crown Office evidently being a further reward for his loyalty. On Ellen's behalf, James Lovegrove repeatedly insisted that Mrs Moyes's former rooms, in a 'very dirty state', should be thoroughly cleansed, while the Office of Works aggressively pursued her publicly owned furniture and fittings right down to the last slop pail and candle.

Only the Select Committee showed a modicum of compassion, deeming it 'right' for Mrs Moyes to receive a gratuity payment of £25. But in June 1873, on Aveland's orders, Elizabeth was cast out of the House of Lords, her home for almost half a century. Within a few years she was dead.[22]

A CAMPAIGN AGAINST JANE JULIA

By the mid-1870s, Lord Aveland, the Office of Works and the Civil Service Commission (among other players) were all jostling for power and patronage in the Palace of Westminster in the name of reforms and efficiency savings. In March 1876, complaints that the Lords chamber was in a filthy state brought the shortcomings of Mrs Bennett's team into sharp focus. Jane hastily recruited some new women Dusters, but they were immediately ousted from their cleaning-up operations by a rival team of men brought in by the Office of Works – a blatant breach of the Housekeeper's custodial powers and duties in the House. But for Jane, far worse was to follow: Aveland had conducted an efficiency review which now recommended that she should be replaced by a male Resident Superintendent.

In July 1876, the Select Committee accepted Aveland's findings and agreed the roles and salaries for his future regime. The new man, on £300 a year, was to take over Jane's duties, including custody of the House. The Housekeeper, female and on £200, was to report to him, along with all the other staff: housemaids to clean and light fires and coal porters to do the heavy work. The Housekeeper would merely supervise the day-to-day work of the cleaners. How Jane would fit into this new order remained for now unresolved. Lord Aveland soon brought in James Scott – another loyalist who was probably a family butler – as his first Resident Superintendent. This was done against the advice of the Civil Service Commissioners, for Scott did not possess 'the requisite knowledge and ability for the proper discharge of his official duties'. Aveland pressured them into accepting Scott.

Arriving in the Lords in August 1876, Scott zealously investigated his new empire. In February 1877, he reported to the Select Committee with an almost indecent relish that 'the Housekeeper, appointed in 1847, is through old age (65) and infirmity, unable to discharge the numerous duties which devolve upon her' – and that only one of the ten housemaids was doing her job in person, all the rest employing deputies. This was in part because 'from old age several are incompetent to discharge their duties', but also as most of them were 'from their social position unsuited for housemaids' work'. The Select Committee took note and agreed to pay off the oldest housemaids, including Mary Anne Mullencamp, heroine of the 1834 fire, still on the books at the age of 86. She was awarded £24 18s 8d. Scott was now able to recruit his own cleaning team.[23]

On top of the death of her ally Sir Augustus Clifford, Black Rod, in February 1877, these criticisms and setbacks clearly proved too much for Jane. Weakened by a bout of bronchitis, in May 1877 she asked to retire, giving her reason as serious ill health. The Select Committee, 'having regard to the efficient manner in which Mrs Bennett has discharged her duties', awarded her a generous pension of £270 a year, matching her salary on retirement.[24]

On 19 July 1877, the doughty Jane Julia Bennett finally handed in her keys to the House of Lords and left her apartment, fifty years after her first warrant of appointment. Her retirement had a domino effect on the other surviving housekeeper posts serving the House of Lords: within a few years, her successor, Ellen Lovegrove, would be the only one left – with her autonomy further diminished.

WOMEN WORKERS IN THE OFFICIAL RESIDENCES

Yet the 1871 and 1881 census returns paint a contrasting picture in which several other women were filling significant – and in some cases prestigious – managerial posts within the new Palace. These roles were located in eight official grace-and-favour residences for the senior staff of the Lords and Commons, along with the palatial Speaker's House. Most of those apartments served as the town houses for their grand occupants, who also maintained large family homes in the country. There were also a dozen or so much smaller dwellings for more lowly live-in workers and their households, which were their sole residences. In their high-Victorian heyday, the official apartments, great and small, collectively occupied no less than a quarter of the new Palace's 8-acre site.

About half of the senior female managers in the grander residences were housekeepers, and the other half were cooks – although the two roles often overlapped, and the terms could be used interchangeably. As an occupant of one of the official residences, Mrs Bennett herself kept a cook, as did Mrs Lovegrove in her turn. Many other servants, predominantly female, were also present in the largest of these establishments – from governesses to ladies' maids, as well as the ubiquitous housemaids. All this made for a sizeable and very visible community of residents, with an extremely high proportion of women.

The most prestigious of the official apartments in the House of Lords, with eighteen rooms spread across seven floors on the southern riverfront of the new Palace, was in 1871 occupied by Jane's ally, Admiral Sir Augustus Clifford. Black Rod since 1832, by this time he was a widower aged 82. Living there too were two of his sons, both holding important posts – William, a rear admiral, and Charles, Tory MP for Newport, Isle of Wight – and two unmarried daughters. Clifford kept twelve servants, eight of them female, headed by a cook and a butler. Yet for all the grandeur of this residence, conditions for family and servants alike were clearly most unpleasant. As Sir Augustus publicly complained in 1867, 'Nothing can be worse than the interior arrangement. The passages are dark and gloomy, and there is scarcely a day when the rooms are not full of smoke and soot, damaging and destroying the public furniture and the property contained within them.'[25] The cause was Charles Barry's defective – and almost unrepairable – heating and ventilation system.

A decade later, in 1881, Black Rod's house was occupied by Clifford's successor, General Sir William Knollys, another elderly widower, with his family and eleven servants: nine female and two male. Overseen by his cook and his butler, this household included no fewer than three 'sick nurses' for Knollys, who was seriously unwell. At the north end of the Palace, the famed proceduralist Sir Thomas Erskine May, Clerk of the House of Commons, was also at his splendid official residence, with his wife, his elderly mother-in-law, a niece, his cook-housekeeper, butler and five more servants, four of them female. Erskine May's deputy, Clerk Assistant Reginald Palgrave, was likewise in his apartment nearby along with five servants, his wife and his family – all women. In their numbers of servants and gender balance, these establishments were broadly characteristic of the town houses of elite families in late-Victorian London. So too was the physical and social separation of the families and their servants, which was far more pronounced than fifty years earlier and was reinforced and perpetuated by the segregated layout of these grand homes.[26]

The amount and quality of official accommodation available to the Palace's lower functionaries was very different from that of the grandees. But theirs were family homes too. In the rooms occupied by James Riddel, Office Keeper of the House of Commons, were in 1881 his wife, his three daughters – two working as elementary teachers and one still at school – and his two sons – one a railway clerk and the other an engine fitter. And Mrs Bennett's nemesis, James Scott, Resident Superintendent of the House of Lords, had with him his wife, his three young daughters (all schoolchildren) and a servant. So despite the focus of the 'Westminster Village' on supporting the work of Parliament, many of the Palace's residents, women and men alike, went out into the world outside its boundaries each day to earn a living or to be educated – doubtless injecting a welcome dose of reality into this cloistered world.

THE LAST YEARS OF JANE JULIA BENNETT

In 1871, during her final years as Housekeeper, Jane Julia Bennett's household was modest: a cook and two female servants. But, fortuitously, living with her also was a new generation of the wider Wright clan: her nieces Elizabeth Wright and Jane Julia Wood (née Wright), together with the younger Jane's husband, Charles Wood, who worked outside the Palace as a clerk, and the couple's infant son, Charles Bennett Wood. On Mrs Bennett's retirement in 1877, the Woods decamped to Chigwell, Essex, where Charles set himself up as a successful and prosperous coal merchant. With them went Jane Julia Bennett who, having recovered her health, lived on with the Wood family in comfortable retirement until her death in 1893, by then in her early eighties.

For over half a century, Jane Julia Bennett had been the most senior – and in her last decade the only – woman to hold a top post, not just in the Lords but in either of the two Houses. The last female manager in the Commons, Sarah Smith, the Deputy Housekeeper, had departed back in 1741.[27] After Jane Julia left the Lords there were no senior women officials in Parliament at all until May Court became Accountant in the 1920s.

The circumstances of Jane Julia's appointment as a child in 1822 and of her rather ignominious departure in 1877 undoubtedly look corrupt when measured against today's codes of standards in public life. Yet she operated in the conditions of her day and faced enormous challenges from her working environment which – despite some slow and limited progress with reforms – was ever more hostile to the notion of females holding administrative responsibilities. She deserves to be remembered and celebrated for her considerable achievements as a woman in charge in an age of men.

In Her Own Words

'In the fitting up of the kitchen it would be desirable there should be two stoves for the Clerks that Members may not be kept waiting 'till others are served.

'A fireplace for a gridiron to dress chops or steaks for Members who may require them.'

'Jane' (Elizabeth Burton), Chief Cook at Bellamy's kitchen, advising Thomas Greene MP, Chief Commissioner for completing the new Palace of Westminster, on kitchen design, 1848

4

CATERING FOR THE MEMBERS: JANE, GODDESS OF BELLAMY'S

In 1835, Charles Dickens, at that time a lobby correspondent in Parliament and writing as 'Boz', cast his satirical eye over Bellamy's kitchen and two of its waiting staff, Nicholas and 'Jane'. Nicholas, a 'steady honest-looking old fellow in black', was the butler. Displaying 'impenetrable calmness', he had since time immemorial been responsible for dispensing fast and simple meals of steak, salad and cheese to hungry MPs, washed down with copious supplies of wine and beer.

But 'as great a character as Nicholas in her way' was 'Jane', a gleefully flirtatious waitress dressed all in black. Not without irony, Dickens dubbed her the 'Hebe of Bellamy's': in Greek mythology, this deity, beautiful daughter of Zeus and the goddess of eternal youth, acted as cupbearer to the gods. 'Her leading features,' Dickens continued, 'are a thorough contempt for the great majority of her visitors, her predominant quality, love of admiration. Jane is no bad hand at repartees and showers them about with a degree of liberality and a total absence of reserve or constraint which occasionally excites no small amazement in the minds of strangers.' It was later patronisingly said that her famed wit 'was an affair of memory, and got by a sort of knack, from her recollection of the *mots* and repartees of the many distinguished, and with her always good-humoured, diners'. This judgement seems to underestimate her abilities and independent spirit. But for all her irreverent behaviour, 'Jane' showed the greatest respect for Nicholas, whom she would eventually succeed as the manager of Bellamy's kitchen.[1]

'Jane' was one of Parliament's greatest characters of the nineteenth century. Her doings were often recounted by the press and her removal in 1851, after many years of loyal – if insubordinate – service, was greeted with dismay by many of her customers. But although she was cast aside as an impediment to the fine dining to which the Commons Kitchen Committee aspired, her legend has lived on. Nicholas – Keynes – was the real name of Bellamy's butler. But, as was widely recognised at the time, 'Jane' used a pseudonym, and her true identity has long been a puzzle. So what can be discovered about her life and career – and the celebrated emporium where she served the Members?

JOHN BELLAMY AND HIS WAITING STAFF

Nicholas and 'Jane' had the good fortune to work for the Bellamys, who were efficient and well organised – and who looked after their staff with assiduous care. The younger John Bellamy had succeeded his father, John, as Deputy Housekeeper to the Commons in 1811, holding the post jointly with his wife, Susan Maria, until her death in 1832. His annual profits of around £640 a year came from a well-run official portfolio of allowances and gratuities, and he drew also from the Treasury a grant of £310 for employing several servants, including male and female cleaners and the waiting staff in his eponymous catering outlet. In 1836, he would be moved on to a fixed salary of £500 for his job of Deputy Housekeeper, with a further allowance of £300 to pay for his servants. These people were, he told a Select Committee in 1833, kept on for the whole year rather than just during the sitting times of the House, for 'they are so valuable to me, that I do not part with them'.[2]

Bellamy's catering establishment consisted of a dining room, kitchen and refreshment room, a scullery and a lobby, all located next door to the prison rooms high up in the Stone Building to the west of the House of Commons. Although his main residence was in Clapham, there were also bedrooms for him and his family next to those for their parliamentary servants in the garrets above Bellamy's kitchens – and cellars for coals, food and drink far below. Much of that space was occupied by the fine wines which he supplied to the Commons as a separate and lucrative enterprise.

John Bellamy kept meticulous records, one of which – a register which was evidently snatched from the 1834 fire as it bears scorch marks on its pages – enables us to track his waiting staff by name over two decades. One constant presence is Nicholas Keynes, butler and catering manager, who had started back in 1801 and would serve until about 1849. Another is 'Jane': Elizabeth Favill, later Burton, baptised at the church of St Nicholas, Lincoln, in 1795 and recruited as Bellamy's resident chief cook in 1817, a role that she would occupy until 1851. In 1834 her salary was £28 a year. After the closure of Bellamy's in 1851, Elizabeth Burton would live out her days in the Westminster area and died in 1862. Her use of a pseudonym, in her case 'Jane', was not unique; in the 1820s at least two other members of the Bellamy's team also had nicknames. It is not known whether these were intended to conceal their real identities from the customers – or were simply a manifestation of the social culture of this celebrated institution.

There is plausible evidence that for all her lively and powerful public persona, Elizabeth Favill led a troubled personal life. In a codicil to his will dated 1837, John Bellamy singled her out under this name for her 'long and faithful service' and left her an annuity of £20. He stipulated that this was 'not to be subject to the debts, control or engagements of any husband she may now have or happen to have hereafter, and for which her receipt alone shall be a sufficient discharge'. This very pointed comment is most likely to relate to Elizabeth's husband since 1820, Samuel Burton. First employed as a waiter at Bellamy's in 1819, he had departed the fold in 1829 – but had evidently waged an aggressive pursuit of his wife's wages ever since, as he was entitled to do by law: a married woman's property and earnings belonged to her husband. This scenario would also explain why John Bellamy, who was clearly very protective of Elizabeth, declined in his accounts to recognise her married surname until after her husband's – probably unlamented – death in 1839.[3]

Bellamy's female waiting staff had already attained legendary status by the mid-1820s. In 1825, a lobby correspondent wrote lasciviously of 'Anne' and 'Jane': 'plump and sleek and clean', they were dishing up steaks 'better than those dispensed by the Houris in paradise, so hot and accurately dressed', along with 'port and sherry and Madeira, so exactly *bodied* for an Englishman's palate'. In 1829, another journalist more prosaically conjured up 'two smart girls, whose briskness and neat attire made up for their want of beauty and for the invasions of time', nonchalantly serving tea to MPs in the corridor outside the dining room. 'They would occasionally turn with petulance, in which they asserted the superiority of their sex to [the men of] rank and opulence with which they were surrounded.'

But while the cooks and waitresses played up to and flirted with the MPs who were rich and famous, all the catering staff showed a marked lack of respect for those who were more impoverished, and especially those from Ireland.[4] This prejudice must have been stoked by the gratuitous slaying of their pet cat by one Irish MP, probably Captain Standish O'Grady, with a kitchen knife, in 1825. One of the waitresses had borne away 'her murdered favourite, watered with the tears that bespoke all that her pity felt, and the loathing hatred which her humble station forbade her to express in louder terms'.[5]

In 1834, Elizabeth Favill ('Jane') had lodgings on site in Bellamy's attics along with five other servants: Nicholas Keynes, Elizabeth Haines, Elizabeth Shaw, Anne Coulthurst and waiter Stuart Ferrin. Bellamy's apartment and possessions would be destroyed in the fire, but apart from losing their uniforms, all of these resident kitchen staff escaped unscathed. So too did Bellamy himself – along with the seventeen cats which lived in his cellars. On being rescued after the flames had died down, these animals 'came purring about him with more than usual docility'.[6]

BELLAMY'S ON THE MOVE

What then became of the cats – or indeed the fine wines in the cellars – is not known, although the latter were insured. But within little more than a week of the fire, enterprising John Bellamy had secured a house in Parliament Street as his headquarters and had requisitioned official furniture for himself and his servants. By the end of December, he was organising the fit-out of some rooms in the Palace for his catering operations. Not far from their previous location, they were above the southern end of the Law Courts, looking out on to St Margaret's Church. With space only for a dining room, kitchen and small bar, they were less capacious than before, although Bellamy's resident servants could once more be accommodated in the garrets above.

In February 1835, the two Houses resumed their sittings in their temporary chambers, and Bellamy's was soon doing a roaring trade again. As Dickens tells us in his famous article about it, this emporium, with Nicholas and 'Jane' singled out for special mention, was serving Members of both Houses and lobby journalists as well as 'strangers', as visitors were known. It could, though, only be accessed from the temporary House of Commons via a steep staircase, prompting many complaints about its inaccessibility.

Consequently, in 1838 it was again relocated, this time to more convenient temporary buildings constructed on top of the medieval chapel of St Mary Undercroft, in the place where the old House of Commons had formerly stood. Bellamy's kitchen staff were cooking their steaks and pies on the very same spot where just four years earlier, Charles Manners Sutton had presided in the Speaker's chair (Figure 2). Meanwhile, in 1837 the Lords had set up its own dining rooms, which it had to shoehorn into its temporary buildings.

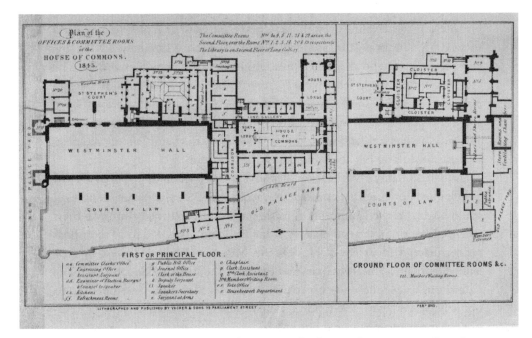

Figure 2: Pocket plan of the House of Commons for the use of MPs, 1843. Bellamy's is at top centre, principal floor level, with the temporary House of Commons nearby.

For the next six years, Bellamy's continued with its old menus, practices and traditions, while the new Palace began to rise up around it. Although John Bellamy considered its temporary sheds to be unsatisfactory, this time because of 'the want of warmth and proper ventilation', these unfavourable conditions did not deter the customers. Radical reformer William Cobbett MP was among others in criticising the malign influence of 'Bellamy's boozing-ken' on the conduct of political business.[7] To keep the service going, Nicholas, Elizabeth Favill/Burton ('Jane') and Anne Coulthurst continued to reside on site, with others – such as waitress Anne Davis, recorded there in 1841 – joining them on a more temporary basis. Other Commons staff living in the Palace were William Ellis, a male servant but later Office Keeper, with his wife and their teenage daughter – together with a watchman and two other male servants. Just like their Lords colleagues nearby, they had no escape from the vast, noisy and, at times, dangerous building site that surrounded them.

The retirement of John Bellamy in 1842 was seen as the end of an era, the press declaring that to eat a beefsteak at Bellamy's had long been a crowning achievement for any man. Although awarded a generous pension – which he would enjoy until his death in 1847 – Bellamy was very disappointed that his role was to be split. Sir William Gosset, Serjeant at Arms, had decided to award the plum post of Deputy Housekeeper to Wilbraham Taylor, his new son-in-law, who also held a prestigious role at Buckingham Palace. The refreshment rooms at least were to stay in the family, for John Bellamy's pleasant but rather ineffectual son Edmund, Assistant Housekeeper since 1827, was permitted to take over his father's allowance of £300 for cleaning and catering services; and he continued to employ the family's long-standing servants, including Nicholas and 'Jane', for these duties.

In 1844, Bellamy's was back on the move again: its temporary sheds needed to be pulled down so that construction work on St Stephen's Porch and Hall could begin. So the Commons' refreshment rooms returned almost to their pre-fire location in the patched-up Stone Building. This was to be their final resting place. Still an irresistible draw for MPs in a hurry, they were by now lauded by their admirers as 'part and parcel of the British Constitution'. The Commons was reputed to ensure that its dullest Members were lined up to opine between 7 p.m. and 8 p.m., 'when Bellamy's kitchen has more attractions than the most eloquent orator'.

Nicholas Keynes was by now far less in evidence and 'Jane' was running the show. It fell to her also to deliver meals to inmates in the prison room nearby, incarcerated – albeit in gentlemanly conditions – because they had fallen foul of the House of Commons. Her taunting put-downs of captive nationalist Irish MP William Smith O'Brien, who in 1846 resolutely refused most of her gastronomic delights on offer, were widely reported. 'What a pity it is, Sir,' she sarcastically observed, 'that a gentleman like you, Sir, should be shut up here when, if you pleased, you might be at liberty in a moment, Sir.'[8] 'Jane' was quite right; all that O'Brien had to do to regain his freedom was agree to serve on a Committee scrutinising a Railway Bill. As this was unconnected with his personal interests, he had strenuously objected on principle, incurring the wrath of the House and his own imprisonment.

THE BATTLE OF THE GRIDIRON

But an existential threat was hanging over Bellamy's. In 1848, the House of Commons set up a Select Committee, at first under the leadership of Augustus Stafford MP, to oversee its catering facilities. This developed into the standing 'Kitchen Committee'. Its membership would change over the decades, but its goals remained constant if perpetually unfulfilled: to create an unrivalled dining experience for MPs which would match the very best that the London clubs had to offer. Edmund Bellamy was soon hauled up for a grilling on the perceived deficiencies of his catering facilities and shocked the Committee by confessing that 'I never was in a Club in my life'.

The Kitchen Committee cast envious eyes across to the House of Lords, where the new Steward William Nichols – imported from clubland at the behest of the Earl of Devon – was planning his services for the lavish new peers' dining room, which was to be equipped with all the most modern cooking facilities. They summoned Nichols and sent him to inspect Bellamy's, which he duly pronounced 'the most inconvenient kitchen I ever saw' – although he suggested minor changes such as bringing in new stoves and replacing the door between the kitchen and the dining room with a hatch. These might, he suggested, allow the menus to be widened somewhat to include soup and fish, pending the completion of the Commons' new kitchens and dining rooms.

Hard-pressed by the Committee, Edmund Bellamy was adamant that his arrangements – and especially the gridiron for cooking meat – were essential for producing the kind of fast meals that Members had wanted ever since the days of his grandfather, particularly given that demand was highly unpredictable. Complaints about services were, he said, very rare and he expressed great pride in his loyal staff of eight women and four men, including Nicholas Keynes and Elizabeth Burton. Most of them had, he said, served his family for many decades and he listed them to the Committee by their names and dates of recruitment. There was, he continued, no capacity or space to extend his menus to include soup and fish: they had in recent times tried bringing back pork chops but that had lasted less than a week.[9]

The Kitchen Committee had no truck with any of this, instead enthusiastically adopting his rival Nichols's reforming recommendations. 'Jane' was clearly thoroughly indignant at Edmund Bellamy's treatment by these Members. She now took the battle for the soul of Bellamy's up to Thomas Greene MP, Chief Commissioner for completing the new Palace of Westminster, whom she knew in person. In June 1848, Edmund Bellamy wrote to Greene: 'At the request of my cook Elizabeth Burton, I beg to hand you a statement of what she considers to be the best for the kitchens in the New Houses of Parliament.' 'Jane' recommended that there should be a single kitchen so that all the work might be done under the eye of 'one responsible person', along with a room for a laundry and for roasting and chopping vegetables. In the kitchen 'it would be desirable there should be two stoves for the Clerks that Members may not be kept waiting 'till others are served'. And – unsurprisingly – vital to the whole operation was 'a fire-place like that now in use, for a gridiron to dress chops and steaks for Members and others who may require them'.[10]

This sensible advice was entirely ignored by Greene and by Charles Barry, the architect of the new Palace. One of the most admired features of Barry's magisterial Reform Club in Pall Mall, built between 1838 and 1841, was the lavish kitchens which he had designed in conjunction with celebrity chef Alexis Soyer. The experience he had gained there had fed into his evolving schemes for the catering facilities at Westminster – and he had already worked with William Nichols to equip the House of Lords' refreshment rooms to the highest possible specifications.

THE LAST DAYS OF BELLAMY'S

The Kitchen Committee now decided to 'rule the roast' itself. The quashing of the Deputy Housekeeper post in 1848 and the sudden death of Edmund Bellamy in 1849 gave its Members a golden opportunity to make changes. They rapidly brought in George Woodhouse, lately steward to the Duke of Beaufort, as Bellamy's replacement. Immediately dispatched to work with Barry on the new Commons kitchen fittings, he soon ordered, among other costly items, 'broiling stoves and hotplates with fuel chambers beneath the same, fitted up in a precisely similar manner to those in the kitchen of the peers' refreshment rooms'.[11]

Meanwhile, the Committee insisted that Woodhouse should introduce soup and fish to the range of dishes on offer at Bellamy's, and 'hauled the cooks over the coals so much that now an MP, or a stranger friend of one, may have a dinner as at a Club, and at much the same prices'. Or that at least was the plan, for Woodhouse 'did not give satisfaction to the Members dining'. His attempts to transform the services seem most unlikely to have commanded the wholehearted support of 'Jane' – especially after her dressing down by the Kitchen Committee. She had at last succeeded Nicholas Keynes after his retirement in about 1849 and appears in triumph in the 1851 census as Elizabeth Burton, resident Housekeeper of the refreshment rooms, House of Commons. From this position she was well able to sabotage her manager's schemes.

For while Woodhouse strove to deliver a fine-dining experience from the inadequate facilities, in Bellamy's kitchen next door things were continuing much as they always had. In this small, plain and 'broiling hot' apartment with 'an immense fire, meat screens, gridirons and a small tub for washing glasses', 'Jane' famously presided, assisted by 'two very unpretending old women' and serving up little other than beer, chops and steaks. Those many Members who shunned the formal delights of the dining room or the tea room preferred by far this 'freer and easier kitchen where they saw or took the strangers they wanted to talk to, and where they enjoyed the sight of the cooking of the meat, afterwards put before them'.

But MPs and journalists alike were all too aware that Bellamy's days were numbered. It might have been 'a corner of the constitution' but it was by now a relic of a bygone age which had to be consigned to oblivion 'along with rotten boroughs and other congenial props of the British institutions'. Its rooms were also urgently needed by the Law Courts next door. And so it was that, when Parliament rose in August 1851, Bellamy's was unceremoniously closed down. On 12 September, its fixtures and fittings were auctioned off, 'Jane's' kitchen range fetching £7 15s amidst noisy jests from crowds of spectators about her former emporium's famous chops.[12]

A new era for parliamentary catering began in February 1852 when Barry's Commons chamber was finally opened, along with the dining rooms, tea rooms and bars for both Houses. In this parallel universe of deferential staff, over-specified and costly equipment and wider menus there was no place for the goddesses of Bellamy's. They now passed into history, although for the next few years rumours circulated that 'Jane' was 'still, we hear, to be seen about the new Houses; no longer a Hebe, but fat and forty; yet still sure of kindly nods from the old members when she happens to meet them'.[13]

The new services were immediately overwhelmed by high levels of demand, many MPs expressing nostalgic regrets for the delicious steaks served up with such brio by 'Jane' and her team. But in its undeviating efforts to make the House of Commons the best club in the world, the Committee of 'political gastronomers' pressed on regardless with its schemes for fine dining. The revelation in 1867 that the beleaguered cooks were adopting the dangerous practice of lighting fires on top of the high-end hotplates instead of underneath them hints at the extreme levels of stress in the Commons' kitchens from sudden spikes in demand.

Catering managers came and went in rapid succession – from 1868 to 1875 the two Refreshment departments were even united under a single Superintendent from the Lords, Frederick Nicholls. Eventually, in 1884, exasperated by the seemingly endless deluge of complaints about the slow service, the Kitchen Committee would bring back not just one grill but two to serve the main Commons dining room – more than thirty long years after the demise of Bellamy's.

VICTORIAN VALUES: CHARLOTTE AND WILLIAM BLADON

Over in the Lords, the opening of the new refreshment rooms in 1852 had signalled a new era of dignity and grandeur. The *Illustrated London News* enthused that they were 'the most luxurious apartments imaginable: the beautiful ceilings, the richly carved doors, screens and panelling, the crimson and green paper-hangings, being extremely striking and harmonious in their *tout ensemble*'.[14] But behind the scenes the challenges were just the same as in the Commons – as was the barely adequate allowance of £300 to employ catering staff. And for Charlotte Bladon, who was soon to be inhabiting this claustrophobic world, events would take a dark turn.

When in 1854 Black Rod, Sir Augustus Clifford, acquired the right to appoint a new superintendent of the refreshment rooms in succession to William Nichols, he turned not to clubland but to someone he knew well: William Bladon, born in 1813 and now his house servant. Soon after his appointment to the Lords in September 1855, Bladon married Jane Charlotte Petitt, known as Charlotte, born in 1823 in Lausanne, Switzerland, and a lady's maid to Clifford's wife. The ceremony took place in November 1853 at St George's, Hanover Square, close to Black Rod's residence. The Bladons soon moved into William's official accommodation in the House of Lords, adjoining the peers' coffee room on the principal floor, where they would live for the next fifteen years. Here Charlotte gave birth to four of the Bladons' five children; sadly, two died here as well. She was also expected to help out in the refreshment rooms and, at times when her husband was unwell, she ran the whole operation on his behalf.

The family's accommodation – in 1859 three bedrooms and a sitting room on the principal floor and a further bedroom for the servants below – was thoroughly inadequate. In 1861, William and Charlotte were living there not just with their two young daughters and a son, but also the five female and two male servants who were attached to the refreshment rooms. Yet William's many complaints to the Lord Great Chamberlain, Lord Willoughby de Eresby, failed to gain them even the small and dark storage room next door to their cramped quarters. This overcrowding can only have compounded Charlotte's extreme marital difficulties, which must have been played out in full view of her family and the servants. For, as she later alleged, ever since the start of their marriage William had treated her 'with great unkindness and cruelty. He frequently in violent and offensive language abused her, and violently assaulted her.'

Bladon's skills were evidently unequal to the very considerable challenges of running the Lords' refreshment rooms. And he was showing increasing signs of money troubles: the Office of Works strongly suspected him of dishonestly using his official facilities for private gain but was never able to build a robust case against him.[15] In May 1868, Bladon related his numerous logistical and cashflow problems to the Select Committee on the Parliament Office and the Office of Black Rod: the great variations in the sitting times of the House; the ever-increasing costs of food and other consumables; and the very high levels of wastage which he had to write off. He asked for an increase in his allowance from £300 to match the new Commons equivalent at £500. Instead, in July 1868 the Committee dismissed him from his post, agreeing to compensate him with a pay-off of £300.

William was now appointed as a Senior Porter to the House of Lords and the family relocated to John Street, Westminster. By April 1871, the Bladons had separated and Charlotte and their three surviving children, Bella, Elizabeth and Margaret, were living in Dover, but William soon 'ceased to supply her with necessities and the means to obtain them'. After her return to John Street, in November 1871 William subjected Charlotte to a severe assault and cast her out. Now desperate, in September 1872 Charlotte petitioned the divorce court for a judicial separation from William on the grounds of domestic violence and desertion. To obtain a divorce she would have needed to prove adultery as well as aggravating factors, but a legally binding separation could at least have given her the maintenance payments that she so badly needed.[16]

William denied these charges and the presiding judge took his word for it, dismissing Charlotte's petition in April 1873. Despite the reforms to the divorce system arising from the Divorce and Matrimonial Causes Act 1857, the odds were still heavily stacked against women. In the early 1870s, an average of 180 divorces were granted each year, under half of them to wives. Only about 100 petitions for legal separation were brought each year, all by women, and more than two-thirds of those were dismissed, as was Charlotte's.[17]

Having fallen on hard times, in 1874–75 Charlotte begged two powerful peers whom she knew from her work in the Lords – the Lord Chamberlain Viscount Sydney and the Duke of Portland – for financial help and assistance in finding her a job. She wrote to Sydney in halting English of her 'distressed position. I am suffering with all deprivation.'[18] Probably through her own efforts, the unfortunate Charlotte did obtain some employment – but eventually, in February 1893 she was consigned to the Greenwich workhouse and then to the London County Lunatic Asylum in Banstead, Surrey, where in July 1893 she died of chronic brain disease and pneumonia.

William, who by 1880 had moved with the couple's three daughters to Millbank Street, had, meanwhile, also been experiencing long-term financial difficulties. In 1882, he was severely reprimanded for taking money for showing visitors round the House of Lords – a major breach of the rules.[19] He died in 1891 and was buried in the Brompton Cemetery. In August 1893, Charlotte was reunited with him there in the family grave – for all eternity.

MARY FURLONG: FRUIT-SELLING AND FEMALE SUFFRAGE

No sooner had Bellamy's disappeared than alternative providers of quick drinks and snacks began to appear in the heart of the new Palace. A new stand selling duty-free alcoholic beverages popped up in Central Lobby, prompting an angry reaction from local traders whose prices were being undercut. When in May 1852 the Lord Great Chamberlain, Lord Willoughby, attempted to close it he was excoriated by MPs as a 'most impertinent functionary', and he hastily backed down.[20]

Nearby – just as in the days of Jane Caroline Drybutter – a fruit-seller, Mary Furlong, was plying her trade. She ran a small but well-established business as a fruit vendor in the Westminster area, working in St Stephen's Hall, Westminster Hall and New Palace Yard with varying degrees of official support, at times calling on Members to support her applications for licences. She was not the only such stallholder in the Palace, but she was the most persistent by far. The second wife (and from 1866 widow) of Patrick Furlong, a watchman in Parliament – one of the men who caused the 1834 fire by overloading the furnaces with tally sticks – Mary also holds a special place in the history of female suffrage.

In 1866, the very first mass suffrage petition, signed by 1,521 women, was presented to the House of Commons by John Stuart Mill, Liberal MP for Westminster. Delivered to Mill in Westminster Hall in person by two of its leading organisers, Emily Davies and Elizabeth Garrett (later Anderson), it proclaimed that 'women are competent, both by law and in fact, to carry on a business, to administer an estate and to fill other positions which ... are usually considered to give a claim to the suffrage'.[21] Davies later recounted how, while waiting for Mill in the Hall, to avoid public outrage over the petition they 'asked an old applewoman to put it behind her stall':[22] she must have been Mary Furlong. This event, which has attained a mythical status, was in 1910 rather fancifully painted by radical artist Bertha Newcombe as marking the dawn of the suffrage movement (Plate 5).

Mary Furlong later emerged from the shadows once more when she inadvertently precipitated a titanic clash over precedence between Lord Aveland, Deputy Lord Great Chamberlain, and Charles Gore, the long-standing Keeper of the old and new Palaces at Westminster. Gore had the right to issue warrants for vendors to trade in Westminster Hall, and in July 1872, clearly frustrated by being repeatedly blocked by him from this prime site, Mary went right over his head and approached Prime Minister William Ewart Gladstone directly. Gladstone's office mistakenly forwarded her letter on to Aveland, who rapidly issued her with a warrant. Delighted, Mrs Furlong wrote to Aveland, 'I humbly venture to tender you my most sincere thanks and earnest gratitude for the kind licence you have given me to pursue my vocation in Westminster Hall during the prorogation of the Houses of Parliament.'

Enraged to discover that Aveland had challenged his powers in this way, Gore insisted that the warrant to Mrs Furlong be rescinded and, when Aveland refused, conducted extremely detailed searches in the public records going right back to the Middle Ages in order to prove his rights. In the face of this antiquarian onslaught, one of Aveland's officials still expressed the hope 'that the poor old woman will be allowed to remain, as at present'. But in March 1873, Aveland decided to concede Gore's privileges except on all solemn occasions such as coronations – and withdrew Mrs Furlong's licence.[23]

Fortunately, Mary Furlong did not go out of business as a result: in 1881 she was still trading as a 'fruit hawker'. And after her death in 1885, the Furlong family maintained its links with Parliament. Family folklore relates that Patrick's daughter-in-law Emma Furlong, a charwoman working in a dining room in 1901, 'sold pies to MPs' in the House of Commons.[24] This brings our tale of catering for the Members in a full circle, from Bellamy's 'Jane' dispensing her famous pies and chops, to the intrepid food vendors of the Furlong family.

About Elizabeth Gully

'Speaker Gully could have chosen no more suitable life companion. She was a lady whose extraordinary charm of manner, sweetness of temper and simplicity of character made her an important factor in the fortunes of her husband.'

Obituary of Elizabeth Gully in the *Daily Telegraph*, 1906

5

THE ADMIRABLE MRS GULLY
AND HER GALLERY

On 8 April 1895, watched by his wife and daughters from the Ladies' Gallery, William Court Gully was elected as Speaker of the House of Commons, a post in which he would serve for the next decade with dignified and inoffensive competence. But:

> Successful as was the tenure of the Chair of the House of Commons by William Court Gully, it would not have been possible but for the splendid qualities of mind and heart of Mrs Gully. A woman of a quite unusual ability and of an inbred tact and sympathy, she filled the great place of Speaker's wife with a beautiful grace. On occasions of ceremony, she played her part by her husband's side regally, and with her knowledge of affairs and of the men and women of the day, she made a splendid hostess.

As remembered later, at the time of her death:

> Removed to the Speaker's House at Westminster, Mrs Gully had socially a very important part to play. There was not merely the holding of receptions, which were always extremely pleasant and popular, but there was also the patronage of the Ladies' Gallery, and of Mrs Gully's Gallery, where the wives of statesmen and other *grandes dames* sat. It is a universal experience that Mrs Gully endeared herself to members of Parliament of all parties without distinction.[1]

Not since the days of Ellen Manners Sutton had a Speaker's wife commanded quite such a keen interest from the newspapers – but where Ellen had attracted a great deal of criticism, Elizabeth Gully enjoyed universal acclaim. Previous Speakers' wives had also been women of ability, with similar levers of influence to deploy, and had served with distinction as consorts to their husbands. However, Elizabeth Gully was even more successful in enhancing her husband's reputation, as well as her own, because she assiduously sought – and obtained – excellent press coverage for him. At the start of his Speakership, this was not least to dispel a scandalous secret from his family's past. But after its end, when two of their own children became embroiled in divorces and one in a child abduction, this high-media profile would come back to bite the respectable Gully family.

A HARD ACT TO FOLLOW

Since 1859, when John Evelyn Denison – Speaker from 1857 to 1872 – had moved from his temporary official house in Eaton Square to his impressive residence in the new Palace at Westminster, the Speaker's House had provided a fitting setting for a regular cycle of grand political dinners and parties. These enabled him to meet and maintain contact with Members from across the House and to gather intelligence about the changing political climate. Continuing this tradition, his successors Henry Brand (in office 1872 to 1884) and Arthur Wellesley Peel (1884 to 1895) had encountered increasing resistance from MPs to the stifling formality of their banquets, for which full court dress was required. Their wives, consorts and châtelaines, Elizabeth Brand and Adelaide Peel, sought to counterbalance this social discord by hosting parties for Members' wives and daughters in addition to their grand receptions which followed some of the Speakers' dinners.[2]

When Adelaide Peel suffered an untimely death in 1890, her eldest daughter, Julia Beatrice Peel, then aged 25, took over many of her duties, which she fulfilled with aplomb. Julia was praised by the press as an excellent conversationalist and a hostess who displayed her 'charming and graceful taste' at the Speaker's House. Her younger brother Arthur, also part of the Peel household, served as a Clerk to the Commons.

Then in 1895 came a great surprise: Miss Peel's engagement was announced to James Rochfort Maguire MP. A wealthy imperialist businessman who was a close friend of Cecil Rhodes, his deeply inept and insensitive activities in South Africa would mark him out for parliamentary and public censure. He was also one of a small group of Irish Parnellite MPs who were actively

disrupting the work of the Commons. His impending marriage to Julia
in April 1895 was thought by some to have precipitated the already ailing
Peel's retirement as Speaker. After a grand society wedding at St Margaret's,
Westminster, and a honeymoon at Waddesdon Manor, the couple went on to
become prominent socialites. In 1899–1900, during the South African War,
they were caught up in and survived the Boer army's siege of the diamond-
mining town of Kimberley, where Julia famously ran the soup kitchen.

As a retiring Speaker, in 1895 Arthur Peel was granted a viscountcy and
– as Lord Peel – recovered his health and would serve with distinction in
the House of Lords until his death in 1912. When William and Elizabeth
Gully succeeded them at the Speaker's House, Peel and his family must have
seemed a daunting act to follow, not least as the Gullys had, until that time,
lived quiet and uneventful lives, out of the public eye.

CONSORT TO THE SPEAKER

In 1865, Gully, then an up-and-coming barrister, married Elizabeth Anne
Walford Selby of Oldbury Place, Ightham, Kent. Their union was famously
happy and successful: as well as producing four daughters and two sons,
Elizabeth was a thoroughly supportive wife. She kept home for William in
Liverpool, where he built up a flourishing commercial practice, and then in
London; she cultivated a wide circle of friends; and she campaigned vigor-
ously in his election campaign in Carlisle in 1886. But following his victory,
for almost a decade thereafter William was regarded as a low-key, retiring
MP. His surprise elevation to the Speakership in April 1895 happened only
because he was put forward by his Liberal colleagues at the last moment – as a
safe pair of hands. His win by 285 votes to 274 in the first contested election
for almost six decades was hard fought. In July, the defeated Conservative
and Unionist Party defied convention by standing against him at the general
election in his constituency of Carlisle, but here too he prevailed.

No sooner had he been elected than – like the Peels – two of the Gullys'
adult children rallied round the family cause. William appointed their
younger son Edward as his Private Secretary, and their youngest daughter
Elizabeth, known to all as Shelley (Figure 3), was also roped in to fill the role
recently vacated by Julia Peel. In regular attendance at her mother's entertainments, Shelley also accompanied her parents on official visits in London
and across the country.

Yet establishing the social and political credentials of William Court Gully
required careful orchestration. For during his contested election and first

Figure 3: Miss Shelley Gully, from *Parliament Past and Present*.

days in the Speakership, 'Bravo Gully!' had been shouted out by his opponents in the chamber and appeared in some press reports – snide references
to a very painful episode from his family's past: an accusation of murder, no
less. William's father was celebrity physician James Manby Gully, famed for
his hydrotherapy clinic in Great Malvern, where he had treated many leading
figures of the age, including Charles Darwin, Charles Dickens and Florence
Nightingale. Among his many lesser-known patients was Florence Ricardo,
almost forty years his junior, with whom he had enjoyed a passionate affair
in 1871–72. In 1875, Florence married Charles Bravo, who turned out to be a
brutal fortune-hunter; and when Bravo was found to have died of antimony
poisoning a year later, James Gully was prime suspect. Even after Dr Gully's
death in 1883, the high-profile and sensational Bravo case – unsolved to this
day – continued to haunt his immediate descendants.

Endowed with charm and determination, acute political antennae and a
flair for publicity, Elizabeth soon mounted a charm offensive on her husband's behalf which swept this scandalous scuttlebutt aside. Key to her
success were her events at the Speaker's House. Her first, a lavish reception on 19 June 1895, with 1,000 invitations and 824 acceptances, was
greeted with great enthusiasm in the newspapers. This was not least because
among the guests, drawn from politics and the cream of London society,
were the Chairman and the Honorary Secretary of the Parliamentary Press
Gallery. 'This is,' it was reported with considerable satisfaction, 'the first
time the Press has been recognised in the festive functions that take place in
Mr Speaker's residence.'[3]

Reporters reciprocated the favour, the *Carlisle Journal* proudly judging
it 'one of the most brilliant functions of an unusually gay London season'.
Mrs Gully received 'the most representative and distinguished company
which has been seen in the Speaker's residence for many years'.[4] The following week, a staggering 1,337 people attended Elizabeth's second reception,
and after this she extended regular invitations to her 'at homes' to journalists
working at Westminster and their wives, as well as hosting prestigious visits
to the Speaker's House for female reporters from local newspapers.

From then on unopposed as Speaker, Gully accrued popular praise for
his 'commanding dignity of presence with a sweetly modulated voice and
splendid face – picturesque and useful qualities which count for much in
the Speaker's chair'.[5] For the next decade, he would exercise his office with
low-key authority and competence, upset only by a significant procedural
stand-off with Irish Nationalist MPs in 1901. And thanks to his wife's efforts,
he would continue to bask in the approbation of the press. The Bravo case
soon became a distant memory and within a few years erroneous rumours

began to circulate that William Gully's father had in fact been John Gully, a famous prize fighter and MP.

MRS GULLY ENTERTAINS

For most of her husband's tenure as Speaker Elizabeth continued to stage high-profile receptions and parties, amplifying their glamour, occasion, exclusivity and social cachet, so that 'a card for Mrs Gully's at home is a passport to good society for the MP'.[6] A significant weapon in her social armoury was the Commons riverfront terrace commanding exclusive views of the River Thames, recently opened up to female visitors: the Speaker's section could now be used for her official events during the summer months. Elizabeth's outdoor teas for all MPs' wives – 'a temple of enchantment for the ambitious'[7] – proved particularly popular and counterbalanced the formality of the Speaker's dinners for their husbands. This was not all, for Mrs Gully also hosted high-profile charitable events at the Speaker's House. In 1902, a sparkling fundraiser in aid of the Westminster Hospital, Broad Sanctuary, featured many leading entertainers of the day – not least music hall comedian Dan Leno, suffragist actress Eva Moore and contralto Clara Butt.[8]

All this activity had an impact on the budgets for the Palace. The Heating and Ventilation Department, asked in 1898 to explain the major increase in the Gullys' consumption of gas for cooking, was adamant that this was because 'the present Speaker entertains more frequently and keeps a larger staff than his predecessor'.[9]

In 1895, Elizabeth Gully was reassuringly portrayed as 'a very charming woman who is of the old school temperament, with nothing of the New Woman about her'.[10] A 'New Woman' was an emotive and divisive term coined by novelist Sarah Grand in 1894, to denote one who 'has proclaimed for herself what was wrong with Home-is-the-Woman's-Sphere and prescribed the remedy'.[11] Yet, as the years went by, the quietly progressive tendencies of Mrs Gully began to show through her reassuring public presence. In common with a few MPs, she employed an – anonymous – female Private Secretary (Figure 4), at this time a rare and elite, although often poorly paid, role for an educated woman.[12] And in 1899 she was one of the first prominent ladies to support the London meeting of the International Congress of Women by publicly offering to host delegates to tea on the Commons terrace.[13] This important umbrella organisation brought together suffrage and other women's groups and advocated for female rights on the basis that 'the adult woman is the equal of the adult man'.

Figure 4: Mrs Gully with her female Private Secretary, from *Parliament Past and Present*.

OF THE SPEAKER'S HOUSE, ITS OCCUPANTS AND NEIGHBOURS

In May 1895, a female journalist writing as 'Penelope' was extremely excited to receive an invitation to visit Elizabeth Gully at the Speaker's House. 'Mrs Gully,' she enthused to her readers, 'who is the EMBODIMENT OF GRACIOUS KINDNESS was anxious that all her friends should see the fine old rooms in which she sat.' Shelley, the Speaker's youngest and unmarried daughter, was in attendance, 'radiant as she stood by her mother's side with her first triumphs of social success, in a lovely gown of brocaded satin of a creamy white tint, holding a lovely bouquet in her hands'. Shelley's brother Edward, the new Speaker's Secretary, was 'anxious to show us the old time-honoured portraits of former Speakers, and to guide us through the fine library where they hang in their robes and insignia of office'. At the end of the tour, 'Penelope' was quick to suggest to Elizabeth that 'her husband's handsome face' and 'fine lineaments' should be added to their number without delay.[14]

The Speaker's House, an even more grandiose re-imagining of its pre-fire predecessor, was an immense asset to its occupants. Originally containing more than sixty rooms, larger than most London clubs, its 'style of magnificence is without a rival in any of the palatial residences of which this country can boast'.[15] At principal-floor level were – and still are – the State Rooms, designed for entertainments on a grand scale and richly adorned with the heraldry and portraits of Speakers past that so impressed 'Penelope' and her posse as well as countless other visitors (Plate 6). On the first floor were two ceremonial bedrooms and six family bedrooms plus dressing rooms and bathrooms. On the top floors there were twelve more bedrooms for the servants, with the kitchens and servants' hall, the butler's pantry and the housekeeper's room at ground and basement levels.

Once significant teething troubles with its heating system had been fixed, the Speaker's House was a comfortable family residence, and well used as such. Yet not until the census night of 31 March 1901 is a Speaker – William Gully himself – recorded at the Palace in person. Then, sixteen people were staying there: William and Elizabeth Gully, their son Edward and daughter Elizabeth (Shelley), their housekeeper, a cook and two kitchen maids, one lady's maid, two housemaids, plus no fewer than two butlers, two footmen and a hall boy aged 17.

The Gully family's immediate neighbour in 1901 was grandee Sir Henry David Erskine, Serjeant at Arms from 1885 to 1915, upon whom the Speaker relied to maintain order in the Commons chamber and the galleries. With Erskine in his suitably imposing official residence were his wife, his son the Assistant Serjeant, his daughter and young grandson, along with a cook and seven female servants, a butler and a footman. Another neighbour of the Speaker at the north end of the Palace, Clerk of the House of Commons Archibald J.S. Milman, was away – but his wife and four daughters were present, with their two manservants, their cook and four more female servants. Although Black Rod had by now been ejected from his residence in the Lords as part of a wider austerity drive by the Treasury, the occupancy patterns in the grand official houses at the Commons end of the 'Westminster Village' were unchanged since 1881.

When William Gully first arrived at the Speaker's House in 1895, he was most fortunate to have as his Clerk of the House – and his neighbour in the Palace – Milman's predecessor, Sir Reginald Douce Palgrave. An experienced, respected and sound proceduralist, Palgrave soon established a strong rapport with Gully, who in a speech at the Mansion House warmly praised him as his 'friend and mentor'.[16] But Sir Reginald's greatest passion was history – especially key people, places and events in parliamentary history, which he was on a mission to popularise. He co-opted the Speaker to his cause, and in 1899 Gully delivered a well-publicised lecture to the Carlisle Literary and Scientific Society honouring his predecessor William Lenthall, who had resisted the tyranny of King Charles I. So impressed was his audience that the ever-supportive newspapers opined 'that Speakers might henceforth contribute to the history of Parliament as well as keeping the House in order'.[17]

There is nothing to suggest that Mrs Gully had any great interest in matters antiquarian, but on his side Sir Reginald was aided and abetted in his historical quests by his resident eldest daughter Mary E. Palgrave. She was a prominent and prolific writer of fanciful historical novels and other romantic tales of a moral and improving nature. In 1898, Mary was delighted to discover the memoirs and other papers of Anne Rickman, an old friend of the Palgrave family, who had just died, and with whom she felt a strong personal connection. She and her father selected and published some choice extracts about Anne's early life in the old Palace in popular magazines.[18] Soon after this, in 1899, the year before he retired, Sir Reginald was thrilled to establish that the site once occupied by the Star Chamber in the old Palace – next to where the Rickmans had lived – corresponded almost exactly with the drawing room in his family's official house. Little did he know that within a few years his residence would be surrendered, and that this cherished space would be repurposed as the Prime Minister's office.

On census day, 2 April 1911, Gully's successor, James Lowther, Conservative MP for Penrith, would also be there with his wife and son, and fourteen servants. Eight of these were female and six were male, now including a valet and two footmen. Another decade later, little seemed to have changed at the Speaker's House following the First World War. On 19 June 1921, newly elected Speaker John Henry Whitley, Liberal MP for Halifax, was in occupation with his wife Marguerita and their 26-year-old daughter Margaret Phyllis, known as Phyllis. Whitley soon relaunched the Speaker's parties and events with Mrs Whitley presiding, ably supported by Phyllis – just like Julia Peel and Shelley Gully before her. But in comparison with the pre-war entertainments, these events were scaled back, with 'a dignified simplicity that suggests the custom … of the United States'.[19] And Phyllis, who had worked in a munitions factory during the war, was a director of the family's cotton-spinning company, S. Whitley and Co., in Halifax. The 1921 census also reveals that the Speaker's establishment had now decreased in size to a housekeeper and six further servants, all female – seemingly a reflection of a shortage of male servants in the wake of the war as well as the Whitleys' more modest style of living.

Further ahead still, after the Second World War, Douglas Clifton Brown would relinquish much of the Speaker's House apart from the impressive State Rooms – today still used for official purposes – and a much-reduced private flat.

WOMEN IN THE CAGE

In 1894, pioneering Black American journalist Ida B. Wells, visiting the Westminster parliament from Chicago, was astonished to observe above the Speaker's chair:

> A wire netting which extended to the ceiling. Behind this there were what I took to be gaily dressed wax figures, presumably of historic personages. Imagine my surprise when I was told that was the Ladies' Gallery, and it was only behind this cage that they were allowed to appear at all in the sacred precincts hitherto devoted to men.[20]

The Commons was the only legislative chamber in the world to conceal its women observers behind bars. In the House of Lords nearby, respectable women were very welcome to attend and observe. In their grand chamber there was a large open gallery strictly reserved for peers' wives ('peeresses'). Any men – including visiting dignitaries – straying into this hallowed space were soon spotted and rapidly ejected by the will of the House. Women were also, at times, admitted to the chamber itself, sitting in the area around the throne, in the boxes and at times overflowing on to the red benches which were normally reserved for the peers. Large numbers of ladies adorned set-piece events such as State Openings and admissions of new peers as part of London's social calendar. Even during the day-to-day proceedings of the House, gorgeously attired women often outnumbered the peers by a considerable margin. In 1910, the Lords chamber was declared 'the most popular assembly in the Empire'.[21]

Yet in the Commons, the long-standing convention that women could not be and therefore were not present had survived intact since the days of the Ventilator. In his Commons chamber, Charles Barry provided generous gallery space for male visitors, peers and the press corps in the body of the chamber. But his Ladies' Gallery lay high up above the Speaker's Chair, famously concealed behind an ornate and heavy metal grille inserted in the window apertures across the front. This inevitably prompted comparisons with a harem, a cage or even a reformatory. When the chamber opened in 1852, the gallery was found to be stiflingly hot and an extremely tight fit for the twenty-one ladies in their crinolines who were attempting to perch on the three rows of upright oak chairs. The ornate metalwork so impeded their view of the chamber that they were rumoured to have wrenched it out of shape to create wider openings. But it was soon established as an important and well-attended political space for women, whose loud discussions were

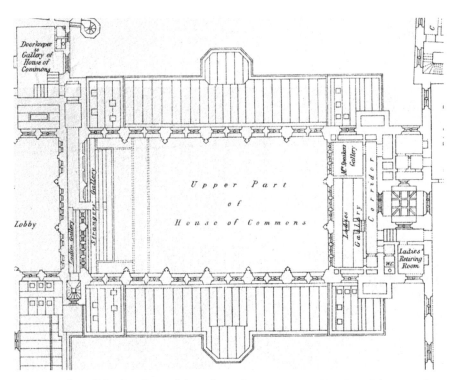

Figure 5: Plan of the first floor of the Palace of Westminster, 1881. Detail showing the main Ladies' Gallery, Mrs Speaker's Gallery next to it, and the Serjeant's Ladies' Gallery at the opposite end.

at times said to drown out the debates from the ears of the press, reporting from their larger and more convenient gallery immediately below.

In the 1860s, the Ladies' Gallery was expanded to accommodate some fifty women, a third of them in the select Speaker's Ladies' Gallery which occupied its eastern portion. The entrance in Commons Court, near the Speaker's House, was guarded by a policeman who checked that the visitors held valid tickets, allocated either by the Speaker's wife or by the Serjeant's team on the instructions of an MP. For popular debates, a ballot was held as places were limited. At the top of a steep staircase, the Ladies' Gallery had its own tea room with uniformed attendants, women's lavatories, cloakrooms and waiting areas, and from 1892 even a hydraulic lift (Figures 5 and 6).

Since the 1860s, many attempts had been made in the House to have the grille removed, invariably defeated by the enduringly defensive and misogynistic views of most MPs. Some of its defenders alleged that the ladies valued the privacy that the screen provided, although if true, that was clearly far from being a majority view. The cage did, though, allow the women to come and go at will, according to the quality of the speeches, and to discuss the

Figure 6: Harry Furniss, *A Corner in the Ladies' Gallery, c.* 1888.

contents. And because of the fiction that they were not present in the part that
lay outside the Speaker's control, they could stay to hear debates on subjects
of a 'delicate character' when all other – male – strangers had been cleared
from the rest of the public galleries. Although invisible in the chamber, the
attendees were regularly listed by name in the press, and from the 1870s female
correspondents began to publish political reports from here. *The Lady*, founded
in 1885, included a regular column, 'from the Ladies' Gallery', humorous in
tone but well informed about the political issues that mattered to women.

More immediately, the caged ladies found ways to make their views
known to the House. In 1868, during a fractious second reading debate on
what was to become the Married Women's Property Act 1870, they rattled

their fans on the grille to signify support for some speakers and audibly hissed at assertions that men should have every right to appropriate and squander their wives' worldly goods.[22] On 5 June 1888, during a debate on a motion to repeal in India the much-hated Contagious Diseases Act – which criminalised women for spreading venereal disease – the ladies 'became greatly excited and so far forgot themselves as to loudly clap their hands'. Speaker Peel sent up a reprimand via the Serjeant, and the ladies apologised.[23] On 1 May 1895, the ladies put up a show of strength in the lobby and the gallery in support of the Parliamentary Franchise (Women) Bill, one clapping so loudly from the cage that she was ejected altogether by the Serjeant – on the orders of Speaker Gully.[24]

Some Members let it be known that the presence of so many demanding women was a major impediment to the business of the House. But for individual MPs their wives could be an enormous support. In 1898, it was said that Liberal grandee Sir William Harcourt, then Leader of the Opposition, 'is very proud of his intelligent wife, and her face is always to be seen in the Ladies' Gallery of the Commons when a great campaign is on'.[25] Noted suffragist campaigner Millicent Fawcett, who served as secretary to her blind husband, MP and political economist Henry Fawcett, endured many uncomfortable hours there observing the proceedings on his behalf, until his death in 1884.

A few MPs' wives or other female observers of particular importance were at times allowed to view the chamber from 'a stand just outside the entrance opposite the Speaker's chair', dubbed the 'Ladies' Nook' or the 'Peephole', from where the visibility was excellent.[26] In 1871, two prominent and respected social campaigners, Josephine Butler and Margaret Pennington, were permitted to witness from here the avid reception in the House of their petition to repeal the Contagious Diseases Acts.[27] And by 1881 up to eight women observers could also be admitted to the small Serjeant's Gallery at the south end of the chamber, high up above the Strangers' Gallery. Like its much larger counterpart opposite, it too was concealed behind a grille (Figure 5).[28] Despite the many discomforts, the numbers of women wanting to view the Commons proceedings often outstripped the number of places available by a huge margin.

MRS GULLY'S GALLERY: PARLIAMENT IN THE PAST

A 'constant attendant at the Parliamentary debates', Elizabeth Gully hosted the crème de la crème of British female society in her exclusive and much-sought-after Speaker's Ladies' Gallery. 'Here have sat all the great women of the day: the Princess of Wales, the Duchess of York, other princesses of our royal family, members of other royal families.' Like her predecessors, Mrs Gully was known to find it a most onerous task to allocate seats, which were in huge demand, but she gained great praise for how this was done.

> [She] made her own rules and saw they were kept. No one ever met with a rough or unkind repulse, but if anyone took an unwarranted liberty, they never again repeated it. It was done in a manner which gained her the love and respect of all to whom she had to dispense this favour.[29]

One of Mrs Gully's greatest challenges in this fiendishly complex balancing act came from Mrs Elizabeth Glynne Gladstone, spouse of Liberal Prime Minister William Ewart Gladstone. Probably the most prominent political wife of the era, Mrs Gladstone had been a frequent presence in the Ladies' Gallery from the 1860s onwards. Widely described as an 'auditor of high distinction', she was there listening keenly to all 'the great historic occasions in which her husband was a central figure', and latterly she often attended for the speeches of their youngest son, Herbert Gladstone, MP for Leeds and his father's Private Secretary.[30] So distinguished was she that a special corner seat on the front right-hand side of the Speaker's Ladies' Gallery was seen as her preserve, and if she materialised unexpectedly, any seating arrangements already carefully finessed by Mrs Gully would have to be changed immediately.

The intense competition for the uncomfortable and caged-off space in the Ladies' Gallery shows just how little had changed for women in Parliament over the previous century. So too does this patronising passage from *Parliament Past and Present*, a substantial and semi-official guidebook published in 1902. Promoting a colourful, picturesque and safe vision, its authors opined that while:

> The obnoxious grille has resisted all efforts to displace it or materially modify it, fair visitors have asserted themselves in other directions in a fashion as would have delighted the aristocratic amazons [of the past]. In the Lobby they are ever much in evidence, and they have special provision made for them in the arrangements of the dining room. But their special province is the Terrace.[31]

So, at the dawn of the Edwardian age, even the most politically competent women – such as Mrs Gully and the stalwarts of the Ladies' Gallery – were excluded from almost all of the Palace of Westminster and were almost all defined only in relation to their menfolk. And as had been the case since 1896, no senior post in either House had a female incumbent. Women had a mountain to climb to be accepted in their own right in the corridors of power.

THE END OF AN ERA: SCANDAL AND SHAME

As *Parliament Past and Present* rolled off the presses, the stress of their official duties was catching up with the Gullys. In 1899, concerns were expressed in the press that Elizabeth, who suffered from heart problems, was often exhausted by her onerous oversight of her Ladies' Gallery and her unremitting social round. And by 1901, William was known to be feeling the strains of presiding over fractious all-night sittings in the Commons chamber. Eventually, on 6 June 1905, he announced his retirement on health grounds and was, as was expected, granted a pension of £4,000 and a peerage. He took as his title Viscount Selby in honour of his wife Elizabeth, whose maiden name it was: a public and fitting tribute to her years of faithful support. Suffering from increasingly severe illness, Elizabeth was now able to move to their country home, Sutton Place, Seaford, in Sussex. But her state of mind and any chances of recovery cannot have been helped by the personal disasters that were by now engulfing two of her children, Shelley and James.

On 24 July 1902, Shelley Gully had married Carleton Salkeld of the 10th Hussars, celebrated as a hero of the South African War, at St Margaret's, Westminster. The wedding reception – one of the Society events of the year – was held at the Speaker's House. More than 400 costly wedding gifts were on display, down to the five silver photograph frames presented by the servants at Westminster. But Shelley soon separated from Carleton and moved back to her parents' home, even accompanying her father at official events. On 20 October 1906, she petitioned for an annulment of her marriage on the grounds that Salkeld was incapable of consummating the marriage 'by reason of his frigidity, impotence or malformation of his parts of generation' which was 'incurable by art or skill'.

Four days later, Carleton in turn sued Shelley for divorce, attesting that his marriage with her had in fact been consummated. He cited as his own cause her frequent adultery with his former fellow officer, the Hon. Edward Brabazon Meade, at the time of the petition based in India with the 10th Hussars. After hearing the two cases together, the judge found for Shelley, granting her an annulment.[32] The allegedly impotent Carleton Salkeld would go on to have five daughters with his second wife, Octavia

Johnstone Douglas, whom he married in 1908; their eldest girl, Catherine, was conceived during their blissful honeymoon journey to the Far East.[33]

In 1906, divorce was still very rare indeed: only 546 petitions were lodged in England and Wales in total.[34] And although the Salkelds' marital travails had taken place out of the public eye, the huge personal upset allied with the social shame and stigma of these unfolding events would have deeply affected Shelley's respectable parents.

Worse still was to follow. In January 1907, Edward Brabazon Meade returned from India and took up a post with the Buckinghamshire Imperial Yeomanry; he and Shelley married in December. Within a few weeks of the wedding, though, in late February 1908, Shelley was discovered in a coma at the Grand Hotel, Brighton. Her new husband was off on a motoring tour, and having checked in alone, she had taken an overdose of the sleeping drug trional. She died a few days later – by misadventure, the coroner directed the inquest jury. This sad episode should, he said, be a warning to women about the dangers of addiction.[35]

Meanwhile, James William Herschell Gully, the Speaker's eldest son, and his wife Ada Isabel, were embroiled in a bitter tug-of-war over their daughter. In 1903, James, a barrister, had left Ada and fled to India with his lover, Miss Dorothy Evelyn Grey. James and Ada's young daughter, Leslie Gully, was made a ward of Chancery in December 1905, with custody awarded to her mother. In May 1906, a further order permitted James, now back in London, timed and supervised visits to see his daughter at the London house of his parents, Lord and Lady Selby – as long as Miss Grey had no contact with her.[36]

But on 1 February 1908, during one of these visits, James Gully abducted the 10-year-old Leslie from his father's London house. He and Miss Grey – posing as a nurse – fled to the Continent with her. This attracted massive press interest in the whereabouts of the granddaughter of the former Speaker, a malign outcome of Mrs Gully's success in raising his public profile. After a week of frantic searching the little girl was discovered by a private detective. Safe and well, she was staying with the errant couple on the island of Waxholm, not far from Stockholm. In a blaze of publicity, Leslie was reunited with her mother, Ada. And after surrendering to the authorities in March, James served a six-week sentence in Brixton Prison for contempt of court: 'a most flagrant breach of the order' and an 'outrageous abuse' of the judge's confidence in the defendant's honour.[37]

Unsurprisingly, in December 1908 Ada brought divorce proceedings against James on the grounds of adultery and desertion, which he did not contest. The judge awarded Ada custody of Leslie and shortened the

customary six months for the final decree to three.[38] That enabled James to
marry Dorothy Grey on 5 August 1909 – just in time, for their first child,
daughter Signe, arrived three months later. She would be followed in 1911 by
their son and heir to the family title, the Hon. Thomas Sutton Evelyn Gully.

The Gully family's unfolding scandals were cast aside when on
15 November 1906 Elizabeth Gully, Lady Selby, died. Lord Selby was said to
have been heartbroken by his loss and there were numerous fulsome tributes
to her in the press. 'Speaker Gully', it was said:

> Could have chosen no more suitable life companion. She was a lady whose
> extraordinary charm of manner, sweetness of temper and simplicity of
> character made her an important factor in the fortunes of her husband
> … Anyone who has talked to her on the subject of debate or on politi-
> cal feeling inside and outside the House must have been struck with her
> shrewd power of observation and her intuitive and quick perception of
> the situation … The entire House mourns the death of one who, by her
> graciousness of heart and mind won universal esteem.[39]

On 6 November 1909, Elizabeth was followed to the grave by her husband.
Generous appreciations poured in praising his tenure as Speaker, and espe-
cially his 'dignity and impartiality' in office.[40] After a memorial service at
St Margaret's, Westminster, his remains were taken on a funeral train to
Brookwood Cemetery, Surrey. Here William Court Gully was laid to rest
in the family vault, alongside Elizabeth and their tragic daughter Shelley.[41]

About Eliza Arscot

'Mrs Goddard again complained to me that Mrs Arscot was so continually worrying and abasing her that it was making her quite ill, and that if it was not for her children's sake she would give up her employment.
   The woman cried bitterly.'

John Kemp Williams, House of Lords Resident Superintendent, recording a complaint by one of the housemaids about Eliza Arscot, Principal Housemaid, in 1901

6

'LOSING THEIR REASON': ELIZA ARSCOT AND HER FELLOW HOUSEKEEPERS

In December 1901, the parish workhouse of St George's, Hanover Square, had a difficult situation to deal with. A new inmate had arrived – a woman called Eliza Arscot, a domestic servant by background. As attendant Annie Churcher reported, 'Eliza Arscot ran into the bathroom and stripped herself naked under the delusion that stuff had been thrown over her. Also that she said she was to be cut up.'[1]

The workhouse was there to provide accommodation for people with no other means of support. Arscot was duly certified under the Lunacy Act 1890 and promptly sent on to a more appropriate institution. She was admitted as an inmate of Hanwell Asylum, a psychiatric hospital in west London, on 21 December 1901. This made her one of 22,155 pauper lunatics (in the parlance of the time) in London that year, her situation a sad but commonplace one. However, there was something unusual about Arscot. Her address on admission was given as 'The Victoria Tower, Westminster', and her occupation, 'Upper Housemaid at the House of Lords'.

In a twist of fate that would surely have horrified Jane Julia Bennett, keeper of the keys, the post of House of Lords Housekeeper had been diminished to the point where its office holder could be banished to a workhouse and lunatic asylum. In Victorian and Edwardian times, women were statistically more likely than men to be deemed 'mad' and confined to an asylum by a patriarchal medical profession or abusive family members. The behaviour of women was often interpreted as irrational and hysterical, in the narrative tradition of Shakespeare's Ophelia and the literary 'mad-woman in the attic', and blamed on female reproductive biology rather than external causes such as poverty and working conditions. Although Arscot's gender influenced her diagnosis and treatment, her class and family background were also crucial, and a fuller picture of her employment situation in the House of Lords is necessary to understand the context of her committal to the asylum.

Eliza Arscot wasn't the first Housekeeper to be considered mad: her predecessor Ellen Lovegrove had also suffered from mental illness. The pattern was noticed and concerns even raised for Arscot's successor, Amelia de Laney. In 1912, when de Laney asked for additional furniture so she could have a companion living with her for the sake of her health and welfare, an Office of Works official remarked, 'I gather that the two previous Principal Housemaids went out of their minds.'[2]

Fortunately, de Laney held on to her sanity, and indeed to her furniture despite the best efforts of the Treasury to remove it. The themes of madness and furniture run through the turbulent lives and careers of the House of Lords Housekeepers in the late nineteenth and early twentieth centuries.

'J.R. LOVEGROVE FOR ELLEN LOVEGROVE'

After the retirement of Jane Julia Bennett in 1877, her title was handed on to Ellen Lovegrove, already Housekeeper to the Crown Office. Born in 1828, Ellen Nash had married the controlling James Lovegrove, then a prosperous stationer, in 1856. In 1874, his seemingly rather menacing 'friendship' with the Deputy Lord Great Chamberlain Lord Aveland – involving money, information or both – had secured him the post of Clerk to Aveland and Ellen her first Housekeeper role. James had clearly been machinating for her further preferment ever since.

As well as succeeding Mrs Bennett in the top job, Ellen soon took on the duties of two further Housekeeper posts, in the Lord Great Chamberlain's Department and the Parliament Office. Yet, although she was still listed as an officer of the House, as Charles Tanner MP opined in the Commons, 'she had nothing to do, and a residence and £200 a year to assist her in doing nothing'.[3] Tanner had a point, for her role was now a shadow of its former self: she reported to the Resident Superintendent, James Scott, and was responsible merely for overseeing cleaning. She had, though, inherited from Mrs Bennett the ground and two top floors of the Housekeeper's handsome official apartment facing into Old Palace Yard, next to the Victoria Tower.

In the 1881 and 1891 censuses Ellen is listed as living there with her husband, James, the head of their household. They kept two servants: a cook and a housemaid.

Claiming a preferential status through his connections with Lord Aveland, James Lovegrove constantly interfered in his wife's duties. On her first appointment in the Crown Office in 1874, he produced a blizzard of letters signed 'J.R. Lovegrove for Ellen Lovegrove' demanding higher pay for her and improvements to their official accommodation, and this pattern continued throughout the couple's time in the Lords. In 1880, again in Ellen's name, James Lovegrove lodged a formal complaint with Colonel William Carington, Lord Aveland's Secretary, against Samuel Hand, the Lords Deputy Serjeant. Hand had, he said, been spotted bringing a woman into his room on more than one occasion – and had even ordered for her 'a hot luncheon from the Refreshment Department'. To this, Colonel Wellington Talbot, the Serjeant, responded, 'I should be glad to know whether it is contrary to the morals of the House to bring one's wife into one's room. It does not appear to me to be a very heinous offence.'[4] This kind of behaviour can hardly have endeared either of the Lovegroves to their colleagues.

But Ellen Lovegrove was able to exercise at least some of her own duties in person, being allowed, in practice, to hire and fire as well as to oversee her staff. In 1878, the most senior, Mary Ann Long, was in a local maternity hospital for her confinement. Ellen arranged an additional temporary allowance of 5 shillings a week for one of the under-housemaids to cover Mary's supervisory work – although in an age when any maternity cover was unheard of, this uplift was to come out of Mrs Long's pay.[5] In 1881, Ellen also secured some sick leave for another housemaid who was ill with 'failing eyesight'.[6]

For more than two decades, James Lovegrove patrolled the corridors of the House of Lords, using his wife's name and his own position to interfere in the business of the Resident Superintendent, James Scott, and to impose petty restrictions in the name of Lord Aveland, who inherited the title Lord Willoughby de Eresby and became Lord Great Chamberlain in his own right from 1888. Lovegrove fell out with senior Commons officials by zealously barring them from bringing visitors to the Lords and drew up detailed rules and regulations for the admission of Queen Victoria's personal guests. In 1889, though, the House agreed a restructuring to save money, apparently initiated by Lord Willoughby. This included phasing out the role of the Housekeeper, who was to be replaced with a 'Chief Housemaid' on £78 a year. This meant that Mrs Lovegrove's post would be extinguished when it was next vacant, and her official residence would be surrendered.[7]

Lord Willoughby became Lord Ancaster in 1892, remaining Lord Great Chamberlain. Meanwhile, the Lovegroves ramped up their reign of terror in the Lords. They had numerous and increasingly toxic disputes with John Bull, James Scott's successor as Resident Superintendent – in 1892, Ellen even refused his orders to curtail the accommodation of one of her housemaids.[8] The pair also insinuated that Bull was taking official coal and other stores for his personal use, while Bull in his turn criticised Emily Reid, one of their housemaids, for drinking alcohol while on duty. Bull soon came to see Lovegrove as 'his bitterest enemy, and one who was regarded in that light not only by him but also by many others who were in the precincts of the House'. Matters came to a head when in June 1896 Bull declined to officiate for Lovegrove while he attended a Coaching Club meeting. This was on the grounds that his absence was a breach of Treasury regulations forbidding officials 'to accept any private employment during office hours'. It was Bull who was summarily and controversially dismissed for disobeying orders – but he brought his enemy down with him. The Lord Great Chamberlain investigated a bitter counter-complaint from Bull in person, and 'found Lovegrove on the Horse Guards; and he has agreed to send in his resignation'. In September 1896, Lovegrove finally left Ancaster's service and retired to Clapham.[9]

The poisonous workplace politics must have taken a considerable toll on Ellen, and by this time her health had broken down. For that reason, on 31 March 1896, six months before her husband's departure, she had already retired on a pension of £103 10s. Her diagnosis was a 'softening of the brain', a term often used at this time to signify senile dementia.[10] She died the following year at home in Clapham, with James by her side. In 1901, he replaced her with a much younger woman, Mary Gertrude Harrison, who took care of him until his own passing in 1909.

THE 'TYRANNY' OF ELIZA ARSCOT

The position of House of Lords Housekeeper had seemingly come to an end with Ellen Lovegrove's retirement, but appearances were deceptive as her supervisory role was still needed. Ellen Lovegrove was replaced by Eliza Arscot, who was given the title of Principal Housemaid rather than Housekeeper. So this element of the 1889 recommendations, at least, was formally implemented, although old habits died hard and Arscot was still sometimes described as Housekeeper. More significantly perhaps, Arscot was not employed on an annual salary as her predecessors had been, but instead on a salary of 30 shillings a week. The weekly wage was a clear indication of the lowered status of the role, which was permanent but precarious, and not pensionable.

Arscot did not get the Housekeeper's residence either, but contrary to the 1889 recommendations, she did manage to live in a small part of it. On her appointment in February 1896, a request was made to the Office of Works by Colonel Carington that she 'be allowed to sleep in a spare room upstairs which formed part of the Housekeeper's apartments but which is now unoccupied'. The request was granted as long as no furniture would be required and 'if it is understood that the girl can be dismissed with a month's notice'.[11] Carington duly assured the Office of Works that the services of the Principal Housemaid could be dispensed with at only a week's notice.

Poor Eliza Arscot's single unfurnished room must have been intolerable, as Colonel Carington's replacement as Secretary to the Lord Great Chamberlain, Yeoman Usher Captain Thomas Dacres Butler, wrote again within a couple of months to request that the room be furnished and that a bedroom be provided, 'which is absolutely necessary for her'.[12] The Office of Works grumbled about it but the work was done and the two rooms were duly furnished and maintained. And so it was that the Principal Housemaid remained resident and is recorded as living there in her two rooms in the 1901 census. As well as her accommodation, she was allocated a scuttle of coal and a bundle of wood a day from the Lords' cellars.

Eliza Arscot was born in 1857, near the border of Cornwall and Devon.[13] She came to London to work as a domestic servant at the age of 16, and arrived at the Lords in 1896 with a good reference from a William Burgess of Piccadilly, saying she had been employed in his family for the past twelve years and was 'capable, industrious, clean, very trustworthy and reliable, and has been an exceptional manageress'.[14] She never married, although the country house tradition of giving all housekeepers the title 'Mrs' meant that she was sometimes called Mrs Arscot.

At first all was well. After John Bull's abrupt departure in June 1896, she was granted a small gratuity for performing the duties of the Resident Superintendent during a ten-day vacancy before the new postholder, John Kemp Williams, arrived in July.

The hiring and firing of housemaids now lay nominally with the Lord Great Chamberlain himself, although in practice this was done on the recommendations of Captain Butler, who kept a list of prospective candidates, mostly widows of soldiers, for when vacancies arose. One such appointment was Mrs Beach in 1899, whom Butler described as 'appears thoroughly fitted', a widow of a sergeant and an Englishwoman, under 40, active, and recommended by Lady Hope.[15] Arscot found fault with Mrs Beach within a short time, writing to Butler:

> Mrs Beach has not carried out her duties satisfactory [*sic*] and does not seem to understand House Work. I consider her a very untidy Housemaid and when I find fault she tells me there is too much to do in the time, if she finds too much now can't think how she will manage in the busy season.[16]

Williams also personally inspected the work and was not satisfied either. Butler agreed, and Mrs Beach was dismissed with a week's notice. In the background, however, a larger negative picture was building up of Arscot's managerial and personal skills. A chronology of incidents was written up by Williams in 1901. Although Williams and Arscot clearly did not get on, and she certainly challenged his authority, the complaints he recorded paint a compelling picture of criticisms from across the staff of the House of Lords, including from her housemaids. It began in February 1897 when a son of housemaid Mrs Ellen Johnson wrote objecting to the treatment of his mother by Arscot, 'complaining of her <u>tyranny</u>, making his mother's existence <u>most wretched</u>, accusing his mother of <u>taking soap off the building</u> and her <u>overbearing manner</u> towards his mother'.[17]

Mrs Johnson did not wish to pursue the complaint. But this was just the beginning. A month later, the long-serving Head Housemaid, Mary Ann Long, reported Arscot for her overbearing manner. Arscot clashed with another housemaid, Mrs Goddard, several times, Goddard saying Arscot had abused her terribly, and if it were not for her children, she would give up her work. 'The woman cried bitterly,' Williams wrote.[18] Others also complained, and one resigned on account of similar treatment.

Nor was it just the housemaids. Williams recorded that scarcely a day passed without reports being brought of her interference with the porters. They claimed she followed them from room to room using irritating language, so they might say something to her that she might report them for; she called them liars and blackguards. Workmen from the Office of Works who were cleaning and polishing furniture in the Lord Chancellor's office complained that she had bullied them and ordered them away. Doorkeepers reported that she accused them of taking towels and tea cloths from their rooms. As the Resident Superintendent, Williams lived close by with his wife, son and four daughters (the oldest of whom worked as a bank clerk) and his family may have found the situation trying too.

Williams referred complaints up the ladder to Butler, who repeatedly cautioned Arscot for her behaviour. In July 1901, she was found to be interfering with the servants of Henry Graham, the Clerk of the Parliaments and the most senior official in the House of Lords. At this point, Butler ordered Arscot to confine herself to the duties appertaining to her office and warned that should anything of the kind be brought to his attention again, it would be reported to the Lord Great Chamberlain. Unfortunately, things still did not improve and in November 1901 Butler escalated the situation. He reported to the new Lord Great Chamberlain George Cholmondeley, 4th Marquess of Cholmondeley, that during the whole of the time he had been in office, complaints to him about Arscot had been a frequent occurrence:

> Her want of tact, her inferior education, and her apparent incapacity to make herself respected by, or to get on with those under her command, render her, in my opinion, unfit for such a post as she now holds. I am extremely reluctant to bring this matter before you, because I believe Mrs Arscot to be a very respectable, hardworking woman and in a different position might be a useful servant. But I think it is not to the advantage of the public service that she should remain as she now is.[19]

The reference to her 'inferior education' shows up an unfavourable comparison between Arscot and her much grander predecessors, with their annual salaries and palatial apartments. The Lords had chosen to downgrade the post, and the result was that it had employed a much humbler working-class woman who perhaps unsurprisingly failed to live up to the unrealistic expectations of colleagues with memories of Jane Julia Bennett and even of Ellen Lovegrove. On 6 December, Arscot was given her final warning by the Lord Great Chamberlain himself: if another well-founded complaint was brought against her, she would receive notice to leave the service of the House of Lords. Arscot was used to dealing with Butler and Williams, and it must have been a terrifying experience for her to be faced with the Lord Great Chamberlain and the very real prospect of losing her job.

LOSING HER REASON

In fact, this may have been the final straw, as her mental illness now emerged. A week later, on 14 December, it became clear that Arscot was behaving strangely and was increasingly unsettled. To his credit, Williams arranged for two trained nurses to look after her, one by day and one by night, and asked Mrs Webberley, one of the housemaids, to stay with her too. But the situation deteriorated from there. Williams sent a telegram to Butler at 10.55 p.m.:

To Captain Butler. Am afraid Mrs Arscot is losing her reason and most anxious to see you today. Resident Supt.

It got worse. At 2.40 a.m., Arscot left her quarters, rang up the servants of Henry Graham and asked to see Lady Margaret (Graham's wife). Thwarted in that, she tried to ring up the quarters of Mr Bowden, the Resident Engineer. The night watch inspector then called Williams out of bed and informed him that 'Mrs A absolutely refused to go back to her quarters'. Williams went out into the courtyard and after about an hour's persuasion got her as far as her own door, but she still refused to enter. About 4 a.m., a physician arrived, Dr Sinclair, who persuaded her to go inside. Williams reported:

She wanted to send the nurse away, and looked terribly wild … She has not been in bed since Friday night and she appears to have nothing in her quarters to eat, as I have sent down 3 dinners today, eggs and milk for nurses. Sinclair is most anxious to see you before further action.

Graham wrote to Butler with his own account: 'The Housekeeper came to my door at 2 o'clock this morning … she had two women with her who evidently had no control over her and the Police had no orders to interfere.' Dr Sinclair's quandary seemed to be the unprecedented situation of how to deal with a pauper lunatic in a royal palace. Graham opined to Butler that, 'for what it is worth, my opinion is that there was no difference between this building and any other'. Arscot was duly removed and passed on to the care of the Westminster Board of Guardians, the body responsible for administering the Poor Law. Her friends and family were informed, and her nephew from Plymouth wrote to object to the possibility of her bank book being handed over to the Guardians. Arscot was admitted to Hanwell Asylum on 21 December, diagnosed with 'Melancholia',[20] although her behaviour was suggestive of a psychotic condition such as schizophrenia rather than a depressive illness.

Hanwell was founded in 1831 as an asylum for paupers and became the London County Asylum in 1889. The number of people admitted to such asylums rose markedly in the late nineteenth century, especially in London, in line with population changes. Living in her two poorly furnished rooms at her workplace, Arscot had no home where family or close friends might care for her, and no money to pay for private care. Asylums were how society coped with people like her, the only alternative to prison or the workhouse. Male doctors frequently blamed female madness on the instability of women's reproductive systems, often linked to pregnancy or childbirth, but in

Figure 7: Eliza Arscot, photographed *c.* 1906. Hanwell
Asylum case book.

Arscot's case it was menopause, with 'change of life' included on her case
notes at admission. Had she been a man, it seems likely that her condition
might have been attributed to the intellectual and economic pressure from
her job and precarious living conditions; but there were no social workers
and no resource for doctors to investigate this.

Over the following years, doctors repeatedly described Arscot as incoher-
ent, garrulous, abusive to nurses, mistaking the identity of people and having
hallucinations such as hearing voices and a crying baby under a mattress – and
talking to pictures hanging on the wall. A recurring theme was delusions of
grandeur, wealth and power, some of which were straightforward ('Thinks
she owns the place'), but other statements read rather differently knowing more about her. 'She calls herself the Principal of the House of Lords,'
one doctor wrote; another, 'she states that she was brought here from the
House of Lords, and that she is the Principal there'. Arscot had, of course,

been Principal Housemaid. However, she also claimed to be appointed by the Queen of England to be 'maid in waiting to the throne', and 'thinks she is heiress of a lot of money', so it is hardly surprising if doctors were sceptical at her descriptions.

Furniture was another recurring theme in the doctors' notes: 'Believes the place belongs to her, that the furniture comes from the House of Lords'. Hallucinations and delusions might typically be associated with disturbing personal experiences, such as her battle to have even one unfurnished room. Also 'she had been bequeathed some houses and unauthorised people were making use of the rents' – perhaps another manifestation of her own uncertain housing situation in the Lords. More disturbing are hints of abuse: 'was told she was to be carried away and burnt or put into a boiling copper'; 'that she was half murdered by some men'; 'that she was nearly murdered at Westminster'; 'says she was murdered by four men and has been brought to life again'.[21]

Alongside the assessment of her mental health, the doctors noted on admission that she was well nourished, though with a cracked, dry tongue and foul breath. Her physical health was deemed over the years as mostly fair to good. A photograph of her from the case book (Figure 7) shows her staring out with huge dark circles around her eyes, wearing a large lace collar. 'She decorates herself with ribbon and works needlework,' one case note read. Yet it was repeatedly recorded that she was a good and hard worker in the wards. Sadly, Eliza Arscot died in the asylum in March 1933, aged 77. The post-mortem verdict was 'Senile decay',[22] which may have simply meant old age.

THE SMALL MATTER OF THE HOUSEMAID'S BED: AMELIA DE LANEY

Back at the House of Lords, the departure of Eliza Arscot led to a resumption of the battle over whether the Principal Housemaid should live on site. Her replacement, Amelia de Laney, was appointed in 1902 and this led to another request for the rooms to be done up. The Office of Works fumed about sanctioning 'squatters as residents', and instead of granting the request, removed her existing furniture on the grounds she should not live in.[23] The Treasury refused to pay for replacement furniture. Terse letters passed backwards and forwards between officials in Parliament and government. Having reached an impasse, Henry Graham, Clerk of the Parliaments, bought replacement furniture at a cost of £85 8s 10d (approximately £6,600 today) with the blessing of the House of Lords Offices Committee, and the Lords reimbursed him from its Fee Fund Account.

The story was reported fully in the newspapers and even picked up by the international press, with *The New York Times* publishing a piece under the inaccurate headline, 'Parsimonious Peers: the struggle between the House of Lords and its Principal Housemaid'.[24] But the Lords was struggling with the Office of Works and the Treasury, not its Housemaid. The incident is interesting not only as an insight into the importance the Lords placed on its resident Housekeeper, but as an example of the House asserting authority over government departments, pushing back over efforts to control it by civil servants. As the Clerk of the Parliaments wrote to the Treasury at the time:

> I do most seriously deplore such a difference of opinion on seemingly so small a matter as a housemaid's bed: but of course the larger question of the jurisdiction of the House over its own premises and servants is involved, and of the right of any Department to swoop down and deprive it practically of the use of any portion of the building assigned to its occupation.[25]

Having established herself, as early as 1903 de Laney made a request to the Office of Works for a bath and a geyser. This request was not granted but some expansion of her quarters took place over the years, for as her census form shows, by 1911 she was living in four rooms rather than Eliza Arscot's two. A telephone branch exchange was set up in the Palace of Westminster from 1907, and de Laney's number was Victoria 6244, ext. 105. In 1911, Miss Amelia Plimmer de Laney was the only female head of household in the Palace of Westminster and the only woman living there to complete and sign her own census form. It shows that she was 62 years old, and under her birthplace she wrote, 'Not sure but I think in London'. Her self-described occupation is not Principal Housemaid, but 'Housekeeper, House of Lords'.

In December 1912, de Laney requested more furniture: a bedstead and bedding, bedroom furniture, carpet, rug, curtains, fender and fireirons.[26] The reason given was so that she might have another bedroom available for a companion who was needed for the sake of her health and welfare. The Office of Works official noted, 'She recently fainted, and it was then realised how helpless she would be in the event of a more serious illness ... I gather that the two previous Principal Housemaids went out of their minds.'[27]

Nothing happened on the furniture front for a year, and when Butler pushed, the Treasury made the excuse that having yet another resident would increase the risk of fire.[28] Government whip William Wedgwood Benn MP (the future Viscount Stansgate and father of Tony Benn) suggested alternative rooms for de Laney in the House of Commons, ostensibly as she would not be so lonely there. Unsurprisingly, given her secure base where she worked in the Lords, 'Miss de Laney entirely declined to take over the rooms as she thinks they are unsuitable and inconvenient on account of their position, and for other reasons'.[29] The Lord Great Chamberlain himself – who was by now Charles Wynn-Carington, Lord Lincolnshire – had to smooth things over and chose to blame the House of Lords Offices Committee who would never agree to move their resident Housekeeper. He explained he had a difficult team to drive and had to be very careful:

> As regards Miss de Laney, I visited her rooms and I find she has 2 bed-rooms (one of which is furnished with her own furniture), a kitchen, a sitting room and a scullery. I told her that I considered her quarters extra-ordinarily good. If she wants any person as [a] companion there is no reason why the second bedroom could not be occupied and I added that it would be absolutely impossible to entertain any application for extra fur-niture or structural alteration, Butler agrees with me. Please consider this letter as confidential.[30]

The request for confidentiality perhaps indicates that Lincolnshire was using the Offices Committee as an excuse. Butler and Lincolnshire were fighting battles over rooms, works and furniture on many other fronts apart from that of the Housekeeper; a letter from Butler to Lincolnshire soon afterwards, following an attempt to take some Lords committee space for the Commons, growled, 'Mr Wedgwood Benn is a very nice young man but if I may say so, a more barefaced attempt to get something for nothing cannot well be imagined.'[31]

Amelia Plimmer de Laney was born in March 1848 in Chelsea, the daughter of Thomas de Laney, a beer seller, and Dorothy, née Plimmer. Orphaned by the age of 9, she then attended the Royal Masonic School for Girls. Here she fared well, for by 1871 she was a lady's maid in the household of Josiah Spode IV, of the pottery family. The role of lady's maid, a personal assistant, indicates that de Laney was of a higher rank of domestic servant than Eliza Arscot had been. Spode died in 1893, leaving de Laney a legacy of £600 (about £49,000 today); by this time, she was working as assistant matron of the Birmingham Workhouse Infirmary.[32] The matron would have been in charge of all nurses and staff in the infirmary, so as assistant matron de Laney may also have had some supervisory responsibility. Initially, she probably lived off Spode's legacy, as she was recorded as a retired matron in the 1901 census, but it must have been insufficient as she arrived to work at the House of Lords soon afterwards. There are no records as to how she came to be appointed, but her connection to the Spodes would have certainly commended her to Butler. Given the circumstances in which Eliza Arscot had departed, de Laney's previous role as a matron must have seemed reassuring, promising an ability to deal with health issues and experience in managing a team of women.

It proved a good appointment, for de Laney was later described by Butler as 'a most kind easy-going person, very much liked by everyone'.[33] Unlike her two predecessors (and her successor, as it turned out), she seems to have maintained good working relations with her own managers and with the team of housemaids that she supervised. Of course, there were incidents, such as the dismissal of housemaid Mrs Frith in 1908. Mrs Frith went absent for several days without a doctor's note, and Williams reported to Butler that the rumour among the staff was that she was married to or living with Marriott, the coal porter, and the cause of her illness was that she was *enceinte* (i.e. pregnant). She was sacked by the Lord Great Chamberlain with a week's notice, because of the unauthorised absence rather than the rumours.[34] But a respectable replacement was found from Butler's list, and apart from squabbles over rooms and furniture, de Laney's tenure as Housekeeper went smoothly.

De Laney served through the First World War and retired from the Lords in 1919 at the age of 71, receiving no pension (a result of the downgrading of the role since Ellen Lovegrove) but a one-off payment of £49 0s 8d: one week's pay for each year of employment, approximately £1,424 today.[35] She initially went to live on her own in Portishead, Somerset. By 1939, she had moved closer to family in Marple, Cheshire, where she was recorded as 'incapacitated', perhaps unsurprisingly as she now would have been aged 91. She died a year later. Her will sheds some light on her later years, with sums of £5 left to 'Sister Josephine of Marple for her great kindness', and £10 to Rugeley Cottage Hospital, as well as larger amounts to her great-nieces and her residual estate to her nephews. Sadly, it is unlikely any of these legacies were paid as her net estate was worth less than £21.

In Her Own Words

'The Members are always telling us what a convenience it would be if the Typewriting Rooms could be anywhere near the Central Hall. Every time the Division bell rings, they have quite a journey to and fro if they are in the middle of dictation.'

May Ashworth, writing to the Serjeant at Arms requesting an improvement in the accommodation for her typing service, 1904

7

THE EVER-YOUTHFUL MISS ASHWORTH: TYPING COMES TO PARLIAMENT

In 1898, a journalist from *Woman's Life* magazine arrived at a fine suite of rooms in 28 Victoria Street, Westminster, just down the road from the Houses of Parliament. She was there to interview Miss May Ashworth, who had held the important position of Typist to the Houses of Parliament since 1895.

Ashworth was only too happy to share insights into life working for Parliament, as well as running her own successful business. While tactfully not mentioning names, she explained how unpredictable the demands of MPs could be, the odd hours and short notice for work, and how important it was to be flexible in such a strange working environment as the House of Commons:

> You see most of our work is done in emergency – without any notice. For instance, an MP rushes into our room and begins at once to dictate something or another … The MPs evince great interest in our work, and often express wonderment at the great speed obtained by the girls.[1]

Ashworth's service could have been a short-term arrangement – it was described as an 'interesting experiment' by the trade press when it began.[2] She had won a contract to provide typing services; it could easily have been taken away and given to another company, had MPs expressed any complaint or dissatisfaction. Yet this did not happen. May Ashworth was to remain the Typist for Parliament for the rest of her life, and her company, Ashworth & Co., continued to provide typing services there after her death in 1928 until well after the Second World War.

Ashworth was a trailblazer and a role model for professional business-women everywhere at this time, let alone in the rarefied surroundings of Parliament. What was the secret of her success? What kind of woman was she? And the big question which the *Woman's Life* journalist may have wondered but had been too polite to ask – how *old* was she?

A CLERGYMAN'S DAUGHTER

To find that out we have to go back to her birth. Mary (known as May) Howard Ashworth was born in the vicarage at Holme Abbey, Cumberland, a parish church which was also a former Cistercian abbey, on 10 February 1863. She was a clergyman's daughter: the first child of the new curate at Holme Cultram, Arthur Ashworth, and his wife Sarah.

Arthur Ashworth, son of a draper, was educated at Magdalen Hall, Oxford (now Hertford College), and held various curacy positions before moving north to become curate of Wigton in Cumberland in 1859. There he met Sarah Bewley, a Wigton native, and they married in 1862. Arthur became curate of neighbouring Holme Cultram in early 1863, and then following a vote by parishioners, was appointed its vicar on 4 January 1865. His health was not good, though, and his active work was given to curates from 1872. The Ashworths brought up their family in the vicarage. Two sons died in infancy, leaving May Ashworth the oldest of five daughters by the time her father died in 1874, when she was just 11 years old.

All the Ashworth daughters were given the middle name Howard. This harked back to Arthur's grandparents, Robert Ashworth of Prescot and Ann Howard of Huyton, Lancashire. The Ashworths were a respectable working-class family of shopkeepers, grocers and drapers. Perhaps the Howard connection had brought money or connections which Arthur wished to recognise, and perhaps this had allowed him to be educated and become a clergyman. Howard was also a resonant name in Cumberland, as the family name of the Earls of Carlisle. Arthur enjoyed good standing and was long remembered locally both as the vicar and as the author of a history of the Abbey of Holme Cultram. The executors of his will were the local Wigton gentry, William Banks of Highmoor House and his sons Henry Pearson Banks and Edwin Hodge Banks.

Arthur left effects of less than £3,000 (equivalent to approximately £187,000 today), which seems to have been enough to keep Sarah living on her own means for the rest of her life, and to provide some kind of elementary education for his daughters. May later talked about being a linguist, having spent some time on the Continent. But there were five daughters, and that money would only go so far. In the end, the Ashworth sisters had to work for a living.

HER OWN BUSINESS

A generation earlier, perhaps May Ashworth would have become a governess or teacher, as few occupations were acceptable for a middle-class woman such as a clergyman's daughter. However, by the 1880s, there were more options, including clerical work – clean, dainty, allowing for only limited contact with social inferiors and men, and available on a wide scale.[3] Ashworth moved to London and became a secretary. She learned shorthand and typing, and in 1888, aged 25, showed huge initiative to set up her own business at a time when, as she said, 'typewriting was practically in its infancy in England'.

It was hard work. As May explained to the *Woman's Life* journalist, 'Though the business paid me from the outset, I had started without any capital, and you know how that hampers one'. She worked from morning to night, with hardly any free time. She spoke proudly of the skills involved and the knowledge gained: learning engineering from an engineer; law from a lawyer; the challenges of typing from Spanish, Latin and other languages. 'I am so fond of work that I never like to leave it, though I do indulge in an occasional spin on my bicycle before breakfast.'

She started as a one-woman service, then began to train her own assistants, educated young gentlewomen, in phonography (Pitman shorthand) and typing. She kept her own stable of staff, while other pupils of hers went out to become secretaries and set up their own businesses elsewhere. She also had premises in the City of London, at St George's House on Eastcheap, from 1891. Her office had window boxes full of flowers, a vase of roses on the writing table and a photograph of her old home, the Rectory in Cumberland, on the mantelpiece. Even at this early point in her career she adopted a flexible approach to her age, doing whatever she thought necessary to remain commercially and socially acceptable. In the 1891 census she trimmed a year off her age, giving it as 27 instead of 28.

In another interview in 1891, she listed the kind of work undertaken. Typing alone consisted of 'Specifications, estimates, balance-sheets, novels,

Figure 8: Miss May H. Ashworth, 1891.

articles, plays, legal work of every description, sermons, business correspondence ... the other day we were called upon to type a pedigree, and
a very troublesome business it proved.' Additionally, there was shorthand
work, reporting medical and literary research work at different libraries,
translations including French, German, Dutch and Italian, and thanks to the
wonders of modern technology, 'typo-filing, by which we can take hundreds of copies from one stencil'.[4]

However, what drew *Woman's Life* and other journalists subsequently
to May Ashworth's door was not just the story of a successful businesswoman

in a new industry, but to hear about the position of Typist to the Houses of Parliament!

TYPEWRITING AND PARLIAMENT

Typewriters had become commercially available in the 1870s, and by the mid-1880s were becoming more commonplace in offices. In 1886, the well-known Irish Nationalist MP Mr T.P. O'Connor asked in the House of Commons if it would be possible to put some typewriting machines into a spare committee room, declaring, 'The type-writer is another of the modern inventions which the House, in its arrangements, seems to be entirely ignorant of.' O'Connor was a journalist by background, clearly used to typing himself, and expressed frustration at having to use ordinary pen and ink. The Treasury minister, George Leveson-Gower, parried the question, saying, 'There is one great objection to typewriters, and it is that they make a good deal of noise.'[5] The question was shelved, Parliament not being quick to adopt new technology. O'Connor had to wait another nine years before a parliamentary typing service was set up in 1895 by Herbert Gladstone MP, First Commissioner of Works.

This was prompted by the report of a Select Committee on House of Commons Accommodation the previous year. Gladstone chaired the Committee and reflected ruefully, 'It has been strongly pressed upon various Members of the Committee, and certainly upon me, that provision should be made for typewriting.'[6] Among many recommendations by the Committee on kitchens, dining rooms and ventilation, was one to convert a room for typewriting. The House of Lords agreed to give up rooms formerly used by Railway Commissioners, and one of those became the Typewriting Room.

Gladstone could have simply put typewriters in a room for MPs to use, as O'Connor had requested back in 1886, but the number of MPs who could themselves type was small. Instead, Gladstone announced to the House of Commons in March 1895 that there would be staff with typing machines at the service of MPs.[7] The new arrangements began on 3 April, and the typing trade was understandably excited by this development. As described in the trade press:

> The First Commissioner of Works [Gladstone] has at length made arrangements whereby a set of clerks will be placed at the disposal of these gentlemen in the room formerly occupied by the Railway Commissioners,

near St Stephen's Hall. At the outset four lady clerks will be prepared to take work according to a scale of charges which has been agreed upon. They are not employed by the Government, but by a private firm at Westminster.[8]

The private firm at Westminster with the lady clerks was Ashworth's.

PROFESSIONAL WOMEN IN 1895

How exceptional was May Ashworth? Typing itself was a gender-free skill on its invention in the mid-nineteenth century, but soon became feminised and allocated as lower-paid mechanical work for women, while men were redeployed in superior career-based grades seen to require intellectual or administrative skill. Shorthand, once a skilled job for male clerks, became linked to typing and similarly feminised.[9] It was therefore not at all unusual to find women working as shorthand typists. More broadly, by the late nineteenth century, women were increasingly employed in secretarial work in the wider world.

May Ashworth's achievement, however, was exceptional in several ways. For a start, she won a competitive contract for her own company. She was unusual in having established her own company but not unique – indeed, there was another school offering 'Business Training for Gentlewomen' just down the road at 5 Victoria Street, Westminster. This was set up by Miss Cecil Gradwell in 1893 with her partner, Miss Octavia Richardson. Gradwell taught typewriting and shorthand, bookkeeping and business training, and worked more widely to publicise the opportunities that secretarial work offered for women. Another enterprising woman with her own business nearby was indexer Miss Nancy Bailey, commissioned by publishers as Indexer of Parliamentary Debates between 1889 and 1901. Other prestigious work included indexing *The Times*, and she trained seventy other women in indexing.[10] Like Ashworth she took steps to reduce her age, appearing as 40 instead of 48 in the 1911 census.

Both Gradwell and Bailey featured in 'Professional Women upon their Professions', a book published in 1895 – the very same year Ashworth won the contract with the House of Commons. The book featured conversations with twenty-five women in areas of work including acting, singing, education, medicine, dentistry, nursing, physical training, stockbroking, librarianship and accountancy.[11] Several of these twenty-five women had had started their own businesses as the only way they could earn a living in their preferred field: the stockbroker because she found she was unable to get the same training as a man in an office, the accountant because she was excluded from the Institute of Accountants. Although the twenty-five women are presented as role models, the impression that they are exceptional and one of very few women in their fields is unmistakable. A conversation with Ashworth would have fitted very well into the series.

Another way in which Ashworth's achievement was extraordinary was because she succeeded in entering the male bastion of Parliament, actually working in the Palace of Westminster. The Commons was not at the forefront of employing professional women. In fact, in 1895 there were no women working in any roles other than as housekeeping or refreshment staff. Clerical staff in both Houses were men. MPs could employ their own staff, and a few may have employed female secretaries but not in any significant numbers until the twentieth century. May Ashworth was the pioneer.

There were questions, of course, about how she won the contract. Her competitors alleged that she had undercut them with rates offered to MPs that were 20 per cent below that recommended by the National Union of Typists. But on examination by the trade press, it became apparent that when setting her scale of charges, she had actually been intelligent enough to take into consideration that she did not need to pay rent, or for heat or lighting, in her room near St Stephen's Hall, and that 20 per cent was a fair discount.

She was also accused of underpaying her staff, although this was fiercely denied. Their minimum starting salary was 25 shillings a week and often topped up by overtime. *Phonographer and Typist* acknowledged that Ashworth was 'well to the fore in all movements aiming at the amelioration of conditions affecting women's labour'.[12] At the end of the day, her male competitors probably could simply not believe they had been beaten to the contract by a woman.

PATRONISED BY BOTH WHIG AND TORY

Several months after work had actually begun, the situation was sufficiently satisfactory for the terms of Ashworth's work to be formally set out in a letter by the Serjeant at Arms:

> That you undertake to keep in the type writing room at the House of Commons as many machines as may be necessary, and to place there, at the disposal of Members, a sufficient staff of skilled operators who shall also be qualified to write shorthand.[13]

Hours were 11 a.m. to 8 p.m., or later as required. The scale of charges (not given) were subject to that 20 per cent discount for accommodation, lighting and warming provided. The public were not to be admitted to the Typewriting Room. Perhaps the Serjeant was wary about the potential conduct of this roomful of young women workers, or maybe potential press interest in the sheer novelty. At any rate, Ashworth made sure to give her interview to *Woman's Life* from her Victoria Street offices.

The arrangement was initially for three years but could be terminated at end of the parliamentary session if not to satisfaction. However, it all proved satisfactory. Ashworth employed an on-site manager, while splitting her own time between Parliament and Victoria Street. As she explained in interviews, 'We are popular with all classes in the House, as you see we are strictly a non-political body and are patronised alike both by Whig and Tory'.[14]

MARRIAGE TO A YOUNGER MAN

In a newspaper interview in 1898, Ashworth advised girls that they should not take paid employment after marriage:

> The advice to girls that I would emphasize is – When you marry, don't, under any but the most exceptional circumstances, consent to work for money or do anymore than the duties of a wife and mother. When a wife once begins to earn money it seems to sap the energy of her husband.[15]

However, that was before she was married herself. On 12 December 1900, May Ashworth married William Paull Jewill-Rogers. Paull (as he was known) was the son of William and Charlotte Rogers, born in 1876 in Swindon, educated at school in Plymouth and then at Wadham College, Oxford. His father was variously a tea merchant, a printer and a hotel proprietor, and Paull had similarly run a hotel, Godstone Hall in Surrey, although this business was dissolved before he married May. Paull seems to have added the name Jewill himself; it came from his grandmother, Eliza Paull Jewill. A hunting man, he drank his namesake drink, Pol Roger champagne, with a gold swizzle stick.

The wedding was at the church of St Paul's, Onslow Square, Kensington, local for them both. Ashworth was living in Queen's Gate at the heart of South Kensington, while Paull was living at Bailey's Hotel in Gloucester Road, where the wedding reception was also held. Bailey's was an elegant and fashionable Victorian hotel, built and run by an MP, Sir James Bailey. It is not known how May and Paull met, but it seems at least possible that it was through this parliamentary connection; perhaps James Bailey used the Parliament typing service, discovered Ashworth lived near his hotel, and invited her to visit it.

The Ashworth family were clearly still remembered up in Wigton, as the *Wigton Advertiser* reported on the wedding of the Reverend Arthur Ashworth's daughter in great detail.[16] The bride wore a lovely gown of white satin and she carried a bouquet of orchids, lilies of the valley and orange blossoms. She was given away by Edwin Hodge Banks, described as her trustee. Banks had been one of the executors of her father's will all those years ago and was still looking out for the Ashworth family. Her sisters also played a prominent role: Beatrice and Evelyn as bridesmaids in pretty frocks of white silk, and Edith as a witness. Edith, now Edith Buckler, had also married in Gloucester Road just a couple of years earlier. Their mother, Sarah, was also present and hosted the wedding reception. The 1901 census shows Paull and May living in Sutton, Surrey, together with her mother and both his parents. So far, so happy ever after.

But there was one rather embarrassing aspect of this wedding. The bride was older than the groom – some thirteen years older. She was 37 and he was 24. She took steps to reduce this gap on the marriage certificate, where her age is given as 34. Her family must have been aware of the subterfuge, but perhaps his were not. The average age for a first marriage in 1900 was 25 for spinsters and 27 for bachelors, so he was younger than average and she considerably older.[17]

Official records can give no hint as to how happy the marriage was in this period, but Rogers family lore is that marriage came as a huge shock to the clergyman's daughter. Legend has it that on honeymoon in Paris, hotel detectives were called to their room because the new wife was screaming that her husband had gone mad! They found the groom sitting calmly in a dressing gown, as he explained that his new bride had been ignorant about what married life entailed.[18] If true, this was not a very auspicious start.

MR AND MRS JEWILL-ROGERS

The wedding also had potential implications for Ashworth & Co. In this period, it was expected that middle-class women would resign paid employment on marriage and this was mandatory in many areas. The marriage bar, as it was known, had been in force in the Post Office and other parts of the Civil Service since their employment of women in clerical and administrative roles in the 1870s.

However, Ashworth was in a different position as she owned her own business. Having set it up herself and achieved so much, including winning the Parliament contract, it is hard to imagine her stepping aside and simply handing the business over to her husband. Instead, she took Paull's name and became Mrs Jewill-Rogers personally, but it appears that she continued to run Ashworth & Co. much as before. The couple are described as 'Partners' on the firm's headed paper in this period, and it tended to be Mrs rather than Mr Jewill-Rogers who corresponded with the Serjeant at Arms as necessary.

There was never enough accommodation in Parliament to satisfy anyone, and battles over office space were constant. The Lords tried to take the Typewriting Room for the use of Black Rod in 1904, leading May to write to the Serjeant. She stressed how important their work was in supporting the work of MPs:

> The work at the House has increased so much recently, especially during the last Session, that we have found it very difficult to manage with the rooms we had … The Members are always telling us what a convenience it would be if the Typewriting Rooms could be anywhere near the Central Hall. Every time the Division bell rings, they have quite a journey to and fro if they are in the middle of dictation.[19]

By now it had become more common for MPs to employ their own staff, including secretaries, who might be men or women. The advent of MPs employing secretaries may have spelt doom for Ashworth & Co. Why would any MP use a typing pool if they had the convenience of their own staff? However, Ashworth's continued to thrive and began to take on more official typing work within Parliament outside that for individual MPs. They started typing up parliamentary debates for Hansard reporters after the establishment of the Official Report in both Houses from 1909, and also began to do some typing for parliamentary committees.

Although Ashworth's described themselves on their headed paper as 'Official Typist-Shorthand Writers to the Houses of Parliament', the reference to shorthand might have been disputed by the ancient company of Gurneys. Gurneys had been official shorthand writers to Parliament since the eighteenth century, and they did not employ any women until after the Second World War. It might also have been disputed by the Hansard reporters employed by the Commons and Lords, also all male, who used shorthand to take notes in the chambers. The kind of shorthand provided by Ashworth's female staff – dictation by MPs in an office environment – apparently could never be extended to recorded official proceedings of Parliament. They could only be entrusted with the more mechanical business of typing it up.

As time went on, May reluctantly entered her forties, putting herself as age 41 instead of 48 in the 1911 census.

THE IMPACT OF WAR

In August 1916, after conscription was extended to married men, Paull applied for a temporary commission in the Royal Garrison Artillery, Anti-Aircraft Home Defence. He was appointed in November and stationed at Droylesden, Manchester. May ran the firm in his absence, although letters exchanged show her consulting him on matters such as charging for committee work. Paull's army career was not perhaps very typical of First World War service: he complained of various ailments which were dismissed by doctors, who deemed him 'too stout and out of condition' and suggested more exercise would be beneficial.[20]

In late 1918, conversations began about a new contract for Ashworth's. It seems the Serjeant initially assumed he would be dealing with Paull, as he wrote to May, 'I am wondering if there is any chance of your husband being on leave in London on any day in the near future.' May replied, 'I have telegraphed my husband begging him to come to town', but this did not apparently happen. A new Memorandum of Agreement was signed by her on 1 February 1919.[21]

Paull finally managed to be demobilised from the army in June 1919, and this marked a completely new phase of life for him. It would appear that the upheaval of war had convinced both him and May that they were better off apart.

THE DIVORCE PANTOMIME

Paull and May's business partnership in Ashworth & Co. was dissolved on 26 August 1919, with May taking responsibility for all debts due and owing, and continuing to run the company. May then initiated divorce proceedings, alleging that conjugal relations had been withdrawn since November 1914.

Under the Matrimonial Causes Act 1857, women divorcing on grounds of adultery not only had to prove their husbands had been unfaithful, but also aggravating factors; in May's case this was desertion. It was necessary to prove the adultery and desertion without apparent collusion. The result was two very carefully written letters to set the scene as they wished the situation to appear in open court. The first by May, addressed to Paull at Cleve Hall, his mother's address, on 18 October 1919:

> Dear Will
>
> For a long time I have made every kind of appeal to you to break off the connection which has brought such unhappiness into our married life, but you have not done so.
>
> When you were demobilised I hoped things might have been different but you only remained at home for a day or two, and then left me, without leaving your address.
>
> I must now ask you to give me a final answer as to whether you intend to return and live with me as my husband or not, as I cannot bear the strain and misery of my position any longer.
>
> If you decide to return, I will do my utmost to make your life happy.
>
> Your wife.

He replied a week later:

> Dear May
>
> I have received your letter asking me to return to you, and am writing to say that I have considered the matter very carefully, and have decided that it is impossible.
>
> No good can possibly be served by trying to continue a life which can only bring unhappiness to both.
>
> Perhaps I am to blame, although for the first twelve years I honestly tried to make you happy.
>
> Our marriage was a mistake on both our parts. Let us try and forget it and make the best of our mistake and start again.
>
> Will.[22]

Armed with this proof of desertion, May then petitioned for divorce on 6 November 1919. The co-respondent was Frances Elizabeth Boardman; May claimed that Paull had lived, co-habited and committed adultery with her on multiple occasions. It took a while to make it through the courts, but the divorce was granted in November 1920 on grounds of adultery and desertion, the decree absolute being issued on 6 June 1921.[23] The way was now free for Paull to marry Frances, which he did immediately. Paull went on to run Cleve Hall Hotel after the death of his parents, and he lived to the ripe old age of 96, dying in 1972.

What the whole divorce pantomime did not show was that Paull and Frances had been in a relationship for at least the previous ten years. Frances Boardman was an Irish nurse, born in Cork in 1886. She had a daughter, Doreen Frances Boardman, born in 1912 in Jersey in the Channel Islands. Doreen's father subsequently died. Frances and Paull apparently began a relationship soon after Doreen's birth as their first child, William Graham Rogers, was born in 1914, also in Jersey. Wartime then interrupted their relationship, but another son, Thomas (Tom) Arthur Rogers, was born amidst the divorce proceedings in Bishops Stortford, Hertfordshire, in September 1920.

It is hard to believe that May would not have been aware of at least some of this, and family memory is that May refused to divorce Paull for many years. It is very likely that divorce would have been scandalous to May, the clergyman's daughter, before the war, and she might have feared it would endanger her position as Typist to the Houses of Parliament. But by 1919 society had changed, and May was also now in a much more secure position. Following her new contract with Parliament and the removal of her husband from their business partnership earlier in the year, she could now divorce him and run her business again as she saw fit.

Perhaps signalling some adjustment to her new life, in the 1921 census she shifted her age closer to reality, giving it as 56 rather than 58. More surprisingly, she listed herself as still married, and with 'home duties' rather than a profession. This might be explained by the fact that she wasn't at home, but staying in a hotel in Budleigh Salterton, Devon, on holiday with her sister Rose. The census return would have been organised by the manageress, Margaret White; it might have been simpler and more respectable to describe herself as a housewife than explain that she was a divorced businesswoman.

ROSE DE BEAR AND THE ASHWORTH GIRLS

May continued to run Ashworth & Co. in Parliament after the war, with staff moving backwards and forwards from her Victoria Street office as required. The 1921 census gives us a snapshot of more than thirty Ashworth's employees across both locations, half of whom were under 21 years old. This shows a strong reliance on training up young girls who would have been cheaper to employ but perhaps also quick and eager to learn. Some were very young indeed, embarking on careers fresh from school and commuting from across

London to the Palace of Westminster each day, perhaps a source of pride to their relatively humble families. These included three apprentice shorthand typists aged just 14, one of whom was based in the Commons – Margaret Ellen Allsopp, a tailor's daughter living in Battersea. At the other end of the spectrum of experience and skill were six women in their forties, including three aged 45: Ethel Marie Anderson, Mary Katherine Anderson[24] and stenographer Margaret Emma Westlake, boarding in St John's Wood. And there was even one man based in Victoria Street – Ivor Bainbridge, translator of languages. He was a British subject but born in Seville, Spain, with a wife born in Switzerland. One can only imagine what it must have been like for him working alongside so many women.

Perhaps the most fascinating Ashworth's employee in 1921, though, was Rose de Bear, secretary, aged 33 and living with her family in Hampstead. Her father, Bernard de Bear, was a famous shorthand writer and teacher. He held the first attested record for the speed of 200 words a minute in shorthand, and for twenty years he was Principal of Pitman Metropolitan School in Holborn, founded in 1870. It advertised itself as 'The Largest and Most Successful Business College in the World', and recorded an attendance of 1,500–1,600 students in 1904.[25] In 1913, Bernard branched out and established his own chain of business schools, the De Bear schools, which had forty-three branches across the UK by the time of his death in 1924, after which the business was bought by John Gregg, inventor of Gregg's shorthand, a rival system to Pitman's.[26] May Ashworth would most certainly have known of Bernard de Bear, and one can only speculate as to how his daughter came to work in her office; presumably Rose was well trained by her father, and perhaps her name was a draw for clients.

Rose de Bear was a secretary at *The Sphere* newspaper before the First World War and subsequently volunteered as a Red Cross nurse. She served from 1916 at the American Hospital for British Soldiers, a convalescent hospital at Caen Wood Towers, Hampstead, then at Tudor House in Hampstead Heath, which operated as a Military Hospital for Jewish soldiers in 1918. She became secretary to the popular novelist, dramatist and poet Sir Hall Caine in 1918, and was apparently the best he ever had – but left because he wanted her to work part-time and she needed a full-time job. Although Ashworth's must have provided job security for a while, after a spell with the Maharajah of Kashmir's staff, she later returned to employment with Hall Caine until his death in 1931.[27] She died in 1981.

Rose also had famous siblings. Her sister Dorothie married an American, and as Dorothie de Bear Bobbe, settled in New York and wrote historical novels including *Abigail Adams: The Second First Lady* and *Mr. and Mrs. John Quincy Adams: An Adventure in Patriotism.* Her brother Archie had an even more colourful career. He was private secretary to Wilfrid Laurier, Prime Minister of Canada, and also to the controversial arms dealer and industrialist Sir Basil Zaharoff. In the First World War, he served first in the Public School Battalion of the Royal Fusiliers and then in the navy (where he was torpedoed in the Channel while being invalided home on a hospital ship). He moved on to music hall, in which he was very successful, becoming well known as a founder of the stage variety revue *The Co-Optimists* and for writing and producing West End shows, including *The Punch Bowl Revue* at the Duke of York's Theatre. In contrast to most of the Ashworth girls, Rose de Bear came from such a sufficiently talented and diverse family that her work in Parliament was almost the least noteworthy aspect of their lives.

ASHWORTH & CO.

After the war Ashworth & Co. continued to operate in Parliament despite increased competition. The House of Lords and House of Commons had begun to directly employ clerical staff, and in February 1924 Eileen Forbes Whittaker opened an 'MP's General Secretary's office', advertised as being 'within the precincts of the Houses of Parliament'. May complained to the Serjeant that this undermined her position, and Whittaker had to publish a correction which clarified that her office was instead 'within convenient distance'.[28]

In 1925, the Lords finally succeeded in claiming the Typewriting Room back from the Commons, despite resistance from the Serjeant and the Speaker. Ashworth's parliamentary operation moved to new accommodation off Westminster Hall, and May wrote to the Serjeant to thank him: 'We are all delighted with the rooms and the skilful way in which the alterations have been carried out and numerous Members have expressed their appreciation.' At this time Ashworth's could boast about 250 MPs as clients, with an average of thirty-five to forty visits to their rooms every day, and working for all departments across the Lords and Commons, as well as assisting some journalists from the Press Gallery and doing some typing work outside their office. The Ashworth's office was open from 10 a.m. to 10 p.m., with fourteen staff working in three shifts. They now had dictation cubicles with glass partitions, used every day by MPs dictating letters and speeches.[29]

In February 1928, May died, aged 65, but Ashworth & Co. continued to operate as official Typists to Parliament under its new principal, Gladys Helen Gowdey, who had worked for Ashworth's for many years and exercised an option in May's will to buy the firm. Miss Gowdey was born in 1885 in Charing Cross Road, London, the daughter of James Cragg Gowdey, a wine merchant born in Barbados to a Scottish family, and Antoinette, née Vollhardt, a Londoner.

Competition continued to increase in the 1930s as the political lobbying agency Watney & Powell came to provide secretarial services in Parliament too. Watney & Powell had been founded in 1911 by Charles Tillotson Watney as the St Stephen's Intelligence Bureau, a press agency specialising in parliamentary news. By the time he linked up with lobbyist Christopher C. Powell to form Watney & Powell in 1930, its political consultancy operations had come to include providing secretarial services for (mostly Conservative) politicians and interest groups.[30]

'SPEAK CLEARLY AND DON'T SMOKE A PIPE': THE TYPISTS OF HANSARD

Another source of competition for Ashworth & Co. was HMSO, His Majesty's Stationery Office, the official publisher for Hansard and other parliamentary publications. Although Ashworth's had initially supplied typing services to Hansard, in December 1923 this was taken over by HMSO, which took on some of Ashworth's 'girls' on a lower salary. Among the staff was Maude (or Maud) Constance Alexander. Born in Walthamstow in 1889, daughter of a printer and one of at least ten children, she started working for Ashworth's around 1915. She and the others were given a special allowance to top up their pay to the rates paid by Ashworth's. Unfortunately, as time passed and their basic pay increased, the special allowance was decreased accordingly, so they never progressed up their pay scale. In 1930, the Association of Women Clerks and Secretaries took up their case, which included complaints about hours and working conditions as well as pay. The Editor of Debates, T.H. Parr, had to provide assurances:

> Steps are being taken to secure that each typist shall have a regular time off for a meal in the evening on the four days Monday to Thursday. It is inaccurate to say that, owing to the strain of heavy work in the past, two girls have broken down ... Regarding drinking water, there is an ample supply quite close, the same water as provided to everyone in the House of Commons.[31]

The poor working conditions probably stemmed from their inconvenient location. The Hansard typists were based in the North Tank Room, a high, leaky attic space above the Upper Committee Corridor, fitted with sound-proof cubicles. They fought long battles, firstly to be taken on as established staff by HMSO, achieved in 1933, and subsequently to be transferred to the House of Commons, which did not happen until 1956. HMSO tried to argue in 1933 that it had given the typists stability whereas their previous employment with Ashworth's had fluctuated. Alexander wrote saying this was completely untrue; they had always had continuous employment with work for the Foreign Office or Treasury when the House of Commons was not sitting, demonstrating the wide range of work that Ashworth's staff undertook.[32] The Hansard typists partly won their case on the basis they were especially skilled workers, as this description shows:

> The fame of girls who have done this work lives long among the reporters. With a clear note and a good memory a Hansard reporter can read back at 80 or 100 words per minute easily. The clever Hansard typist welcomes this speed, and her fingers find the keys with a dexterity and accuracy that amazes the spectator. All she asks is 'Speak clearly and don't smoke a pipe.'[33]

In November 1942, Hansard staff listed in an inventory of staff for wartime evacuation planning purposes included five women, all typists. The most senior of these was Maude Alexander, the last survivor from the Ashworth days, by now aged 53. Another was Bessie Bloy, daughter of a coal porter from Streatham; she had previously worked as a typist for the biologist and longevity expert Dr Maurice Ernest.

After the war, it appears that HMSO began to use Hansard as a training ground for younger, less-experienced women. *Our Hansard*, published in 1950, declared snobbishly that they arrive 'as average – and sometimes less than average – copying typists. They reach eventually if they can withstand the breaking-in process, a high speed as dictation typists and acquire a much-enlarged vocabulary.' They then returned to HMSO and new girls arrived in their place, 'which gives rise to much internal friction'.[34] In 1956, the typists were finally transferred to the employment of the House of Commons, thus presumably relieving the friction, although only three of the six staff wanted to transfer: the supervisor and two of the younger staff.[35] By now, the supervisor was Bessie Bloy; Maude Alexander had died in 1955, aged 66. Bloy was made MBE following her retirement as Superintendent of Hansard Typists in 1968.

ASHWORTH & CO.: THE FINAL YEARS

Ashworth & Co. continued to provide services to Parliament through the Second World War. In 1939, when it was considered whether Ashworth's should be included on the Parliament staff evacuation planning list, it caused some consternation among the staff as to whether they would be taken over by the government and whether they would get any work (and therefore pay) during recesses. Miss Gowdey gave the Serjeant at Arms a list of six 'skeleton staff' names, but it was decided that with the likelihood of the House only sitting one or two days a week there would not be sufficient work to justify them coming.[36] The evacuation did not happen and Ashworth's remained based in their offices in Westminster Hall throughout the Blitz. In 1943, when there was no heating, it was noted, 'The girls at the moment are wrapped up in their coats and are doing their best to make themselves comfortable but in very difficult circumstances.'[37]

Ashworth's was taken over some time after 1945, although the name lived stubbornly on within Parliament and on its headed paper: 'Norma Skemp Ltd (incorporating Ashworth & Co)'. Norma Skemp Ltd occupied the same premises at 28 Victoria Street. Norma Skemp, a Women's Royal Naval Service (WRNS) officer during the Second World War, had set up her own business in Westminster and grown it from nothing in a very similar way to May Ashworth.

Under May Ashworth's professional ownership and management, and her female successors, Ashworth & Co. successfully provided official typing and translation services for MPs, peers and parliamentary offices from 1895 until at least 1965, with the name recognised within Parliament as the typing pool well into the 1970s.[38] May consistently promoted women throughout her life, and indeed after her death. In her will, she gave £20 to every 'lady' who had been her employment for at least five years, and £50 if they had been there for ten. And in 1939, on the death of her last surviving sister, Ethel, her residuary estate went to the Professional Classes Aid Council, 'to be earmarked and applied for the assistance of Women applicants only'.

In Her Own Words

'Patience. 36 hours here. Will they ever go. I am so thirsty. Nearly 26 hours have gone, and I have found water. Thank God. E W Davison April 1910. Rebellion against tyrants in obedience with God.'

Emily Wilding Davison's inscription inside a ventilation
shaft in the House of Commons, 1910

8

FOR ONE NIGHT ONLY?
EMILY WILDING DAVISON IN
THE CUPBOARD

On 3 April 1911, Dr John Esmonde MP rose to ask a rather unusual question in the House of Commons. Apparently, a lady had been found in the crypt.

> **Dr. ESMONDE:** May I ask the hon. Member for Southampton whether it is true that a lady has been found in the crypt, and, if so, when she got there, and what he proposes doing?

> **Mr. DUDLEY WARD:** I have just been informed that a lady was found in the crypt this morning. I have not yet had time to make myself fully acquainted with the circumstances. Presumably the lady went there in order to avoid the Census. The only step I propose to take at present is to inform the President of the Local Government Board so that she may be enumerated with the rest of the population.[1]

The crypt in the Palace of Westminster, properly called the Chapel of St Mary Undercroft, was – and is – a Royal Peculiar, meaning it is under the jurisdiction of the monarch rather than a bishop. Dudley Ward, MP for Southampton, held the office of Treasurer of the Royal Household, which is why he answered the question. And 'the lady', was, of course, suffragette Emily Wilding Davison who was, according to legend, resident in Parliament for just one night. Dudley Ward ensured she was indeed enumerated with the rest of the population, the Clerk of Works recording on the census form that she was, 'Found hiding in crypt of Westminster Hall since Saturday'.[2] This meant she had in fact been there for two nights.

Davison was away from home not only to avoid the census but also to make a political point; if she was to be recorded anywhere, she wanted to be present in the House of Commons to make her claim for equal political rights in the heart of democracy. This was the most dramatic and eye-catching of many protests by Davison and other suffragettes within the Palace of Westminster: women using their bodies to disrupt and physically challenge the boundaries and control of parliamentary space and participation. Activity had moved from the constraints of the nineteenth-century Ventilator, through the gilded cage of the Ladies' Gallery, to direct and physical resistance deep within the building. Parliament had symbolic value as the centre of democracy and also as a physical space which excluded women from decision-making and power.[3]

Yet Davison was not the only woman at the Palace that night: the census records show sixty-seven other female residents were there too, by right. One of these was Amelia de Laney, House of Lords Housekeeper, the only female head of household in the Palace of Westminster, and the only woman living there to complete and sign her own form. There were also seven female staff living and working in the House of Commons Refreshment Department; seventeen women resident in the household of a husband or father; and forty-two women servants in the households of male officials. Their presence in Parliament on census night may be less well known than Davison's, but their stories also shed light on the operations of Parliament and their importance should not be underestimated. Finally, although we can only guess at what most women working in Parliament may have thought of Emily Wilding Davison, the defaced census form for Ethel Marie Anderson, Typing Manager in the House of Commons, brilliantly illuminates the strong opinions on suffrage in one family.

BANNED FROM CENTRAL HALL

Following the first mass suffrage petition hidden underneath Mrs Furlong's apple cart in 1866, through decades of dogged but unsuccessful peaceful campaigning, the votes for women movement took a new turn in the early twentieth century with the formation of the WSPU, the Women's Social and Political Union, by Emmeline Pankhurst and others in Manchester in 1903. The WSPU believed in 'Deeds Not Words', and from 1905 adopted tactics of direct action which began with shouting in public meetings and escalated over the years to include window-smashing, chaining themselves to railings and ultimately arson and bombing. These women became known as 'suffragettes', in contrast to Millicent Fawcett's non-militant campaigners, the 'suffragists', although the distinction was not firm and many women belonged to more than one organisation.

Suffragette action in the Palace of Westminster began in 1906 with demonstrations initially in the Ladies' Gallery and then in Central Lobby. Known also in this period as Central Hall, Central Lobby lies at the heart of Parliament between the House of Commons and House of Lords. Most visitors would enter via St Stephen's Hall, walk through to Central Lobby, and wait there to see Members, perhaps for meetings, social reasons, or to get a card to watch debates from the Ladies' Gallery. However, the disruption from suffragettes became so great that on 14 February 1907, women were banned from Central Lobby and confined to St Stephen's Hall; suffragette activity then moved to St Stephen's Hall instead.

The Central Lobby ban remained in force for eleven years, rescinded only after the first votes for women were granted in February 1918. It was inconvenient for female visitors, especially those not accompanied by male relatives, friends and colleagues. Although the rules were rigorously enforced for solo women who might have been suffragettes, it is likely that they were bent on occasion for those accompanied by respectable men, such as this occasion reported by the police in April 1908:

A Mr Baddeley a private Secretary to the Admiralty entered the Central Hall from St Stephen's Hall accompanied by a lady. PC Robins the Constable on duty at the door informed him that he was not allowed to take a lady in, he replied 'it is ridiculous I am a Secretary and I am going to the Back of Chair', and insisted upon going. To prevent a scene occurring the Constable allowed him to proceed.[4]

The unnamed lady does not appear to have had an official role, but the ban would also have had an impact on the many women who were in Parliament for business reasons. The regulations issued by the Speaker acknowledged this:

During the sittings of Committees Ladies having business in the Committee Rooms will be allowed to proceed to the Committee Room corridor but will not be permitted to remain in the Central Hall (unless accompanied by a Member).

Lady-Secretaries of Members wishing to proceed to the room set apart for their use in the Old Crown Office will be permitted to do so.

These regulations are to take effect ¾ of an hour before the Meeting of the House.[5]

What this showed was that because Central Lobby was so central, some women had to be allowed to pass through it – as long as they didn't stop! Women who had business in committee rooms might have been giving expert evidence, attending in secretarial capacities or observing proceedings. 'Lady-Secretaries' of Members would have included suffragette Margaret Travers Symons, Secretary to Labour Leader Keir Hardie, who carried out a very high-profile demonstration in Parliament. On 13 October 1908, Symons asked Thomas Idris MP, a friend of her father, to get her a ticket to the Ladies' Gallery. While she waited, he left her looking through the peephole or 'Ladies' Nook', the observation post and window in the outer door to the House of Commons chamber used frequently by women. From there, Symons managed to run in and interrupt a debate, exclaiming, 'Leave off discussing the children's question, and turn your attention to the women first', thus becoming the first woman to 'speak' in the House of Commons.[6] She was formally excluded from the building for this and wrote a grovelling if qualified letter of apology to the Speaker in 1910: 'This I have regretted on account of the inconvenience it has caused my employer, Mr Keir Hardie, in connection with my secretarial work.'[7] She was readmitted.

Although most of the suffrage campaigners were concerned with the House of Commons, the regulations also affected women visiting the House of Lords. The Lord Great Chamberlain controlled security down at the Lords' end of the building and as late as 1916 refused to allow Emmeline Pankhurst into Peers' Lobby when she arrived with a deputation of nine women to see Lord Grey, apparently regarding the Greek statesman, Eleftherios Venizelos. She spent an hour and half waiting in St Stephen's Hall, 'created a disturbance by behaving in a disorderly manner' and was then banned indefinitely from the building by agreement of the Speaker and the Lord Great Chamberlain.[8]

The Central Lobby regulations are silent as to any exceptions for women working for Parliament such as Miss Ashworth and her team, or living on site in households, so there was probably not much impact on them. The regulations would not have been applied when the House was not sitting, when women were there to clean the banned area, or to those passing through it on the way to work in kitchens or offices – or simply pausing in a grand space that was also part of their home. Women familiar with the layout of the Palace would have been able to take alternative routes through the building to avoid Central Lobby while the House was sitting. This would have included women staff – and also Emily Wilding Davison.

EMILY WILDING DAVISON IN THE PALACE OF WESTMINSTER

Emily Wilding Davison is, of course, a famous suffragette, today probably second only in public memory to Emmeline Pankhurst. Davison is known principally as the suffragette martyr; she died in June 1913 following a collision with the king's horse at the Epsom Derby. This deed and her funeral, with a procession attended by 50,000 spectators, reverberated on newsreels around the world. It has continued to resonate through history and popular culture ever since, for example featuring heavily in the 2015 film *Suffragette*. However, in 1911 she was a more peripheral figure in the movement. She was an extremely active and militant member of the WSPU, arrested multiple times, imprisoned, on hunger strike, forcibly fed, yet apt to break from the herd and do her own thing, and protest in her own way. Of this, the census protest was an excellent example – but not the first. For Davison knew the Palace of Westminster well. Police reports show that she was found there on at least five other occasions and had even been – ineffectively – banned from the building.

The Serjeant at Arms was formally responsible for security in the House of Commons. The Metropolitan Police were responsible for providing that security, meaning that each time suffragettes breached the Palace defences, the long-suffering Chief of Police, Inspector Charles Scantlebury, had to pen yet another report to the Serjeant's office explaining what had happened. The Assistant Serjeant, Walter Hugh Erskine, was the recipient of these reports and he must have come to shake his head each time he saw Davison's name.

Davison's first recorded demonstration in Parliament was on 30 March 1909, when a group of WSPU suffragettes led by 65-year-old Georgiana Solomon attempted to present a petition. When refused, 'a number of women in colours and sashes dashed at the entrance and made a determined effort to get past Police'. Although just one of a larger group, Emily Davison is at the top of the list of names of the eleven women and one man who were arrested.[9]

The following year, Davison chose to act alone – and this time she hid, in a manner much more like her later census protest. On 3 April 1910, she was found in a ventilation shaft at 6.30 p.m., having concealed herself there for two nights. Davison gave an account of how she entered the building on a tour, slipped away from the public areas through a door marked 'Private', and entered a ventilation shaft, climbing two ladders to settle down on some planks used by workmen. It was filthy and very uncomfortable, initially overwhelmingly hot from the pipework and then cold overnight when the pipes were switched off:

> There came a period of hideous, awful waiting. The time wore away so slowly, for I had nothing to do but read my guide to the Houses of Parliament ... Big Ben kept me informed of the slow progress of time ... I dozed occasionally and listened for the Abbey afternoon service bells.[10]

She managed some sleep, although she was scared of falling down the shaft. For provisions, she had brought two bananas, some chocolate and lozenges for a cold. After initially suffering great thirst, she managed to find some water the following day, and after that she felt capable of waiting for days if necessary. Eventually, she was found by a policeman on night patrol – 'the poor constable was terror-stricken, so that he nearly dropped his lantern' – and arrested.[11] The police report to the Serjeant relates that the constable, PC 438 Thorndike, asked, 'What are you doing here?' She replied, 'I am a suffragette and my ambition is to get into the House to ask a question.' The report adds:

> The following was found written in pencil on a window pane inside the shaft. EWD April 3rd 1910. Patience. 36 hours here. Will they ever go. I am so thirsty. Nearly 26 hours have gone, and I have found water. Thank God. E W Davison April 1910. Rebellion against tyrants in obedience with God.[12]

The authorities released her without charge. Davison speculated that this was because she would have had to appear before the House of Commons itself, which seems unlikely. No damage had been done, and if any charge had been issued, it is likely that the Serjeant at Arms and the Westminster Police would have been severely embarrassed at having to admit she had managed to hide unnoticed for so long. This occasion proved to be a practice run for her later stay in the crypt chapel.

Soon after stowing away in the ventilation shaft, Davison appeared at the other end of the building, throwing stones to break a window in the Crown Office, House of Lords, on 23 June 1910. She attached labels to the stones, which were found inside the room where she had broken the windows.

They were addressed to 'Mr Asquith', the prime minister, and read, 'Give full facilities to the New Bill for woman's suffrage'; 'Indignant womanhood will take this insult, be wise'; 'Be wise in time, women will not be trifled with'.[13] Davison's reference to the new bill for 'woman's suffrage' relates to the first Conciliation Bill being proposed in Parliament at this time, which would have given the vote to approximately a million women.

As a direct result of these protests, Davison was banned from the building. The Speaker of the House of Commons, James W. Lowther, wrote to the Serjeant at Arms:

> A lady who breaks the windows of the Crown Office and gets into our ventilating shaft is evidently not a desirable personage to have hanging about St. Stephen's Hall so her name had better go on the Index Expurgatorius.[14]

The Index Expurgatorius was a list of people banned from the building. Naturally, no such list could keep Davison out and, a few months later, she was back. A major suffragette protest took place outside the building on 18 November 1910, which became known as 'Black Friday' because of the violence and brutality shown by the police against female protestors in Parliament Square. Davison's reaction to this came the following day and as close to the Commons as she could get. She threw a hammer through a window between the House of Commons chamber and a division lobby. Her action was witnessed by a police officer and she was immediately arrested. Again, labels were found attached to the hammer: 'Be wise and promise the further facilities at once the women are demanding'; 'Do justice before the General Election or judgment will surely fall'.[15]

She was subsequently fined and, as was usual with suffragettes, opted to go to prison rather than pay. The police report noted at the trial on 30 November that she was 'unrepresented by any of the Women's Social and Political Union they do not acknowledge her',[16] showing she was very much acting of her own accord rather than in response to any direction. After a week of hunger striking and forcible feeding, she was released. Judgement did not fall at the General Election in December, where Asquith's Liberal government was re-elected again.

CENSUS NIGHT RESIDENT

A few months later came census night, 2 April 1911. Suffrage campaigners approached the census in different ways. Suffragists, those using peaceful methods of campaigning, such as the National Union of Women's Suffrage Societies led by Millicent Fawcett, abided by the census and completed their forms as required by law. They wanted to act as good citizens and saw this as strengthening their case for the vote. Some militant campaigners also chose to comply in full, perhaps wanting to support the wider aims of the census, which included providing accurate data for social and welfare reforms. However, many members of the WSPU and the Women's Freedom League adopted tactics of civil disobedience. Some resisted, for example by defacing their forms, writing 'Votes for Women', 'No Vote No Census' in large letters – one of these women was Mary Jane Anderson, of whom more below. Others chose to evade, attempting to avoid being recorded by hiding in darkened houses, cycling, caravanning or going skating all night on the Aldwych rink.[17]

Davison's protest was unique in that she used her evasion to make a political point. She did not want to be at home, at her lodgings in Russell Square (although her landlady did also record her there, despite her absence – an irony, when many suffragettes were evading the census, that Davison was recorded twice). She wanted to be present in the House of Commons, the place she had targeted so many times over the last few years that perhaps it also felt like home. Armed with her prior knowledge of the building, a bottle of water and some biscuits, Davison peeled off from a visitor tour during the afternoon of 1 April.

Public access to the crypt chapel – which had been 'bedizened with gold' in the 1860s and was a popular visitor attraction – was, in theory, tightly controlled. In 1885, a bomb planted by Irish separatists, believed to have been posing as visitors, had exploded near the top of its narrow access stairs, and for the next decade it was closed altogether for security reasons. In 1911, it was open on Saturdays for pre-booked public tours, or as Emily would have known, it could be accessed for the frequent large groups, of up to forty people, hosted by an MP. The subsequent police report assured authorities that the crypt was checked by police on Saturday, 1 April at 4 p.m. after the last of the public had gone through, but that seven parties with Members as guides went through the crypt after that. Davison was with one of those.[18] She went to hide in a little storeroom at the back of the crypt. As described in the suffragette newspaper *Votes for Women*:

A NIGHT IN GUY FAWKES' CUPBOARD
Armed with some provisions, Miss Davison took up her position in a cupboard of about five foot by six foot. What at first sight appeared to be a

mere timber room was in reality a spot of great historic interest, for on the wall were written the words 'Guy Fawkes was killed here.'[19]

Guy Fawkes was not, of course, killed in this cupboard, which is a post-1834 fire creation dating from around 1857; he was found with thirty-six barrels of gunpowder in an undercroft beneath the House of Lords in 1605 and executed nearby in Old Palace Yard. Nevertheless, this is what the cupboard was known for in 1911. Davison stayed in the cupboard for two nights, taking occasional short walks around the chapel to stretch her legs. She was nearly discovered when an MP threw open the door to show the 'Guy Fawkes' cupboard to a visiting group but managed to hide behind boxes. She was eventually discovered there on the morning of Monday, 3 April by Joseph Medynski, a workman from the Office of Works. She was taken to nearby Cannon Row police station, refused to give her name or say how she got there, and released after a few hours in the matron's room. The police explained that they were not responsible for patrolling the crypt at night and so were not to blame.[20] No charges were brought as no damage was done.

The police readily identified her as Davison from her previous actions in Parliament and the First Commissioner of Works (William Lygon, Earl Beauchamp) instructed that she be recorded on the census. This was done by Percy Edgar Ridge, Clerk of Works, who had completed his own census form at home in Surbiton and presumably arrived at work the next day only to find himself given this additional task. Unsurprisingly, in the circumstances, Davison's Parliament census form is filled with inaccuracies. Her surname is misspelt as 'Davidson' throughout; her age is given as 35 instead of 38; her occupation as school teacher, a profession she had left several years previously to dedicate herself full-time to activism (her landlady's alternative form described her more accurately as political secretary); and her birthplace as 'Long Worsley' (her family were from Longhorsley, Northumberland, but she was born in Blackheath, London).

Davison's final appearance in Parliament came a couple of months later, when she was found on a staircase in the middle of the night near the House of Commons Library on 26 June 1911. At 2.23 a.m., a police officer spotted her as she scaled a 3ft railing at the Members' staircase.[21] He followed her up the stairs and found that she was bare-footed. Following her arrest, a Bow Street magistrate said there was no evidence to show that she went to the House of Commons to attack anybody and he did not think she had committed any offence to bring her within the criminal law. He discharged her, saying she must be more careful in future.[22] Davison refused to give any undertaking not to go there again, but in fact she does not seem to have troubled the Palace authorities after this episode.

'DO NOT COUNT ONLY A WIFE': THE ANDERSONS

Another remarkable – and previously unrecognised – piece of suffrage history jumps out from the parliamentary census forms for 1911. Ethel Marie Anderson, employed by Ashworth & Co. as Manager of the House of Commons Typing Office, aged 35, was living with her mother Mary Jane Anderson, aged 58, at 4 Whitehall Gardens, Gunnersbury, Chiswick. Mary Jane completed their form, scrawling across the middle 'Votes for Women'. This was later struck through in red ink by the census enumerator (Plate 7).

Expressed in her own words, Mary Jane's rage permeates each section of the form. In the first column for the names of the people being enumerated, she writes, 'The Superior Male as head is away' – this referred to her husband, John Joseph Anderson, who was staying in a hotel in Pembrokeshire that night. In the next column, for relationship to the head of the house, she has written, 'Do not count only a Wife'. She has scribbled through some of these words herself, apparently wanting to ensure her name and position as 'Wife' was in fact clear on the form. Her daughter's details below are also clear and unannotated. But in the next column for profession or occupation, Mary Jane lets rip with, 'Housekeeper Cook General Servant Mother payment for which is no <u>wages</u> no <u>Vote</u>'. Wages for housework would become a prominent campaign by feminists in the 1970s, but 'wages for wives' was also a demand by some women's rights activists in this period, and here is an ordinary housewife seething at the injustice of her situation back in 1911. In the final column for any infirmity to be described, Mary Jane has one last broadside: 'Being of Female Parentage must be feeble minded consequently no Vote'.

As the census form also records, both Mary Jane and Ethel Marie were born in the United States of America. So, who were the Andersons and how did they come to be resident in the United Kingdom in 1911?

John Joseph Anderson, their 'superior male' husband and father, was born in 1847 into a prominent Baptist family with strong local roots in Long Sutton, Lincolnshire, and Wisbech, Cambridgeshire. One of the six children of Charles Anderson and Katharine Anderson, née Butterfield, John Joseph was variously recorded over the years as a draper, auctioneer, merchant, superintendent of coal agents and commercial traveller. He journeyed to the USA probably before 1871, and in 1874 married Mary Jane Keenan at the Philadelphia Monthly Meeting, a Quaker body; he was aged 26 and she 21. The couple had two children born in Pittsburgh, Pennsylvania: Ethel Marie – who would go on to be Typing Manager in the House of Commons – in September 1875, and Cyrus Victor in August 1877. The family then moved to the UK before their third child Royston was born in Wisbech in 1879, relocating to London before 1901. There is nothing to suggest that any of them even visited the USA after that, and although Cyrus served in the US Army between 1918 and 1919, he was based in England throughout.

Mary Jane may have known of women's suffrage from her childhood in America: the movement in the USA formally originated in the Seneca Falls Convention in 1848, before she was born, and the Pennsylvania Women's Suffrage Association had its first annual meeting in Philadelphia in 1870. Her daughter's job in the Commons would certainly have provided both of them with an insight into the movement's goals and progress in Britain. And although she may never have had an occupation other than 'Housewife Cook General Servant and Mother', Mary Jane must have been delighted that her daughter was able to enjoy opportunities that had not been open to her. For Ethel became a Typist at Ashworth & Co., possibly one of May Ashworth's original employees based in Parliament as early as 1895, when she would have been 20 years old. Certainly, she was a secretary in a typing office in 1901, probably Ashworth's. In 1911 she was manager of Ashworth's House of Commons Typing Office, and in 1921 she had risen to be manager of Ashworth's Victoria Street operation.

It is not known if Ethel shared her mother's views on votes for women, but the family do appear to have been close-knit. Her brothers moved on to have their own families, but Ethel never married and continued to live with her parents. In 1922, they moved from Whitehall Gardens to 13 Oxford Road nearby in Chiswick; Mary Jane died in 1927 and John Joseph in 1936, Ethel remaining in the family home. She was still living there and working at Ashworth's in 1939 when she was recorded as 'Book Keeper, Typing Dept, House of Commons'. By this time, May Ashworth had died and the company had been taken over by Gladys Gowdey, but Ethel had reason to be loyal; under the terms of Ashworth's will, Gowdey had to pay Ethel £50 a year from company profits for the rest of Ethel's life, as a condition of buying the firm. May Ashworth clearly valued Ethel Marie Anderson highly to support her in this way.

One of Ethel's cousins, Mary Katherine Anderson, also worked at Ashworth's. She was born in Wisbech in March 1876 to Charles Benjamin Anderson, brother of John Joseph, and Alice Ann Anderson, née Mason. Alice farmed 66 acres in Leicestershire and probably passed these lands on to her daughter when she died in 1893, for in 1911 Mary Katherine was a 'land owner', living in Wisbech with her father. The First World War brought a change of direction, as in 1921 she was a clerk working for Ashworth & Co. in Victoria Street – another parliamentary family connection, as she was managed by (and had evidently been recruited by) her cousin Ethel. Ashworth's may well have been a springboard for Mary Katherine's career, as she went on to serve in the Ministry of Pensions. She passed away in 1947, followed by Ethel in 1956.

AN OLD RETAINED SERVANT: MARTHA KING

Apart from Davison, the most notable woman living in Parliament who was recorded in the 1911 census was Amelia de Laney, House of Lords Housekeeper and the only female head of household who filled out her own form.[23] A larger all-female household, however, was that of the seven servants living and working in the House of Commons Refreshment Department. Their census form was completed by their manager, Charles Frederick King, who had previously lived in the Palace but by 1911 was resident with his family elsewhere. They were four milk room maids, one tea room maid and two housemaids. Ten beds were available so perhaps there were vacancies, or some staff were simply staying elsewhere that night. The women ranged in age from 43-year-old Ada Hammond to Dorothy Coulson who was just 15.

The tea room maid was Martha Ann King, who had a very long career in the Commons. Born in 1873 in Penge, Kent, she is mentioned in a Select Committee report in 1916 as a wine dispenser who had worked there for nineteen years.[24] Kitchen Committee minutes in the late 1930s record her as an 'old retained servant' who enjoyed an annual Christmas gift of poultry. She finally retired on 31 December 1938, with a £40 gratuity and a pension.[25] By this time, she would have been 65 and had worked in the Commons for forty-one years. Tragically, the advent of the Second World War meant she did not get to enjoy retirement for long; she died on 13 September 1940 in hospital following bombing where she lived in Barkworth Road, Camberwell. The Commonwealth War Graves Commission lists her as one of more than 1,000 civilian war dead in Camberwell. Although the war memorials in the Palace of Westminster include civilian war deaths, they do not include the recently retired Martha King, despite the length of her service. The Kitchen Committee did at least note her death in its minutes: killed by enemy action.[26]

It is not known what de Laney, King or any other woman living or working in Parliament in 1911 thought about Davison's stay, or suffragette action in their midst. Unlike Mary Jane Anderson, they gave no hint on their census forms. It is likely that some of the family members of officials may have supported suffrage generally, although probably not militant activity. For example, Lettice Ilbert, daughter of Clerk of the House, Sir Courtenay Ilbert, was an active suffragist, although by 1911 she had married Oxford academic H.A.L. Fisher (later an MP) and was not resident in Parliament with her father.[27] Others may have been anti-suffrage. Horatia Erskine, wife of Assistant Serjeant Walter H. Erskine who received all the police reports, a resident on census night, was a friend and biographer of Mary Sumner, founder of the Mother's Union, and shared Sumner's view that caring for children gave women a more exalted status than the achievement of political rights.[28]

Another long-serving member of staff noted in the Commons Refreshment Department along with King in 1916 was 'Miss Pankhurst at the Press Gallery Bar, 17 years'.[29] Tantalising prospect as it is to think of a Miss Pankhurst concocting suffragette work while serving drinks to journalists in Parliament, there is, sadly, no evidence that she was related to her suffragette namesakes. Born in 1879 in St Martin-in-the-Fields, London, Mary Elizabeth Pankhurst was resident as a waitress in the Commons in 1901 and recorded as Manageress of the Press Gallery Bar, House of Commons in 1911 while living with her mother nearby in Pimlico. However, Pankhurst did not manage anything like Martha King's length of service; by 1921 she had moved on and was working as a waitress in a tea room on Pall Mall. She married in 1941 and died in 1954.

REMEMBERED IN THE PALACE

Many other suffragette protests took place in the Palace of Westminster apart from those by Emily Wilding Davison. Perhaps most notably, on 28 October 1908, three suffragettes from the Women's Freedom League – Helen Fox, Muriel Matters and Violet Tillard – carried out a protest in the Ladies' Gallery, in what became known as the Grille Incident. In the same Ladies' Gallery that Ida B. Wells had been so astonished to find in the UK House of Commons, where previous generations of women had painstakingly peered down at debates, strained their eyes, rattled their fans, and hissed and clapped at proceedings, suffragettes now took things a step further.

Matters and Fox chained themselves to a section of the much-hated grille, which ran across the windows along the front of the gallery, concealing the women from the view of MPs in the chamber far below. Meanwhile, Tillard manoeuvred a 'proclamation' banner through gaps in the grille and into the chamber, causing a tremendous uproar that interrupted proceedings. That section of the grille had to be taken out of the window aperture and – doubtless with great difficulty – removed to a committee room where the locks were filed off to release the suffragettes. The Ladies' Gallery was closed for some time afterwards. Simultaneous protests took place by other women in St Stephen's Hall and by men in the Strangers' Gallery. Women were challenging both the physical and metaphorical barriers which excluded them from democratic proceedings in the Palace of Westminster.

Following a petition by the London Society for Women's Service, referring to the Ladies' Gallery as 'a custom which is merely a survival of a more picturesque age', the grille was finally removed from the Ladies' Gallery windows and the Strangers' Gallery opened to women in August 1917.[30] By this time, the Representation of the People Bill was progressing through the House of Commons and it was clear that some women would soon get the vote.

Women could now choose between the Strangers' Gallery or the Ladies' Gallery, although they still did not have equal access to other galleries, let alone all areas of the building such as dining rooms, with many constraints remaining. Yet it was a big step forward and recognised as such at the time. The grilles were placed in Central Lobby, where they can be seen today, a small brass plaque recording their former purpose placed there by suffrage supporter Sir Alfred Mond MP, First Commissioner of Works. Women were allowed back into Central Lobby from 1918, and most of the exclusions of individuals from the building were quietly cancelled in 1922. The Ladies' Gallery remained in existence until it was destroyed, along with the rest of the House of Commons chamber, by bombing in the Second World War.

Much later, another plaque was put up to record Emily Wilding Davison's stay on census night. Davison's contribution to the British suffrage movement was huge, and today she is remembered in memorials, plaques, names of buildings and statues in Epsom, Morpeth, Royal Holloway and elsewhere, as well as in many productions on stage and screen. Her lasting legacy within Parliament, however, was to make the crypt chapel cupboard famous, no longer for an invented connection to Guy Fawkes but for her stay there on census night. Having sneaked in with a tour group, it is perhaps ironic that she then became part of the attraction herself. Visitors seem to have been solemnly counted in and out to ensure none were able to emulate her

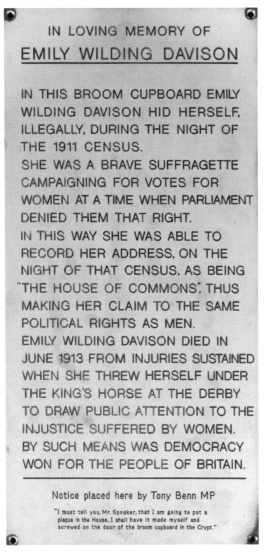

IN LOVING MEMORY OF
EMILY WILDING DAVISON

IN THIS BROOM CUPBOARD EMILY
WILDING DAVISON HID HERSELF,
ILLEGALLY, DURING THE NIGHT OF
THE 1911 CENSUS.
SHE WAS A BRAVE SUFFRAGETTE
CAMPAIGNING FOR VOTES FOR
WOMEN AT A TIME WHEN PARLIAMENT
DENIED THEM THAT RIGHT.
IN THIS WAY SHE WAS ABLE TO
RECORD HER ADDRESS, ON THE
NIGHT OF THAT CENSUS, AS BEING
"THE HOUSE OF COMMONS". THUS
MAKING HER CLAIM TO THE SAME
POLITICAL RIGHTS AS MEN.
EMILY WILDING DAVISON DIED IN
JUNE 1913 FROM INJURIES SUSTAINED
WHEN SHE THREW HERSELF UNDER
THE KING'S HORSE AT THE DERBY
TO DRAW PUBLIC ATTENTION TO THE
INJUSTICE SUFFERED BY WOMEN.
BY SUCH MEANS WAS DEMOCRACY
WON FOR THE PEOPLE OF BRITAIN.

Notice placed here by Tony Benn MP

"I must tell you, Mr. Speaker, that I am going to put a
plaque in the House, I shall have it made myself and
screwed on the door of the broom cupboard in the Crypt."

Figure 9: Tony Benn's plaque to Emily Wilding
Davison, 1991.

stay, which can only have been a tourist gimmick for such a tiny space. In
1924, a copy of her memorial leaflet was sent to the Keeper of the Crypt,
with a note: 'It might interest your many visitors to see the picture of the
Suffragette when you tell the story of why you count them in and out. One
bye [*sic*] one.'[31]

Today, the cupboard is still strongly associated with Davison, and in 1991 a
plaque to her (Figure 9) was put up by Tony Benn MP, who spoke about it
as follows:

I have put up several plaques – quite illegally, without permission; I screwed them up myself. One was in the broom cupboard to commemorate Emily Wilding Davison, and another celebrated the people who fought for democracy and those who run the House. If one walks around this place, one sees statues of people, not one of whom believed in democracy, votes for women or anything else. We have to be sure that we are a workshop and not a museum.[32]

Benn was assisted by Jeremy Corbyn MP, who recalled many years later, on the centenary of the first votes for women in 2018 (by which time Corbyn was the leader of the Labour Party):

I met him [Benn] when the House finished one evening, went to his car, picked up the toolbox, the plaque and some tools and an electric drill ... I thought, 'Oh my goodness, how do I explain to a policeman what I'm doing walking through Parliament carrying an electric drill at 11 o'clock at night?'[33]

One can only assume that Davison would have approved and may have felt similarly nervous on the various occasions she smuggled in a hammer or stones to break windows, or brought provisions to facilitate a longer stay.

Davison's plaque is still there today, admired by the small numbers of people who can visit the chapel and peek into the cupboard. However, every visitor to Parliament can view a much larger monument to the women's suffrage movement, which celebrates the many rather than the few. *New Dawn*, a light sculpture by artist Mary Branson, sits in Westminster Hall above the entrance to St Stephen's Hall, the doorway used by generations of suffrage campaigners (Plate 8). It was commissioned by the Speaker's Advisory Committee on Works of Art and installed in 2016 on the 150th anniversary of the presentation of the first mass women's suffrage petition – the one hidden underneath Mary Furlong's apple cart. It is made of 168 hand-blown glass disks incorporating colours of the major suffrage organisations, mounted on a circular portcullis, its lighting ebbing and flowing with the tidal Thames. In a building where the contribution of women over the centuries is almost entirely invisible, *New Dawn* is a beautiful and glowing permanent tribute.

In Her Own Words

'I am desirous of joining the London Chamber of Commerce but have to produce three references before I become a member.'

Vera Goldsmith, former Girl Porter in the House of Commons, writing to the Serjeant at Arms, 1920

9

A WARTIME INNOVATION:
THE GIRL PORTERS

In April 1917, with Britain in its third year of the Great War, Walter Hugh
Erskine, Assistant Serjeant at Arms, sat down and took a deep breath to write
to James Lowther, Speaker of the House of Commons:

> As it is an innovation, I think perhaps I ought to let you know that I have
> been obliged to appoint four temporary Girl-Porters to take the places
> of four Porters in my department who, in turn, will do the work of four
> Messengers called to the Colours.[1]

'Called to the Colours' meant the men had been called up to join the
armed forces. This showed that conscription had finally caught up with the
Serjeant's staff. In 1916, Parliament had passed the Military Services Act,
which meant all men aged between 18 and 41 had to enlist. Initially, this was
restricted to unmarried men and childless widowers, but was then extended
to married men. There were some exceptions for certain classes of essential
worker but manual labour in the Serjeant at Arms Department was not sufficiently essential: the men had to go and fight.

However, their work still had to be done. The 'Westminster Village' was
part of the Home Front, the civilian population of a nation at war. The House
of Commons and House of Lords sat throughout the war, passing legislation
such as the Defence of the Realm Acts. MPs and peers debated issues such as
defence and conscription, trouble in Ireland and votes for men and women.
Women continued working in existing roles in Parliament throughout

the war to make this possible, including housekeepers, cooks, waitresses, barmaids, telephone operators and Ashworth's shorthand and typing team.

In wider society, where men were called up, women stepped up to do work traditionally done by men. Approximately 1 million of them entered the workforce for the first time during the war, with others moving from more traditional spheres of women's work such as domestic service to new areas such as munitions. The Speaker and the Serjeant would have been well aware of this; women were working in visible roles in public transport, factories, farms and even in the armed forces, in the women's auxiliary services.

In Parliament itself, change was slow; indeed, for the first few years of war, there was no visible change. In the House of Lords, the messenger staff were mostly old soldiers, all above military age, and there was therefore no need to employ any Girl Porters. But some younger men in the House of Commons were called up to serve and by early 1917 the portering staff had been reduced to two. Things were desperate. Walter Erskine had to resort to women – indeed, to girls. The youngest was just 14 years old.

There is no reply from the Speaker to Erskine's letter, no record as to what he thought about the 'innovation' of Girl Porters. But Speaker Lowther had been very impressed by the war work of his daughter Mildred, Principal in the Army Pay Office since 1916. He was also fresh from chairing the Speaker's Conference on Electoral Reform, which reported in January 1917 and recommended, among other things, that some measure of women's suffrage should be conferred. This led directly to the Representation of the People Bill, introduced in May 1917, which would eventually give the parliamentary vote to women over the age of 30 who met the qualification for the local government franchise – effectively a minimum property qualification. The Girl Porters were far too young to vote themselves, of course, but perhaps the Speaker might have seen their employment as another sign of a changing society in which women would play a greater public role.

THE ROLE OF THE GIRL PORTERS

The Girl Porters were Elsie and Mabel Clark (aged 16 and 14), Dorothy Hart (18) and Vera Goldsmith (16). Erskine was responsible for recruiting the girls and he drafted their job description as follows:

> Their duties would be to deliver letters etc. from the various Offices in the House of Commons, and their hours of duty would be from 10 am to 6 pm on week days, except Saturdays, with a reasonable time off for meals.

Figure 10: War Office workers: a supervisor, an indoor messenger and an outdoor messenger.

The wages would be 9/s per week for a girl of 14–16 years of age, and 12/s per week for one of 16–18, with 1/s per week War Bonus in addition in both cases, and these would be paid during the Session and adjournment of Parliament but not during such time as it is prorogued. Uniform would also be supplied.[2]

Their job titles in Parliament were 'Girl Porters' but they were also called 'Girl Messengers' as this more closely reflected the work they did. They wore the same uniform of brown drill overalls and hats worn by War Office Girl Messengers, and indeed Hart and Goldsmith had previously worked as War Office Girl Messengers (Figure 10). The salaries were also the same as those received by girls of similar ages at the War Office.

Members of Parliament may have been startled to see these Girl Porters walking around the House of Commons with their deliveries at first. But outside Parliament, the Post Office had employed many women for decades in roles such as sorting clerks and telegraphists, and the war brought more visible opportunities for some women, including delivering mail in some urban areas and working as telegraph messengers. In Whitehall, the same was true. Civil Service historian Hilda Martindale wrote:

> No picture of the employment of women in the Civil Service during the war would be complete without reference to the girl messengers who, in their brown overalls, flooded Government Departments and did their best, often with considerable success, to cope with work formerly done by hoary-headed old men.[3]

So it was not surprising that down the road at Westminster, the House of Commons found itself forced down the same path.

THE ASSISTANT SERJEANT AT ARMS AND HIS STAFF

Like many staff in Parliament, Walter Erskine was from a parliamentary family – his father was Sir Henry David Erskine, a former Serjeant at Arms. Born in Scotland in April 1870, Walter lived with his family and a host of domestic servants in the Serjeant's residence in the House of Commons while his father held this post between 1885 and 1915.

Walter might perhaps have hoped to follow in his father's footsteps and become Serjeant in 1915, but it was not to be. The new man appointed was Admiral Sir Colin Richard Keppel. Keppel came from a very distinguished naval background with many years' service as equerry to the royal family; it is not surprising that practical matters such as the appointment and management of the Girl Porters was left to his assistant, Walter.

Before the war, the Serjeant at Arms Department employed seventy-one men in a wide variety of roles, including doorkeeper, attendant, messenger, porter and cleaner. Some were permanent employees and others – known as sessional staff – had jobs only when Parliament was in session. Some men volunteered at the start of the war, such as sessional cleaner Corporal Reginald Lanchbery who signed up for service with the 8th Royal Highlanders (the Black Watch) in December 1914 and became the only one of the Serjeant's staff to be killed in action, on 17 July 1916 at the Battle of the Somme.

Others understandably preferred to work in the Commons as long as they were able. Initially, it was sufficient simply for Erskine to certify that all the men were essential, but as the war progressed he found himself under increasing pressure to account for all the Serjeant's male staff and to provide lists of all those still working in Parliament, with explanations as to why they were exempt. Some explanations were straightforward; many men were simply above recruitment age (41 initially, later raised to 51) or were unfit (Nightwatchman W. Cotter had only one leg, for example). Others went off to war but were later discharged unfit and returned to their old jobs, such as Alfred Carter, who lost an eye as well as suffering gunshot wounds.

Others were more complex cases. Erskine decided early on that Samuel Clark, a porter who was also Elsie and Mabel's uncle, could be spared for war service. Before conscription, under the 'Derby Scheme' introduced by Lord Derby in October 1915, men were asked to attest to their willingness to serve and then wait to be called up. Samuel duly attested for war service at Southwark Town Hall on 1 December 1915 and was called up on 13 June 1916, but then told to return home. The note in the Serjeant's file states this was presumably because he was a widower with a child. Samuel's wife, Mary Ann, had died in 1911, leaving him alone to look after their 3-year-old daughter, Vera. Samuel continued to work for the Serjeant through the rest of the war.

However, with every eligible man called up, there were vacancies in the Serjeant's team. Erskine shuffled the men around between roles, and ultimately had to recruit women, whom he had previously employed only as housemaids and cleaners. He was clearly very worried about the ability of female porters to undertake the tasks assigned to them. As well as penning his letter to the Speaker, he wrote to all Heads of Offices in the House of Commons in April 1917, 'I venture to express the hope that … you will be able to arrange for your Office Messengers to take a greater share in carrying heavy boxes and books.'

A PARLIAMENTARY FAMILY: THE CLARKS

So who were the Girl Porters? All four were from working-class families and would have worked for a living regardless of the war. Without the war, however, they would never have ended up as porters in the 'Westminster Village'.

Like Erskine himself, two of the Girl Porters, Elsie and Mabel Clark, were from a parliamentary family – albeit not nearly such a grand one as the Erskines. The Clark girls were recommended to Erskine as 'nieces of Porter Clark'. Their uncle Samuel was the younger brother of their father, John. Samuel Clark had started in the Serjeant at Arms Department as a cleaner in 1898 at the age of 19 and was promoted to porter in 1912. Elsie and

Mabel would have known their uncle well, as he lived with them when they were young children before he married in 1907. It is also likely that, after he became a widower in 1911, he and their cousin Vera moved back in with them and their mother.

Elsie and Mabel had another reason to know the parliamentary area, as their father, John, had been a police constable with his beat just down the road. Previously a draper's porter (portering clearly ran in the family), John Clark joined the Metropolitan Police in 1890 and was assigned to 'Division A', the Whitehall area, in 1891. He married Olive Kate Lavers at St Anne's Church, Soho, Westminster, in 1894 and they had seven children. Elsie Rose Clark and Mabel Edith Clark were born at the family home in 66 Russell Gardens, Boniface Street: Elsie on 19 October 1900 and Mabel on 30 December 1902. They had two older brothers, Ernest and Alfred, and three younger siblings followed. Boniface Street was very close to Whitehall and Westminster, in an area just south of Westminster Bridge 'largely tenanted by police'. By the time the First World War began, the family had moved to 130 Penton Place, Walworth, inhabited by 'mechanics, labourers, printers, clerks'.[4]

Unfortunately, John's police career was cut short at the age of 44. He resigned from the Metropolitan Police in March 1914, having been certified as medically unfit, and died from 'general paralysis of the insane' (a crippling and terminal disease, linked to syphilis) at Long Grove Asylum in Epsom, Surrey, in October 1914. This left Olive as a widowed mother of five children aged 14 and under, with no income. There was no such thing as a widow's pension in those days (not until the Widows', Orphans' and Old Age Contributory Benefits Act 1925, long campaigned for by women's organisations and championed by early women MPs, including Nancy Astor) and no such thing as child benefit (not until the Family Allowances Act 1945, the culmination of a lifetime's work by Eleanor Rathbone MP). Parliament would eventually pass the Police Pensions Act 1921, which gave police widows such as Olive a pension of £30 per annum with an allowance of £10 per child – but in 1914 she was not entitled to anything except a small gratuity. For many widowed women with young families, the only option would have been the Poor Law and the workhouse, which was a huge stigma.

Fortunately, charitable help was at hand for Olive in the form of the Metropolitan & City Police Orphanage in Strawberry Hill, Twickenham. The object of the orphanage was 'to afford relief to destitute orphans of members of the Metropolitan and City of London police forces; to provide them with clothing, maintenance, and education, to place them out in situations where the prospect of an honest livelihood shall be secured'.[5] On John's resignation from the police, the orphanage initially paid compassionate allowances of £10 (approximately £592 today) per child per year to Olive for Elsie, Mabel and their three younger siblings – this must have been a lifeline for the family. The allowances stopped for Elsie in October 1914 (around the time her father died, alas) and Mabel in December 1916, when they reached the age of 14 and became old enough to leave school and start work. The allowances stopped for the three youngest children, one by one, when they were admitted to the orphanage – Harold in November 1914 at the age of 10, Hilda aged 8 in 1916 and Jack aged 8 in 1918. One can only speculate as to how Olive felt about this, but it may have been a positive opportunity for such a poor family: the orphanage had excellent facilities including classrooms, playing fields, swimming pool, gymnasium and dormitories; medical, dental and ophthalmic care; and later its own hospital. The orphanage, together with the Melbourne Police Commission, later sponsored Jack's immigration to Australia and oversaw his welfare there, including an emergency operation for appendicitis.[6]

Of Olive's two grown-up children, Ernest was a barrister's clerk before the war while Alfred was yet another porter, at the Army & Navy Stores. Ernest married in February 1915 (a first child following within a year), which would initially have exempted him from military service. Although conscription was extended to married men in May 1916, there is no record of Ernest serving even after that; he later followed in his father's footsteps and became a railway policeman for the Great Western Railway. However, Alfred joined the army in April 1915, aged 18, serving as a private in the Middlesex Regiment, and was tragically killed in action on 1 July 1916 during the Battle of the Somme. His body was never found; his army service record notes him as missing, presumed dead. The army did not even order his personal effects to be returned to his mother until June 1917 – it must have been an appalling period of uncertainty for the family. Today, Alfred's name is on the Thiepval Memorial.

There was also a financial implication from Alfred's death. Olive received a separation allowance and a portion of Alfred's pay while he was serving. Although not generous (10s 3d a week, approximately £30 today), it might have made all the difference to such a poor family. But it ceased on his death.

So in the midst of this family tragedy in 1916, there were also financial pressures. Elsie and Mabel both went out to work to do their bit. Before coming to the House of Commons in 1917, Elsie had previously worked at a company called Spicer Bros for eight months and then at a leather merchant called Carpenter Bros for five weeks. And although Mabel Clark was only 14 years old, she had worked at a printing and advertising company called Johnson

Riddle & Co. Ltd for three and a half months. Both girls got good references from their companies, Johnson Riddle writing that Mabel's 'conduct has been satisfactory in every way', and Carpenter Bros that Elsie was 'quiet and industrious and punctual. And we think her quite suitable as a messenger.'

Erskine read the references and was presumably also assured by Porter Clark that his nieces would be worthy employees of the House of Commons. Erskine duly wrote to Olive to offer them jobs, and she accepted on behalf of her young daughters.

THE DRESSMAKERS: DOROTHY HART AND VERA GOLDSMITH

The other two Girl Porters, Dorothy Hart and Vera Goldsmith, had no parliamentary family connections. Both worked for dressmakers before 1914, an industry hit very hard by the outbreak of war. Laid off by their employers, they came to work as messengers at the War Office and were recommended for work in Parliament by the War Office.

Dorothy Gladys Hart was the oldest of the four Girl Porters, born on 18 May 1898 in Clapham, London. Her father, John, was a journeyman plumber and lead worker, and during the war he worked in a munitions works in Wareham. This large factory in Holton Heath made cordite for the Royal Navy during the war. Dorothy's head teacher described her as 'honest, truthful, industrious and punctual & regular at her work. She was a sensible and intelligent girl.' Dorothy left school in 1912 aged 14 and went to work for a local costumier, Mrs Alice Pearce. The occupation of dressmaker or seamstress was a common one for working-class women, likely to involve long hours bent over sewing machines in factories, work rooms and shops. However, Mrs Pearce ran her business out of her home in Clapham, so perhaps it was not so bad an environment. Also, as a costumier, Mrs Pearce may have specialised in making costumes for plays or other theatrical productions, so Dorothy may have seen some of her work on view on the stage.

Such a business would, of course, have suffered at the outbreak of war. Mrs Pearce wrote in Dorothy's reference: 'She left me May 1916. The war has hit my business very badly hence the reason for my workers leaving.' Dorothy found a job at Peter Robinson High Class General Drapers. Although their flagship store was in Oxford Street, she was employed in one of their factory work rooms. It may have been a difficult environment after sewing costumes at Mrs Pearce's house. After three months, Dorothy applied to work as a Girl Messenger at the War Office, where she was employed from 23 October 1916 by Emily Moore Hamilton, Superintendent of Girl Messengers. Dorothy was one of several girls Hamilton recommended to Erskine as suitable to work in the House of Commons and described by her as a 'good steady worker'.

The last Girl Porter, Veronica (known as Vera) Agnes Goldsmith was born on 24 October 1900 in Croydon, Surrey. Her father, William, was a journeyman gas fitter. Vera had three siblings, including an older brother, Algernon, who served as a corporal in the Essex Regiment during the war. Vera's head teacher wrote her a reference: 'She is absolutely honest and truthful, fairly intelligent, industrious, punctual and regular at her work and sensible in behaviour.' After school, Vera worked for three months for a dressmaker in Croydon, but the business was wound up and she applied to be a Girl Messenger at the War Office, where she was employed from 15 December 1916, aged 16. Vera was then recommended by Hamilton to Erskine as a 'good and willing worker'.

We have no pictures of any of the Girl Porters, although in the records there are tiny hints of their appearance. Dorothy Hart was described as 'nice-looking' in a note by Hamilton, which might perhaps have influenced Erskine's decision to hire her. And while she was working in the House of Commons in December 1917, a request came in for Goldsmith to be photographed in her uniform by the National War Museum (now the Imperial War Museum) for their record of women's work. Erskine queried why Goldsmith, pointing out that Hart was most senior of the girls, and Hamilton replied that they had asked 'specially for a young girl with hair down'. Sadly, no photograph can be traced of Goldsmith, with her hair down or otherwise.

THE INFLUENZA PANDEMIC

The four Girl Porters were employed in the House of Commons from April 1917 through to the end of the war and beyond. Erskine was very pleased with their work, but however successful they were, they must always have been aware that they were temporary, doing the jobs of men on active service. Armistice Day on 11 November 1918 doubtless signalled rejoicing at the end of the war, and yet was also a clear milestone in their employment; it could only be a matter of time now before the men returned and they would lose their jobs.

Yet one of the girls would not live to see this happen. One week after the Armistice, Mabel Clark died on 19 November 1918 from influenza and double pneumonia, aged just 15. So the Girl Porters' story is not just one of wartime opportunity for working-class young women, but also shows parliamentary staff touched by a global pandemic. Mabel was a victim of the 1918 influenza pandemic which killed approximately 228,000 people in the UK and many millions across the world. The virus came to the UK with returning soldiers in several waves; Mabel died at the peak of the worst wave in autumn 1918.

Perhaps she or Elsie heard the House of Commons debating the epidemic for the first time on 30 October 1918, when the effect on children and whether schools should be closed was one subject discussed.[7] Maybe they worried about their younger brothers and sister away from home in the orphanage, where 150 children (out of 248) contracted influenza that year – it caused some anxiety but all the children recovered, comparing very favourably with the general population.[8] It was young Mabel, working in the heart of Parliament, who succumbed. She died at the family home in Penton Place with her mother Olive present at her death. Olive, having lost one of her sons to the war, now lost a daughter to the pandemic.

THE RESTORATION OF PRE-WAR PRACTICES

After the death of Mabel, the other three girls continued in post until male staff began to return from the armed forces to their previous posts. Erskine had to dispense with their services in March 1919. By this time, his doubts and fears about the employment of girls had been completely allayed. He wrote to Miss Tupp, the new Superintendent of Girl Messengers at the War Office, on 4 March 1919:

> Hart, Goldsmith and Elsie Clark (now aged 20, 18 and 18 respectively) are each anxious to continue in similar employment when they leave here on 22nd inst and I have promised that that I would write to ask you if you could arrange for their transfer to some other Government Department. It is impossible for me to speak too highly of the way these three girls have done their work while at the House of Commons, and their conduct has been exemplary throughout.[9]

Tupp did take the three in as messengers at the War Office immediately afterwards, but this too would have been of limited duration. There was now great pressure in society and Parliament for returning servicemen to be given jobs. The Restoration of Pre-War Practices Act passed in June 1919 ensured that women were formally removed from many wartime jobs. Girl Porters and Girl Messengers in Parliament and government had to seek alternative ways to earn a living.

There was never any prospect of the Girl Porters continuing to work in Parliament after the war; their work was by definition temporary, and the war was an episode in their working lives rather than transformative overall. Nevertheless, they are an excellent example of how the war led to new opportunities in roles beyond those previously defined as 'women's work', through substitution of male labour with female labour in Parliament itself.

LIFE AFTER PARLIAMENT

So what became of the Girl Porters? Elsie Clark left London and went to live with her 77-year-old grandmother, Susan Clark, in Sherston, Wiltshire, along with her cousin Vera. They are recorded there in 1921 with Elsie, aged 20, helping at home, and Vera, aged 13, at school. Elsie next appears in records in 1933, when she married John Henry William Balch, a driver in the RAF during the First World War. They had a son, Reginald, in 1935 and ran the Red Lion Inn, Wincanton, Somerset, for many years after the retirement of Balch's father. Elsie's uncle, Samuel Clark, kept up the parliamentary connection, continuing to work in the House of Commons until his retirement in April 1939 aged 60, by which time he had been promoted to Assistant Superintendent in the Members' Waiting Room. He then went to live with his daughter Vera, by now married but still living in Sherston, and he died in 1942. Elsie Balch died in 1975, aged 75.

Dorothy Hart went back to her previous profession of dressmaking. Erskine wrote a glowing reference for her in February 1920:

> She gave the utmost satisfaction, both as regards her work as a messenger and her personal conduct. I have, of course, no knowledge of her capabilities as a dressmaker, but should be very glad to hear that she has obtained the employment she desires.

The parliamentary connection may have helped. She did indeed get the job, working for 'Isobel' (famous fashion designer Madame Isobel) at 4 Maddox Street, just off Regent Street in the West End. However, this potentially glamorous career did not last long. In 1925, Hart married William Haddock, an engineer from Birmingham. They had three children, one of whom died in infancy, and lived in the West Midlands. Dorothy Haddock died in Greenwich in 1980, having reached the ripe old age of 82.

In contrast, Vera Goldsmith did not go back to dressmaking; unlike Hart, she had not spent much time in that profession. Instead, Goldsmith became part of a wider pattern of work followed by working-class young women after 1918, moving from more traditional female jobs such as domestic service and dressmaking towards office and retail work. Erskine wrote a reference for her for the Food Control Office in Croydon in August 1919, saying she was 'quick, intelligent, gave complete satisfaction'. Food control would have been important at this time as rationing of foods such as sugar, butter and meat was introduced early in 1918 and some foods continued to be rationed until 1920.

In 1920, Goldsmith wrote to Erskine to ask for a reference as she wished to become a member of the London Chamber of Commerce. The London Chamber of Commerce was founded in 1881 to represent the interests of the London trading community and assist its members in resolving day-to-day trading problems. There is no evidence to show that Goldsmith succeeded in becoming a member, but her interest in it may indicate she wanted to pursue a professional career in business and not simply an administrative role. Frustratingly, there is no sign of this ambition being fulfilled. By 1921, Goldsmith was working as a shop assistant at D.P. Roberts, a chemist's, in Croydon. She died in 1950 in Purley, Coulson, Surrey, aged 49, having worked as a 'butcher's cashier' for many years. She never married and died intestate.

And what became of their employer? Walter H. Erskine was promoted from Assistant to Deputy Serjeant in 1929. He retired in 1940 and died in 1948, aged 77. He was made CBE in the New Years' Honours list of January 1936. By coincidence, this was the same list in which former suffragette leader Christabel Pankhurst was made Dame Commander. As the honours were conferred by King Edward VIII in the white and gold throne room at Buckingham Palace the following month, Erskine must have reflected ruefully on the irony that, after the suffragettes had made his life so difficult for so many years, one of their leaders had ended up receiving a high state honour alongside him.

In Her Own Words

'There is no sensation of mystery about it. It just did not pay. Prestige attached to the appointment may have been all right, but nobody can afford to run a business at a loss. That is all there is to it.'

Maude Waddell, explaining why she gave up the
House of Lords catering contract after less than a year, 1939

10

THE MONSTROUS REGIMENT: WOMEN MANAGERS IN THE LORDS

On 14 December 1926, under the headline 'WOMAN'S POST IN LORDS', a Miss H.F.M. Court was pictured on the front cover of the *Daily Mirror*. It reported she had been appointed head of the Costings and Accounts Department in the House of Lords from 1 February next, the first woman to hold this post. This news was widely reported, and not always positively. The *Western Daily Press* described it as 'another instance of the increasing invasion by women'. And it must have been a slow news day at the *Aberdeen Press*, whose shrill headline evoked the misogynist rhetoric of John Knox's sixteenth-century book *The First Blast of the Trumpet against the Monstrous Regiment of Women*:

> 'The Monstrous Regiment'
> The few die-hard anti-feminists who are left may fly to John Knox for con-solation in the latest shock they have received, for 'the monstrous regiment of women' has captured one of the high administrative posts in the House of Lords staff. Miss H F M Court has been made head of the Costings and Accounts department. Her assistants will be two women.[1]

Court would eventually be joined by another woman manager, Maude Waddell, appointed to run the House of Lords Refreshment Department in December 1938. Although Waddell did not hold the contract for long, her replacement, Elsie Hoath, would carry the baton of female leadership in the Lords well beyond the Second World War.

THE HOUSE OF MEN

The Lords may well have feared a monstrous regiment in the 1920s as it was not, of course, a House of Lords and Ladies. In contrast to the House of Commons, where Nancy Astor had become the first woman MP to take her seat at Westminster in 1919, the House of Lords had no women peers. In this period, the Lords was almost entirely made up of men who had inherited their titles, and although there were a few hereditary women peers, they were not allowed to sit in the Upper House. In 1925, only a year before Miss Court's appointment, Lady Rhondda, a great feminist campaigner and hereditary woman peer, had finally failed to take her seat in the Lords in a test case which had dragged on in the Committee for Privileges for several years.[2] Women did not sit in the Lords until 1958, when the Life Peerages Act 1958 allowed both men and women to become peers for their lifetime. Full equality did not arrive for another five years, when, by the Peerage Act 1963, hereditary women peers were finally allowed to sit.

However, women were involved with the House of Lords in other ways. Many aristocratic women exerted substantial influence over male relatives and high society as political hostesses. Other women lobbied, petitioned and sought to influence the work of the Lords, as they had done for centuries. As well as female housekeepers and kitchen staff, the Lords would have observed women newly appearing in other working roles. Miss Ashworth's first Typewriting Room was on the west front at the House of Lords' end of the Palace of Westminster, and she supplied her typing services to Lords' offices as well as Commons' offices from the early twentieth century. And from 1918, Miss Court was one of a small enclave of women working for the Lords in the Accounts Department.

Accountancy was a male-dominated profession in this era. Although women worked in bookkeeping and on the fringes of accountancy from the mid-nineteenth century, they were barred from men's professional bodies and unable to become chartered accountants, which greatly limited their career progression. Admission to professions such as law and accountancy was one of many areas targeted for change by suffrage campaigners. Following partial suffrage in 1918 and continued campaigning, this situation was changed by the Sex Disqualification (Removal) Act 1919, after which Mary Harris

Smith became the first chartered accountant in England and Wales. She had campaigned to join the profession since 1887! However, even after 1919, the total number of women accountants remained tiny for decades.

It is therefore noteworthy that the House of Lords, a house of men, had come to employ a woman accountant at such an early date. As with the Girl Porters in the House of Commons, the reason lies back in societal changes caused by the First World War and another parliamentary family connection – this time, the Courts.

A PARLIAMENTARY FAMILY: THE COURTS

Hannah Frances Mary Court (known as 'May') and her brother Robert Ambrey Court were twins who successively worked for the House of Lords: Robert between 1903 and 1917, May between 1918 and 1943.

Their link to the Lords was their father, Thomas Ambrey Court. Thomas was the son of another Thomas Ambrey Court, a grocer from Hereford. Thomas senior was appointed a local magistrate in 1859. This was controversial. It was even contested in the House of Commons, where it was presented as part of an attempt to pack the Hereford magistrates' bench with Tories – but there was also prejudice against him as a retail tradesman. Described in the Commons as a 'respectable grocer in a large way of business',[3] he was proud to proclaim himself as a magistrate in the census two years later. This important role in the local justice system would have given him and his family significant local standing.

If the Courts were keen to increase their social position then they must have been pleased when Thomas junior (Thomas the Younger, as the family called him) moved to London to work for the House of Lords from 1873, aged 23. He was employed initially as a Copyist – a junior position, essential in an era before photocopying or other mechanical methods of duplicating documents were widely available (and well before Miss Ashworth's typing service came to Parliament). By 1881, he was able to describe himself on the census as 'Principal, Copying Dept, House of Lords'.

A few years after he started working at the Lords, Thomas married Hannah Mackean Walkinshaw. Hannah was born in Stand, Lancashire, to a Scottish family. Her grandfather Daniel Walkinshaw was manager of the City of Glasgow Life Assurance Company, and a trust fund was set up as part of her marriage settlement on her marriage to Thomas in 1877. Although not enough to support the family on its own, as all the Court children went out to work, the money must have been a useful supplement for an aspirational middle-class family. The trust fund was still in existence and able to pay out small sums on Thomas's death in 1921.

Thomas and Hannah had four children. The oldest, Cecil, was born in 1879. The twins, May and Robert, arrived a year later, born on 13 December 1880 in Balham. May was the elder, her time of birth recorded as 7 p.m. on her birth certificate with Robert following at 8.45 p.m. There was then a gap before their younger brother Edward (Ted) was born in 1887.

Sadly, their mother, Hannah, died in 1895. After her death, Thomas remarried and had one further surviving daughter, Phyllis, born in 1901, before being widowed again and remarrying again. Meanwhile, the House of Lords decided to merge its Copying and Accounting Offices in 1899, and Thomas arrived at the top of his career ladder in 1903, becoming Receiver of Fees, Accountant and Examiner of Acts, and head of the Accounting and Copying Department. In 1911, the House of Lords Offices Committee granted him a rise in salary to £650 a year (approximately £50,000 today).

His children found their own paths, at home and abroad. Cecil and Edward both immigrated to Canada in the early twentieth century, but the twins stayed close to London. Robert was educated privately and came to work with his father in the House of Lords in 1899 as a Copyist, aged 18. He married Violet Louise Bolton in 1908, they had a son, Richard Ambrey Court, born in 1910, and the family lived first in Twickenham and later in Cheam, Surrey. He began to progress through the department and by 1914 he was Assistant Examiner of Acts.

Meanwhile, his twin sister May worked initially as a junior teacher. In 1901, she was living and working in Mary Maynard's 'Ladies' Boarding School' in Wandsworth – a small establishment with nine girl pupils resident along with an all-female staff of teachers and domestic servants. Perhaps teaching was not for May, though, as ten years later she was recorded as an 'embroideress in decorative society needlework'. It appears that she was also mixing with higher society who might be attracted to her needlework, as on census night she was a visitor in Sloane Square, staying with Margaret Graeme Maxtone-Graham. The Maxtone-Grahams were Scottish gentry.

Both teaching and embroidery were among very few occupations open to middle-class women in this period, and thus far, all the Court family jobs were typical of gender roles. But then the war came.

THE FIRST WORLD WAR

As soon as war was declared, Robert was quick to volunteer as an officer – one of eight clerks of military age in the House of Lords who were given permission by the Clerk of the Parliaments to serve. Robert was the perfect candidate. He already had four years' service with the Territorial Force, in the Honourable Artillery Company Infantry Battalion, and started drilling with an 'Old Boys' Corps' at the outbreak of war. He applied for a temporary commission in the regular army for the period of the war and the commanding officer nominating him asked for him to be posted to his own regiment as a lieutenant, saying, 'I am convinced he would make a good officer.'[4]

He progressed through the ranks, starting as a lieutenant on 1 December 1914 and becoming a captain in September 1915, and later an acting major. He saw action in Gallipolli, France and Egypt.[5] Sadly, Robert Ambrey Court was killed in action on 26 April 1917, near Bapaume, Pas-de-Calais, France, aged 36. He is buried at the British cemetery at Hermies in France. His name is inscribed on Parliament's war memorials in the Royal Gallery in the House of Lords and on the Recording Angel memorial in Westminster Hall. The House of Lords paid a gratuity of £470 (approximately £26,700 today) to his widow, Violet, which was more than she got from the army and the gross value of his estate put together.

Figure 11: Robert Ambrey Court, *c.* 1914.   Figure 12: Hannah Frances Mary 'May' Court, 1922.

One can only speculate as to how desolate Robert's death must have left his widow, his 7-year-old son, his twin sister May, and his 67-year-old father Thomas. Thomas had already lost his youngest son the year before. Edward had returned to England and married in 1915 but had died while serving with the 1st Canadian Mounted Rifles Battalion in the Battle of the Somme, on 1 October 1916.

Thomas must have hoped that Robert would make it through the war, return to work in the House of Lords and succeed him as House of Lords Accountant. This was not to be. However, just under a year later, May followed in his footsteps and came to work in the House of Lords. Perhaps this would have been some small consolation for the Court family. She was not actually given her brother's job, but his death had provided a vacancy and an employment opportunity in the House of Lords Accounting and Copying Department.

FROM LADY CLERICAL ASSISTANT TO ACCOUNTANT

On 1 April 1918, May Court was appointed as the first of two 'Lady Clerical Assistants' in the House of Lords, with Miss Mabel Evelyn Waterman appointed three months later. They were put on a salary scale of £110 rising to £250. Court was 35 years old; Waterman was 23.

Waterman, a gardener's daughter, was born in Streatham, close to the Court family in Balham. By 1911, Waterman was living in Wandsworth, and employed as an apprentice typist at the age of 15 – an excellent example of a woman who might otherwise have become a domestic servant taking advantage of typing as a new job opportunity. Court must have turned to clerical work after the outbreak of war, when the market for decorative society needlework collapsed. Certainly, the Lords employed Court because of her family connection. Court and Waterman were the first women directly employed by the House of Lords apart from in housekeeping, cleaning or catering roles, other female typists having been employed via Ashworth's agency. They were appointed during shortages of male labour near the end of the First World War. But, unlike many women wartime workers, such as the Girl Porters in the House of Commons, both Court and Waterman kept their jobs after the war and were quickly promoted.

Thomas Ambrey Court retired aged 69, after forty-five years' service, and was replaced as Receiver of Fees, Accountant and Examiner of Acts by Hubert Percy Norris on 1 March 1919. We can assume that Thomas was happy enough with this, as he wrote his will at this time and affectionately

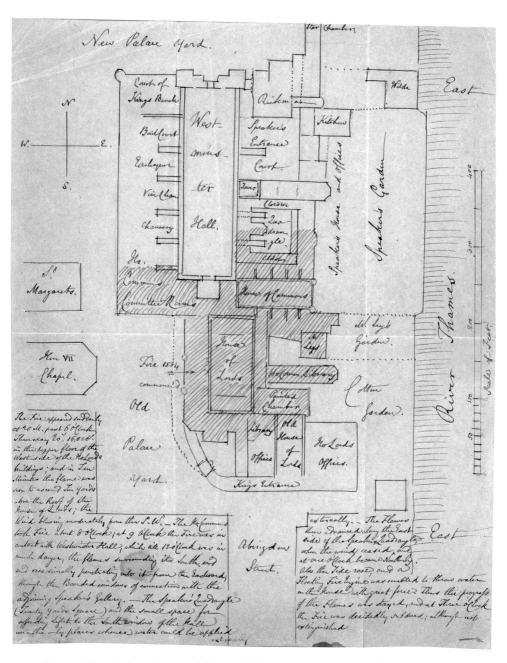

Plate 1: Sketch plan of the old Palace of Westminster, 1834, by John Rickman, showing the extent of the fire.

Plate 2: Anne Rickman, *Our House in New Palace Yard*, watercolour, 1832.

Plate 3: Sketch of the Ventilator in the roof of the former St Stephen's Chapel, from where women were allowed to view the proceedings of the old House of Commons. Pencil drawing by Frances Rickman, 1834.

Plate 4: *The Destruction of the Houses of Lords and Commons by Fire on the 16th of October 1834*, William Heath, colour lithograph.

Plate 5: Painting of Elizabeth Garrett and Emily Davies presenting the 1866 women's suffrage petition, by Bertha Newcombe, 1910.

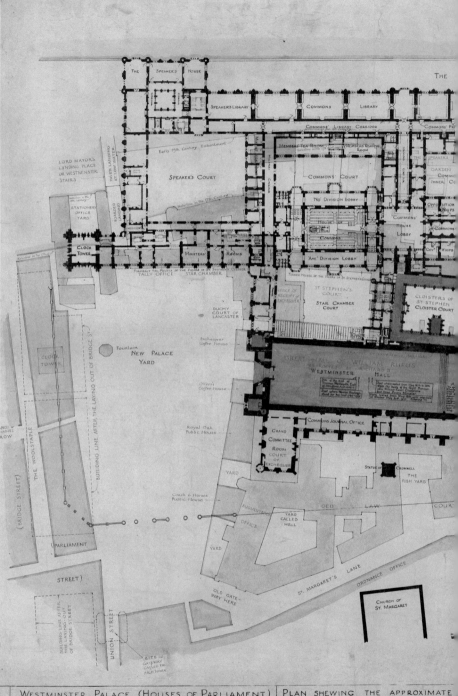

THE

THE SPEAKER'S HOUSE

SPEAKER'S LIBRARY

COMMONS LIBRARY

COMMONS' LIBRARY CORRIDOR

COMMONS' PA

LORD MAYORS
LANDING PLACE
OR WESTMINSTER
STAIRS

Early 19th Century Embankment

MEMBERS TEA ROOM

MEMBERS READING
ROOM

THE
SPEAKER'S

GARDEN

COMMON
INNER CO

STATIONERS
OFFICE
YARD

SPEAKER'S COURT

COMMONS' COURT

CLOCK
TOWER

Waterline in the 17th Century

'NO' DIVISION LOBBY

HOUSE OF
COMMONS

OPPOSITION
WHIPS

COMMONS'
HOUSE
LOBBY

COMMONS

MINISTERS' ROOMS

'AYE' DIVISION LOBBY

GOVT WHIPS

FORMERLY THE HOUSES OF THE VICARS OF ST STEPHEN'S COLLEGE
TALLY OFFICE   STAR CHAMBER

FORMERLY THE HOUSES OF THE VICARS OF ST STEPHEN'S COLLEGE

VEALE OF
RECEIPT OF
EXCHEQUER

ST STEPHEN'S
COURT

STAR CHAMBER
COURT

CLOISTERS OF
ST STEPHEN
CLOISTER COURT

DUCHY
COURT OF
LANCASTER

Exchequer
Coffee House

CLOCK
TOWER

Fountain   NEW PALACE
YARD

Oliver's
Coffee House

GREAT HALL OF WILLIAM RUFUS
WESTMINSTER   RICHARD II
HALL

Royal Oak
Public House

COMMONS JOURNAL OFFICE

GRAND
COMMITTEE
ROOM
COURT
OF
EXCHEQUER

STATUE OF CROMWELL
THE
FISH YARD

(BRIDGE STREET)

THE WOOLSTAPLE

BUILDING LINE AFTER THE LAYING OUT OF BRIDGE ST.

Coach & Horses
Public House

YARD

OLD   LAW   COURT

(PARLIAMENT

AUGMENTATION
OFFICE

YARD
CALLED
HELL

YARD

STREET)

OLD GATE-
WAY HERE

ST. MARGARET'S LANE

ORDNANCE OFFICE

CHURCH OF
ST MARGARET

BUILDING LINE AFTER
THE LAYING OUT
OF BRIDGE STREET

UNION STREET

SITE OF
GATEWAY
CALLED THE
HIGH TOWER

WESTMINSTER PALACE (HOUSES OF PARLIAMENT)   PLAN SHEWING THE APPROXIMATE
OF THE BUILDINGS OF THE PALACE AN

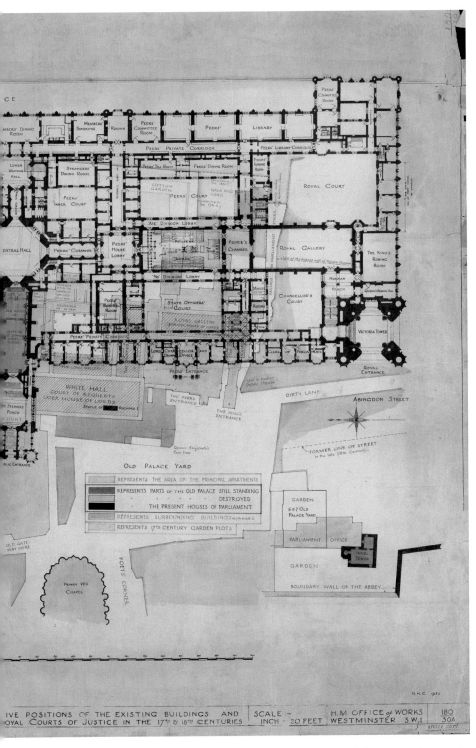

Plate 6: Plan of the New Palace of Westminster, principal floor, superimposed on a reconstruction of the old Palace. Drawn by G.F. Checkley for the Ministry of Works in 1932.

CENSUS OF ENGLAND AND

Before writing on this Schedule please read the Examples and the Instructions given on the other side of the paper, a...

The contents of the Schedule will be treated as confidential. Strict care will be taken that no information is disclosed with regard to individual persons.

than the preparation of Statistical Ta...

NAME AND SURNAME	RELATIONSHIP to Head of Family.	AGE (last Birthday) and SEX.		PARTICULARS as to MARRIAGE.					PROF of Person
		Ages of Males.	Ages of Females.		Completed years the present Marriage has lasted.	Total Children Born Alive.	Children still Living.	Children who have Died.	Personal Occupation.
1.	2.	3.	4.	5.	6.	7.	8.	9.	10.
1 The Salvation Hall									
2 Mary Jane Anderson	Wife		58	Married	37	3	3		
3 Ethel Marie Anderson	Daughter		35	Single					Manager of House

(To be filled up by the Enumerator.)

	Males.	Females.	Persons.
Total	—	2	2

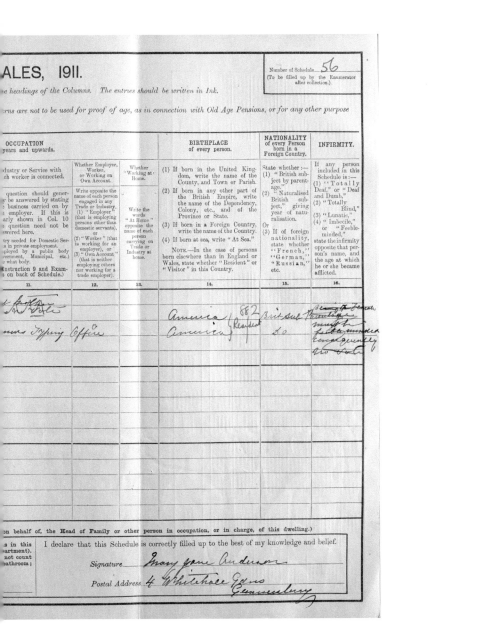

OCCUPATION years and upwards.			BIRTHPLACE of every person.	NATIONALITY of every Person born in a Foreign Country.	INFIRMITY.
dustry or Service with ch worker is connected.	Whether Employer, Worker, or Working on Own Account.	Whether Working at Home.	(1) If born in the United Kingdom, write the name of the County, and Town or Parish.	State whether :— (1) "British subject by parentage,"	If any person included in this Schedule is :— (1) "Totally
question should generally be answered by stating business carried on by employer. If this is arly shown in Col. 10 question need not be wered here. try needed for Domestic Service in private employment. ployed by a public body vernment, Municipal, etc.) Instruction 9 and Examson back of Schedule.)	Write opposite the name of each person engaged in any Trade or Industry, (1) "Employer" (that is employing persons other than domestic servants), or (2) "Worker" (that is working for an employer), or (3) "Own Account" (that is neither employing others nor working for a trade employer).	Write the words "At Home" opposite the name of each person carrying on Trade or Industry at home.	(2) If born in any other part of the British Empire, write the name of the Dependency, Colony, etc., and of the Province or State. (3) If born in a Foreign Country, write the name of the Country. (4) If born at sea, write "At Sea." NOTE.—In the case of persons born elsewhere than in England or Wales, state whether "Resident" or "Visitor" in this Country.	(2) "Naturalised British subject," giving year of naturalisation. Or (3) If of foreign nationality, state whether "French," "German," "Russian," etc.	Deaf," or "Deaf and Dumb," (2) "Totally Blind," (3) "Lunatic," (4) "Imbecile," or "Feebleminded," state the infirmity opposite that person's name, and the age at which he or she became afflicted.
11.	12.	13.	14.	15.	16.
			America 1882	British	
nns Typing Office			America	Do	

Plate 7: Census form of Mary Jane Anderson and Ethel Marie Anderson, 1911.

Plate 8: *New Dawn*, sculpture by Mary Branson.

bequeathed £50 to 'my old colleague' Norris. However, only three months later, on 1 June 1919, the word 'Accountant' was removed from Norris's title. He remained Receiver of Fees and Examiner of Acts, but May Court was made Accountant and put on the same salary range as him – £200 p.a. rising to £500. Even though she was presumably paid less than him at this point, to be put on the same pay scale as a man, and after only a year of service, was a rare and remarkable example of equal pay in this period. It was also an unusual role for a woman to hold: the House of Commons Accountants were all male at this time.

Waterman was made Assistant Examiner of Acts at the same time, and both Court and Waterman were listed as House of Lords senior staff from 1919. Another woman, Winifred Mary Bird, was appointed as a Lady Clerical Assistant in 1920 to replace Court in that role. Thomas died in 1921, having seen his daughter succeed him as House of Lords Accountant – not a situation he can possibly have dreamt of when the twins were born back in 1880! And when his old colleague H.P. Norris announced his retirement in 1926, the House of Lords took the opportunity to rearrange the duties among existing officers. May Court became head of the Accounting and Copying Department, with the title Receiver of Fees and Accountant; Mabel Waterman was promoted to Examiner of Acts.

ACCOUNTANT TO THE LORDS

For nine years following Norris's retirement in 1926, no men worked in the Accounting and Copying Department. It was at this time that the press, responding perhaps to a hostile tip-off from within the Lords, dubbed Court's team the 'Monstrous Regiment', declaring:

> They will be three lonely women, for in no other department or office in the House of Lords do women hold the higher appointments. Their duties, however, are intricate enough to keep them from brooding over their solitary grandeur.[6]

These 'intricate duties' were set out in a statement by the House of Lords to the Treasury in 1924.[7] As Accountant, Court was responsible for all work in connection with payments and keeping and rendering of accounts. She performed all calculations, paid salaries, pensions and other fees, counter-signed cheques, corresponded with the Treasury and ensured information was printed and laid before the House as necessary.

Court's work was certainly managerial and professional with significant financial responsibility, although there is no evidence that she or anyone else in her department ever had any accountancy qualifications. She was not one of the very few female chartered accountants (there were just six in England and Wales in 1925, and only sixty-one by 1935).[8] Furthermore, all was not plain sailing in the Accounting and Copying Department. In 1929–30 the Treasury carried out a major audit on the House of Lords Security Fund and Fee Fund, and discovered a long-running deficit of nearly £6,000 – a huge amount of money, equivalent to about £275,000 today.

The Treasury investigation must have been extremely difficult for Court, not just because of her own position but also because the long-running nature of the deficit shone the light on her father too. It would have been a great relief to her when the Treasury decided that the situation was due to 'misappropriations' before 1902, and 'It may confidently be said that no one of the last three Accountants [Thomas Ambrey Court, Percy Norris and Miss Court] has embezzled funds'. Each of them in turn ought to have reported the past embezzlement but it was not necessary to discipline Miss Court, who had in fact kept better records than her predecessors. The Treasury conclusion was:

> As to disciplinary action the real culprits are dead, and I doubt as regards Miss Court whether more than an expression of displeasure is necessary. She must have lived for some years in dread of disclosure of unhappy incidents of the past of which she had no clear understanding and which she suspected might involve her father's honour.[9]

The Treasury straightened up the financial situation in the House of Lords, closing the Fee Fund, and recording in the 1931 Estimates: 'Reimbursement of security monies £6,000. Sum required to make good loss in the years preceding 1902 discovered in the course of a recent investigation.' Miss Court could now relax: her reputation, and that of her father, was safe.

ALL THE SINGLE LADIES

Court was not alone in her work. As the 'Monstrous Regiment' article declared in 1926, she was one of 'three lonely women'. The three at this point were Court, Waterman and Winifred Phipps; they were joined shortly afterwards by Miss D.C. Hood, making an office of four.

Perhaps the press called the women 'lonely' because they were all single and had to remain so as the marriage bar compelled them to resign paid work if they married. All turnover in Court's department over the years was due to resignations on marriage. Each one was reported to the House of Lords Offices Committee who approved marriage gratuities – one-off payments related to salary and service length. This may or may not have been much compensation for the loss of a salary.

Among Court's staff were the Phipps sisters. Winifred Mary Jacintha Phipps had been appointed to replace Winifred Bird in 1924, aged 20. She was daughter of Major Frederick Reginald Phipps and his wife Lucy. Her father was an eminent engineer; he had been Borough Surveyor in Basingstoke before the war and was awarded an OBE for his service in the Royal Engineers. In 1924, he was Senior Engineering Inspector at the Ministry of Transport. The House of Lords would have been pleased to employ the daughter of such a respectable man. He merited an obituary in *The Times* on his death in 1927. In fact, they were so pleased that the next time a vacancy occurred in 1930, they appointed another of his daughters, Alicia Nelly Phipps. Alicia was younger sister to Winifred – another parliamentary family connection coming into play.

In 1936, Mabel Waterman resigned to marry after seventeen years' service. As well as receiving a marriage gratuity, she was given a dinner service and needlework table as wedding presents by 'Friends and Colleagues of the bride at the House of Lords' – and her old boss H.P. Norris also sent a cheque.[10] Waterman's departure marked a big change in the gender balance of the Accounts Department as a male Assistant Accountant was appointed in her place: Percy Johnson, previously clerical officer in the Public Trustee Office. Court remained in charge, however, and he reported to her. Winifred Phipps became Examiner of Local Acts at the same time; she was put on the same salary scale as Johnson and at a higher entry point than him.

The Phipps sisters both resigned on marriage in 1939, having worked together in the House of Lords for ten years. Other women appointed under Court's leadership who did not marry went on to have long careers in the House of Lords administration. These were Rosalys Joan Griffith, employed from 1936 to 1963; Rosalind Clara Evernden, from 1939 to 1971; and Joan Parnell Culverwell, from 1939 to 1976.

THE LATER YEARS

May Court lived at 85 Chelsea Gardens, Chelsea, for many years. During the Second World War, she was a Reserve Fire Spotter in Chelsea. In 1942, she was awarded an OBE for her services to the House of Lords. She retired on 1 July 1944 aged 63, by which time her salary was £750 per annum, having worked for the House for twenty-six years. Court was replaced by her deputy, Percy Johnson, and his new deputy was also a man. This ended the female management of the House of Lords Accounting and Copying Department, although Griffith, Evernden and Culverwell continued in their subordinate roles.

Less than a year after her retirement, May Court died on 19 April 1945 at Knaresborough Place, Kensington, of carcinoma of the uterus and cardiac failure. She never married and had no children; she left her estate to her stepmother Elizabeth and aunt Cornelia, and after their deaths to her nephew Robert Ambrey Court (son of Cecil). Today, her descendants still treasure her OBE and proudly remember her achievements. Although Court's promotion in 1926 was reported in the press, unlike Miss Ashworth, it seems she never gave an interview and records give scant clues as to her personality. It is only thanks to family memory that we know that she was known as May.

Court's pioneering career in the House of Lords was initially made possible by family connections and wartime expediencies. However, her subsequent success, rising rapidly from Typist to Accountant, and then to a long tenure as head of department, managing both male and female staff, was exceptional for a woman of her time and undoubtedly due to her own abilities.

CRISIS IN THE KITCHENS: MAUDE WADDELL

There was one other department in the Lords apart from the Accounting Department which in 1939 was managed by a woman: the House of Lords Refreshment Department. This was headed first by Maude Waddell and then by Elsie Hoath, who were very different kinds of people with completely contrasting work experiences.

In December 1938, the kitchens were in crisis. The House of Lords caterer, A.J. Carpenter, had gone into liquidation. As for previous generations, it seemed impossible for anyone to run a business profitably given the unpredictable parliamentary timetable, working around recesses and prorogation and erratic sitting times. The Lords interviewed caterers from the Savoy, Selfridges, Army & Navy, Fortnum & Mason – none wanted the contract unless they had a guarantee against loss, which the Lords was not willing to give. Only one firm was up for the job, which was Jane Brown, of Exhibition Road, South Kensington. This was managed by Miss Waddell, who ran a small restaurant and held the catering contract for the Natural History Museum. It wasn't the Savoy, but would have to do. Waddell proposed to provide 'waiters and not waitresses and to have a lady superintendent instead of a man'. She was given a year's contract.[11]

Born in Ireland in 1893 to an Irish mother and a Scottish father, Maude Evelyn Waddell was brought up in Scotland, one of at least seven children. She was an orderly in the Scottish Women's Hospital Unit serving with the French Red Cross in 1916, and became an officer in the Women's Auxiliary Army Corps after its formation in 1917.[12] Scottish Women's Hospitals (SWH) was an offshoot of the Scottish Federation of Women's Suffrage Societies and the largest of several organisations set up by women doctors who offered their services to the War Office but were turned down. Its Scottish founder, Dr Elsie Inglis, was told by the British government to 'go home and sit still', instead of which she offered her services direct to other Allied countries.[13] Units were established in France, Serbia, Salonika, Corsica, Macedonia, Russia and Romania. Waddell worked in the SWH kitchens in Rouen and became interested in catering as a result.

Although Waddell was not at all famous, she was living with a woman who was. Elsie Bowerman, suffragette and survivor of the *Titanic*, had also worked as an orderly with SWH in the First World War, serving in Serbia, Romania and Russia, where she witnessed the Russian Revolution.[14] It is possible that they met each other through the SWH, but certainly they knew each other soon after the war through the Women's Guild of Empire, an organisation opposed to communism and fascism, which Bowerman co-founded with Flora Drummond in 1919. Waddell was Secretary when Bowerman was Honorary Secretary in the 1920s.[15] In 1939, Bowerman and Waddell were listed as living together in Kensington, London (Bowerman as a retired barrister and Waddell as a caterer). At this time, Bowerman had just helped Lady Reading found the Women's Voluntary Service and Waddell had been running Jane Brown for about ten years.[16]

Waddell and Bowerman were living together at Batchelors, Cowbeech Hill, in Sussex at the time of Waddell's death aged 62 in 1955. In her will, Waddell left the bulk of her estate to her family but all her personal possessions including furniture to Bowerman. Today, Batchelors is Grade II listed and Historic England was proud to recognise Bowerman's connection with the building as part of their 'Herstories' project – researching properties connected with the suffrage struggle – in 2018.[17] Waddell's long association with Bowerman, however, appears to have been completely unnoticed by everyone. The entry for Bowerman on *Encyclopaedia Titanica* states that there is no mention of a relationship or intimate friendship with anyone in her correspondence but also mentions an interesting anecdote about Bowerman refurbishing a flat she owned in St Leonard's, Hastings, in the 1950s because a 'close lady friend' was coming to live with her. Soon afterwards, her tenants were shocked to find her sobbing on the stairs: her friend had died suddenly.[18] This seems very likely to have been Waddell.

As part of her application to the Lords in 1939, Waddell supplied a list of personal referees which included Cicely Stanhope and Nina Butler, both awarded the MBE for their services to the Red Cross in the war. Butler lived in the Lords for many years; she was the daughter of Thomas Dacres Butler, Secretary to the Lord Great Chamberlain between 1892 and 1929 (and employer of Eliza Arscot and her fellow Housekeepers). Nina's sister, Hersey, another keen Voluntary Aid Detachment (VAD) nurse, even had her wedding reception in the Robing Room in the House of Lords in 1919 with Nina as a bridesmaid. Waddell must have hoped that such a personal connection would commend her to the House of Lords. Her other referees were respectable men such as R.L. Atkinson, Assistant Keeper of Public Records and secretary to the Historical Manuscripts Commission; Colonel E.E.B. Mackintosh, director of the Science Museum; and Father Maryon-Wilson, future 12th Baronet Maryon-Wilson. One mystery is why the company was called 'Jane Brown' when no such woman is anywhere evident. Perhaps Waddell inherited the name when she began running the restaurant on Exhibition Road, or simply chose it as a respectable English woman's name.

In her application letter, Waddell stressed to the Lords that she was a high-class speciality caterer. Following first-class honours at the Edinburgh School of Cookery, she trained under 'Monsieur Michelet (chef to the late Tsar)' in France, specialising in haute cuisine. She provided a list of balls, receptions and parties she had catered for, which, as well as many occasions at the Science Museum, also included trade shows, the Eton & Harrow Match and events attended by Queen Mary and the Duke of Connaught. Although it is understandable that Waddell thought the House of Lords contract would be a logical progression from all this, in fact it shows the reason for the situation turning sour very quickly. After only eight months, Waddell handed in her notice in August 1939 in view of financial losses sustained.

Waddell found that providing routine meals for Members of the House of Lords was very different from catering for high-class events. As a newspaper headline succinctly put it, 'Peers Content with Cup of Tea'.[19] Although

Waddell had managed to cater for some fancy events, including a visit by the French President Albert Lebrun, who addressed both Houses of Parliament in Westminster Hall in March 1939 (and who appeared to have a special liking for plum cake), she found that most luncheons were served to Law Lords, members of their staff and law witnesses, and with the House sitting so irregularly and infrequently there was not much demand for dinners. As she explained:

> On one occasion when Lord Halifax was expected to make an important pronouncement on foreign affairs, and everything pointed to a full attendance of peers, I made special arrangements to meet probable demands. The House rose at eight o' clock and only two remained. I was left with a whole lot of material on my hands. Nobody can run a business like that at a profit.[20]

The House of Lords Offices Committee heard that the final straw was that she had expected to get the contract to provide catering for the Lord Chancellor's Breakfast, but had been disappointed. The relationship went from bad to worse, as she claimed a refund for additional wages paid in lieu of housing accommodation. It appeared that the refurbishment of her rooms by the Office of Works had taken so long she had never been able to move staff in before deciding to terminate the contract.[21] It was a sorry end to Waddell's association with the House of Lords. She continued to run Jane Brown restaurant and may have benefited from her connection to Parliament, brief though it was. In September 1939 'Jane Brown' was listed as giving a radio programme on the BBC Home Service on 'Cooking for large numbers'.[22]

MISS HOATH TO THE RESCUE

Fortunately, a saviour was at hand in the House of Lords: Miss Hoath took over the operation. Elsie Winifred Hoath was born in 1897 in Brenchley, Kent, daughter of a shoemaker and youngest of seven brothers and sisters. Her working life before the Lords is unknown. Her two brothers served in and survived the First World War and her sister Lilian was a Red Cross nurse. Two other sisters, Rosa and Kathleen, are noted as Red Cross volunteers in 1939. But all that can be said about Elsie is that she took the reins so promptly at Waddell's departure in August 1939 that she must have been working in Parliament in some capacity already, perhaps in the Commons or employed by Jane Brown in the Lords. Certainly, Hoath had taken over by late September 1939 as she is recorded as Catering Manageress in the 1939 Register, resident in the Lords along with her assistant Marie Preece, presumably living in the same rooms that the Office of Works had taken so long to refurbish for Waddell. By this time, the Second World War had been declared, and nobody in the Lords would have wanted to start interviewing caterers again.

In January 1940, it was reported to the House of Lords Offices Committee Refreshment Sub-Committee that Hoath had balanced the current accounts and was paying off outstanding debts. She was congratulated and asked to carry on indefinitely until amalgamation with the Commons Refreshment Department might be achieved. This amalgamation never happened.

The admirable work of Hoath carried on through the war and beyond. She and her team regularly received praise and even a bonus. Hoath and Preece lived on site throughout the war and helped with fire watching at the Palace of Westminster; both were awarded the Defence Medal for civilian service.[23] The key to Hoath's success seems to have been to concentrate on providing basic food to peers rather than fine dining, enabling her to be more flexible when the political situation required it. During the Suez Crisis debate in 1956, Earl Fortescue commented there were so many Lords still wanting to speak that 'it is suggested that we sit through dinner. Dinner can be provided here, but it would be convenient if those noble Lords who want it would let Miss Hoath know.'[24]

In 1961, Hoath wrote to the Refreshment Sub-Committee of her intention to retire, saying, 'I do not feel equal to working another summer here.' Aged 64, she was entitled to a small state pension but no work pension, and the Clerk of the Parliaments reminded the Committee of 'the great debt the House owes Miss Hoath for her reliability, loyalty and hard work, particularly during the last war'. A collection raised a retirement fund, paid half in cash and half to buy an annuity, as well as a watch, presented to her at a luncheon on 18 July. At the insistence of Lady Reading, 'The Committee agreed that a woman should be appointed rather than a man', and Miss M. Riddell, of Marks and Spencer catering department, was duly hired.[25]

When scraping together a retirement income for Hoath, Lady Reading and the other lords seemed unaware that Hoath was not a single spinster but a widow. She had married Thomas F. O'Halloran, himself a widower with two adult children, Patrick and Margaret, in 1945; he died in 1949. She did not use her married name at work and was always known as Miss Hoath. Although the formal marriage bar was lifted in 1946, she may well have still felt threatened by revealing her new status, or perhaps she feared an informal bar, or simply that attitudes to her in the Lords might change if she was known to be a married woman, even a widow. Elsie O'Halloran died in Tunbridge Wells, Kent, in 1983 aged 86.

In Her Own Words

'We fully appreciate being retained during the War, may we be allowed to state that during that time we have done the extra duties of both male and female cleaners ... [but now] employment is almost an impossibility as employers will not engage us for short periods ... May we be allowed to point out that we have to be mothers as well as fathers to our children and in times like these it is a terrible trial.'

Petition to the Serjeant at Arms from eight
female sessional cleaners in the House of Commons, 1919

11

MISS BELL AND HER BELL:
THE LATER HOUSEKEEPERS

Beside an unobtrusive doorway near Chancellor's Gate in the House of Lords is a doorbell, known as 'Miss Bell's Bell'. The bell itself, a small white button marked PRESS in an elaborate ironwork surround, is a Pugin original, made when the Palace, with its large array of residences, was designed in the mid-nineteenth century. The wooden sign above, 'Miss C. Bell', is a later addition (Figure 13). Clearly this was once Miss Bell's front door – but who was she?

Catherine Leece Bell was the last resident Housekeeper or Principal Housemaid of the House of Lords, retiring in 1948. She is now completely forgotten, so those who notice the bell today may wonder idly who she was. Her doorbell remains as material evidence that women worked in the building, and in particular signifies that this doorway once led to the palatial apartments of the Housekeeper of the House of Lords. One thing never changed though, as battles over the Housekeeper's furniture raged on.

DOMESTIC SERVICE IN PARLIAMENT
BETWEEN THE WARS

Although increasing numbers of women were taking up employment in offices, shops and factories in the interwar period, domestic service still predominated within the female labour market in Britain. In 1931, the sector accounted for around 24 per cent of women in work and about 8 per cent of the entire workforce. Nationally, in 1931 around 60 per cent of female

Figure 13: Miss Bell's bell, photographed in 2022.

servants 'lived in' at their place of work, as Miss Bell did in the Lords. Although some men did enter domestic service, particularly after the First World War, 'the sector was so firmly feminised that most employers found the prospect of male servants alarming or ridiculous' and men were mostly employed in institutions such as schools rather than in households.[1] The House of Lords, reflecting life in the stately home, employed only women as housekeepers or housemaids. But in the Commons, which more closely resembled a government department, both men and women were employed as cleaners – although the men were on better terms than the women. Most of the female Commons cleaners were not on permanent contracts, which led to much distress and poverty.

In the Commons, there was no equivalent of Miss Bell's front door; women housekeepers, housemaids and cleaners were not resident unless attached to one of the officials' households. Yet they were very much present – and often employed through the informal system of parliamentary families. A traditional reliance on familial recruitment networks to find jobs from the most senior to the most junior posts continued to be as strong in the Palace of Westminster as in the outside world. And in an echo of the Girl Porters during the First World War, the Second World War led to additional opportunities for women with good connections in Parliament to be employed as porters and cleaners.

GRANDEES, MINOR OFFICIALS AND SERVANTS WHO LIVED ON SITE

In the interwar era, a number of minor officials still lived on site at the Palace of Westminster in order to keep its vital services functioning. At the Lords' end, on the census night of 19 June 1921, these included Janet Elizabeth Rogers, Miss Bell's predecessor as Housekeeper; George Canter, Turncock (controlling the water supply), with his wife and daughter; and William Bowden, Electrical Engineer, as well as his wife, daughter and a son who worked for Messrs Mowlem as a carpenter in the Palace of Westminster. Resident Superintendent Thomas Whitehead was also present in his seven-room apartment, with his sister Lucretia, as was Catering Manager Walter Barrow, a contractor, with his wife, daughter and two cooks attached to the Refreshment Department. Over in the Commons, three Office Keepers were resident, one with a son serving Parliament as a messenger. And the famed Commons Kitchen Committee, still going strong, employed nine living-in female servants. Resident Engineer William Bradshaw was also present with his wife Berthe, although now minus their two children and the two servants that had been recorded in 1911.

While constantly trying to bear down on their bills for heating, lighting and furniture, the Treasury grudgingly recognised the requirement for official accommodation for these essential workers. In its long-standing campaign to rid the Palace of as many resident grandees as possible and save money, it had encountered several major setbacks; by 1921, however, its officials had succeeded in ensuring that five official residences for senior staff had been surrendered and turned over to other uses.

Four grand residences remained, where each family was supported by a number of servants, the vast majority female. Most notable of those was the Speaker's House, which Treasury officials accepted as being out of bounds for any significant cost-saving measures. In 1921 it was, as already noted, occupied by John Henry Whitley, his wife, daughter and seven servants, all women. Next door to the Speaker was the Serjeant's house with twenty-five rooms, where the eminent retired Admiral Sir Colin Richard Keppel was present, along with his wife and eight servants – one man and the rest women. Keppel, who served as Serjeant to the House of Commons from 1915 to 1935, was supported by the Deputy Serjeant, Francis Russell Gosset, who also lived on site. The son of an earlier Serjeant who had been born and brought up in the Palace, Gosset was a familiar figure at Westminster for half a century, helping to maintain order in the chamber first as Assistant Serjeant and then as Deputy Serjeant from 1885 to 1929. He and his wife, Mary, kept four servants: a butler, a cook/housekeeper and two maids, all occupying his set of fourteen rooms above St Stephen's Porch, the main entrance to the Commons on the west front of the Palace.

Over in the Lords, a number of official suites were available for short-term use by senior staff, but by 1921 only one grand residence – with twenty-two rooms – was left. Its occupant was Captain Sir Thomas Dacres Butler, Yeoman Usher of the Black Rod from 1892 and additionally, from 1896, Secretary to the Lord Great Chamberlain. With him in 1921 were his wife, his daughter Nina, a female visitor, and one male and five female servants, a slight decrease from a decade earlier. Ever since his arrival, the Treasury had quibbled with his insistence that his house be furnished at public expense, as 'there are no official rooms in the ordinary sense of the word. The office work … is carried on outside his residence.' But the Treasury did, in the end, cover the costs of fitting out his state rooms, kitchen, scullery and house-keeper's room and five bedrooms, two of these for his servants. Here his household remained in some style until he retired in 1929.[2]

THE PLIGHT OF THE SESSIONAL CLEANERS

Housekeeping in the House of Commons was managed by the Serjeant at Arms Department, with several resident male Office Keepers, akin to the Lords' Resident Superintendent, responsible for various parts of the building. Two non-resident women worked for these Office Keepers as housemaids, known also as housekeepers, with an additional eight women employed as sessional cleaners, allocated particular rooms, passages and stairways to keep clean. Although the title never conveyed the power and prestige it did in the Lords, some Commons housekeepers had long tenures.

The record might well be held by Mrs Hart, who died in 1916 after a staggering forty-eight years' service, first as a female sessional cleaner and then from 1893 as a housemaid. Born Eliza Letitia Gould in 1845, she married Joseph Hart, a cabman, in 1867 and had at least five children before being widowed in 1882. She lived close to the Palace of Westminster all her life; her father was a House of Commons messenger and her son Charles

Figure 14: Mr and Mrs Hills, photographed by Benjamin Stone, 1904.

came to work as a warehouseman's assistant in Parliament. This was very typical as many jobs were held by members of extended parliamentary families, with husbands, wives, sons and daughters often employed together or in succession.

Another example was Mr and Mrs Hills, who were recorded together for posterity by the MP and photographer Sir Benjamin Stone in 1904. John Hills was a messenger, who died after forty-three years' service. His wife,

Catherine, was a housekeeper between 1880 and 1912; she was granted a gratuity on her husband's death and a pension on retirement, and died in 1925 at
the age of 76.

Although the housekeepers had permanent, established jobs and were usually awarded pensions, this status was not enjoyed by other female cleaning
staff, however long and exemplary their service might be. One curious example of this was Catherine Mossenton, who had been widowed in 1893 and
gone on to chalk up seventeen years' satisfactory service as a sessional
cleaner. Her husband, George, had variously worked as an omnibus driver,
groom and stableman before his death, a presumably respectable working-
class livelihood after serving nine months of hard labour in Wandsworth
for embezzlement at the age of 15. On her retirement in 1915, she wrote to
the Serjeant asking for money, but was refused. She died in 1917, curiously
not quite in the poverty-stricken situation that one might assume from her
request. Her net estate was worth £782 (about £46,000 today) and among
small bequests to family members were a silver bracelet, a gold watch, brooch
and earrings, and some clearly valued books conveying a good level of education – six volumes of *Old and New London* and a *Fox's Illustrated Book of
Martyrs*. Possessions like these would have been well out of reach for humbler
working-class families such as that of the Girl Porters Elsie and Mabel Clark.

More immediately problematic for the Serjeant than retirees was the
situation for working cleaners who were paid weekly and thrown out of
work and into poverty every time the House of Commons went into recess.
Debate with the Treasury on this subject began in 1896, when the Serjeant
wrote to say that, although Lords cleaners were employed all year round,
Commons sessional cleaners were not, and this caused considerable hardship.
The Treasury, which controlled the purse strings, was not convinced. The
stand-off went on throughout the First World War and beyond. A petition
to the Serjeant from female sessional cleaners in 1919 read:

> We fully appreciate being retained during the War, may we be allowed
> to state that during that time we have done the extra duties of both male
> and female cleaners … [but now] employment is almost an impossibility
> as employers will not engage us for short periods … Of course the War
> Widows have their pensions, which are totally inadequate to keep them
> otherwise they would not be at work … May we be allowed to point out
> that we have to be mothers as well as fathers to our children and in times
> like these it is a terrible trial.
>
>   M. Holland, M. Ross, E.L. Walsh, R. Harris, J. Champ, E. Exford,
>   H. Gunter, M. Russell.[3]

The female sessional cleaners were all married or widows. Some of the signatories were war widows, such as Elizabeth Exford, whose husband George Osman Exford was killed in action in the Battle of Jutland in 1916. Others were married but may have still been adversely affected by the war. Emily Louisa Walsh, another signatory, was the wife of a male cleaner, Thomas Mortimer Walsh. In 1913, a weekly allowance of 10 shillings had been made to Emily for a year because Thomas was suffering from a relapse of a nervous condition and she was having a very hard struggle with their two young children.[4] The sympathetic treatment of this male employee can be contrasted with that of Eliza Arscot, consigned to an asylum only a decade earlier. Thomas went on to serve in the army during the First World War, which cannot have helped his nervous condition. He was noted as 'out of work' in 1921 while his wife was now working for the Serjeant as a cleaner, presumably having been employed in his place and supporting the family on her own – no wonder she signed the petition. They both went on to live a long time, however. Thomas died in 1946 aged 69, while Emily ended her days in 1966, having lived to the ripe old age of 90.

Male sessional cleaners were in a similar situation, but the Commons made efforts to find them alternative paid work throughout recesses. From 1921, it was agreed that the male sessional cleaners could be paid all year round, but the women were excluded by the Treasury from this new benefit. The assumption was that female cleaners would find it easier than men to find other work during recesses, but that was not the case; the periods of time were too short. The Serjeant repeatedly requested funding for retention fees and sick pay, but Treasury officials repeatedly refused to pay for work that was not done.[5] It appears that workarounds were found instead: in 1938, it was noted that three senior women sessional cleaners were employed also as attendants in the ladies' cloakroom to take them up into full-time employment.

After the departure of the temporary Girl Porters of the First World War, the Serjeant at Arms Department only employed women as housekeepers and cleaners – until the advent of the Second World War meant that the men were called up and necessitated the employment of women as porters again. This time, there does not seem to have been anything like the same angst over what the women would wear and what duties they would perform, but as with the Clark family in the First World War, parliamentary family connections came into play. Long-serving Office Keeper and army veteran William Munsie (who had enlisted in the Scots Guards back in 1903 at the age of 18) died in October 1941, after which his daughters, Mrs Janet Eileen Edwell and Mrs Joyce V. Clark, were employed as female porters from December, not having previously worked in the Commons; they had husbands serving in the armed forces. The Serjeant's Department was clearly keen to support the Munsie family, as in 1944 their mother Clara Violet Munsie also began working as a cleaner. Edwell's husband was killed in action in 1940. She remarried in 1945 but kept her porter job and was later made a female cleaner.

A third temporary female porter, Grace Phyllis Coulber, was appointed in May 1942, directly after her porter husband Servais St Joseph Coulber had been called up by the RAF. She was made redundant in 1946 when he returned from active duty, a clear example of a wife substituting for her husband. The fourth and last temporary female porter, Miss Teresa Mary O'Grady, was the only one without an obvious parliamentary connection. She was employed from September 1942 and discharged in December 1945.

THE MATRON HOUSEKEEPER: JANET ROGERS

Meanwhile, over in the House of Lords, following the retirement of Amelia de Laney, Captain Thomas Dacres Butler appointed Janet Rogers in her place as Housekeeper in June 1919. Like de Laney, Rogers was paid a weekly wage (39 shillings a week by 1928, worth about £80 today), and her post was not established or pensionable. But at least nobody seems to have challenged her right to live on site. An inventory of the Housekeeper's furniture the month before shows an impressive list covering her sitting room, bedroom, hall, kitchen and toilet suite, with additional items received in August including a dinner set, tea set, cutlery and bed linen.[6] In January 1922, Rogers requested a bath but this was roundly ignored by the Office of Works for years. Butler wrote occasional letters expressing the hope that the bath might be provided and that he understood there was no structural difficulty, all to no avail. Only when the price was reduced from £180 to £40 did they relent.[7]

Janet Elizabeth Rogers was born in 1862 in Bridgnorth, Shropshire. Her father Charles was a minister in the Catholic Apostolic Church, a Protestant sect formed in the 1830s. Rogers may have had a precarious childhood as her father was not always employed and the family were living on charity in 1881. Her career before the Lords is not known and she is absent from the 1901 and 1911 censuses. However, following in the footsteps of former infirmary matron Amelia de Laney, Rogers recorded herself as 'Matron Housekeeper' to the Lords in the 1921 census, and had a visitor staying with her, Ellen Beatrice Greenwood, who was a retired nurse from Queen Alexandra's Military Nursing Service for India. It is likely that Rogers also had a nursing background, maybe working overseas with Greenwood, which would explain her earlier census absences. Military backgrounds were preferred in the Department of the Lord Great Chamberlain, and Captain Butler may well have favoured a former military nurse who could act as a matron and housekeeper.

Rogers' tenure as Housekeeper was not as smooth as de Laney's. Within a few months, the housemaids were up in arms, and fourteen of them wrote a joint letter to Butler complaining about her 'harassing manner'. He must have had flashbacks to the long list of complaints about Eliza Arscot twenty years earlier and wondered if a similar fate was in store. The housemaids noted their length of service, which ranged from a few months to thirty years in the case of Mrs Emma Burton. Top of the list of complainants was a Mrs Amelia Whitehead.[8] Rogers retaliated with a written statement:

> I have always tried to be most careful, as I know how very difficult these people are now. To Mrs Whitehead I was more severe perhaps: because she will not properly clean out one of the cellars ... Ever since I came all the women very much resented supervision ... and found as I tell you, Mrs Gibbons and Mrs Leslie having a sit down breakfast, and most, if not all the others in the habit of making tea and standing about talking to the Policemen.[9]

Butler referred the matter up to the Lord Great Chamberlain, explaining he did not feel he could ignore a complaint from fourteen of his sixteen house-maids, but opining that 'no doubt there is something to be said on both sides'.[10] It may have just taken some time for the housemaids to get used to their new manager after the easy-going de Laney.[11]

Rogers also had some trouble with Thomas Whitehead, the Resident Superintendent who had replaced Williams in 1910. She remarked during a skirmish with another housemaid in 1923, 'I have been told: both by Sir Thomas [Butler] and also before by Miss de Laney that Mr Whitehead has nothing whatsoever to do with the women – if this could be made quite plain it might make things easier.'[12] Thomas Whitehead, an army pensioner, was unmarried and lived on site with his sister Lucretia, but it is likely that Amelia Whitehead and Thomas were also related in some way, which would have soured the relationship with Rogers. Both Whiteheads subsequently retired in 1927.

The House of Lords housemaids were employed permanently and throughout the year, and although they were mostly not entitled to pensions, they received gratuities on retirement consisting of one week's pay and 75 per cent bonus for each year's service. In some cases, previous service in government departments was also taken into account. Although nobody seems to have had a length of service to rival Mrs Hart's forty-eight years in the Commons, the record in the Lords seems to have been held by Emma Burton, who retired in 1929 after thirty-nine years' service with a gratuity of £47.

In May 1928, Rogers was ill and seriously thought about retiring. Consideration was given to her successor and names flooded in, but a doctor approved her to carry on to the end of the year. She and Butler were both pleased about this, but it was probably an unwise decision as Rogers did not make it to the end of the year. Sadly, she died in post in the Housekeeper's quarters on 30 October 1928, of heart disease and gastritis.

THE LAST OF THE RESIDENT HOUSEKEEPERS

Following the death of Janet Rogers, Catherine Bell took over the post of House of Lords Housekeeper in December 1928. Bell had expressed her interest several months earlier when Rogers had been ill, writing to Butler, 'I have had a long chat with Miss Rogers and now quite understand the duties of the post.'[13] Competition was stiff, as Butler had a pool of twenty-one candidates to consider, each listed with their age and number of supporting letters. At 54 years old, Bell was the oldest candidate. She also mustered nine letters of support; the second-placed candidate had an impressive eleven, although most applicants had just one or two.

Catherine Leece Bell was born in 1874 in Bootle, Cumberland, daughter of a station master. After her father's death, her mother supported the family as proprietor of a temperance hotel. A hospital nurse by background, Bell followed the matronly tradition of Amelia de Laney and Janet Rogers. She trained at the Nightingale training school at St Thomas's Hospital between 1898 and 1902, afterwards working in private nursing, including at a hospital in Marylebone. During the First World War, she was sister in charge of Inchcape Hospital, a convalescent hospital for officers set up by Lady Inchcape in Mayfair. Among Bell's referees at her appointment were the matron at the Nightingale training school, who described her as 'a woman of wide experience and broad outlook', and also the eminently respectable Claud Schuster, long-standing Permanent Secretary to the Lord Chancellor, who wrote, 'She nursed my wife once and showed herself extremely capable, tactful and pleasant.'[14]

It is certain that by now Butler was looking for another nurse-matron-housekeeper in the mould of de Laney and Rogers, as two names crossed off the list of applicants were marked as 'no medical experience'. As it turned out, Bell was one of the last appointments made by Captain Thomas Dacres Butler, who retired from the Lords in July 1929 after an impressive thirty-three years' service as Secretary to the Lord Great Chamberlain and thirty-eight years as Yeoman Usher. A constant presence for many years, battling on behalf of the Lords and its staff for rooms and furniture alongside his glittering ceremonial duties for State Openings and other such occasions, he had known all the Housekeepers from Ellen Lovegrove through Eliza Arscot and Janet Rogers – and now Catherine Bell.

Inevitably, Bell's appointment was accompanied by a request for furniture. By now, the Lord Great Chamberlain's office seems to have given up importuning the Office of Works to pay for it, instead simply applying directly to the House of Lords itself. In May 1930, the Lords Offices Committee approved £40 to be paid to the Housekeeper for furnishing her rooms, followed a year later by a payment of £10 for carpets and further sums of £10 for furniture in 1933 and 1939. Bell was also awarded small increases in her salary, and in 1938 she received a month's pay after being incapacitated by an accident while on duty. The Second World War led to the appointment of an additional housemaid for the Air Raid Precautions (ARP) refuges which were constructed on site, along with, in 1942, two temporary housemaids 'owing to difficulty of filling vacancies on the porters' staff', who continued to be employed as such well after the war ended.[15] It seems that rather than employing female porters as in the Commons, the Lords preferred to call them housemaids and to get them to do the same work.

Bell left office in 1948, by which time she was being paid £4 9s a week. She was not entitled to a pension but did get a retirement gratuity of £104 6s 6d – approximately £3,709 today. She died in Millom, Cumberland, in 1953. By now, society had moved on again; domestic service was no longer the largest employer of women. In 1921, 23 per cent of young women had worked in domestic service, but by 1951 it was just 5 per cent. For the Lords, the time had at last come to complete the reform of its Housekeeper post in line with the recommendations of 1889. At Catherine Bell's retirement, the post of resident Housekeeper was finally abolished, replaced by an additional payment to the Head Housemaid. And so ended the long reign of the Lords Housekeepers, with 'Miss Bell's bell' the only relic of their existence today.

In Her Own Words

'With regard to my present staff here … most of them with the best will in the world cannot afford to give voluntary service, and it is my duty to try and look after their interests.'

Edythe Mary Thomson, Commandant of the British Red Cross Nurses at the Palace of Westminster First Aid Post, 1939

12

EXPERT SHOTS AND
DRAGONS: PARLIAMENT
AT WAR

On 3 September 1939, Prime Minister Neville Chamberlain made his famous radio broadcast declaring that Britain was now at war with Germany. Along with the rest of the country, the authorities at the Palace of Westminster immediately swung into action, in particular to prepare for air raids. Gas attacks were feared imminently, and within a day or so, a team of thirty-five female nurses from the British Red Cross Society arrived to support the Houses of Parliament by running first aid points set up at refuges across the Palace. The advent of aerial warfare the following year made their presence essential. These nurses were just a few of the many women who were to play a crucial yet almost invisible part in Parliament's war effort over the next six years.

Female MPs such as Edith Summerskill and Mavis Tate pressed for women to play their part in the war effort nationally, in roles such as fire watching, the Home Guard and in munitions factories. Alongside them, but with little public credit or acclaim, women staff came forward to perform those exact roles on site, defending the Palace of Westminster so the MPs and peers could continue to sit, legislate and scrutinise the work of government through-out the war. Unseen heroines include Edythe Thomson, Commandant of the Red Cross nurses; six women auxiliaries in the Palace of Westminster Home Guard; and Vera Michel, Welfare Officer for the dozens of women who worked in the Westminster Munitions Unit in the basement. The most tragic story was that of Barbara Shuttleworth, fire watcher and Home Guard auxiliary, who was stalked and murdered by a Polish RAF officer following a wartime liaison.

PARLIAMENT DURING THE SECOND WORLD WAR

As with the First World War, the Palace of Westminster was part of the Home Front in the Second World War, part of the civilian population of a nation at war, but a major difference was that for the first time the UK was now subject to air raids on a large scale. Along with other cities, towns, ports, railways, bridges and other targets across the UK, London was attacked by German bombers in a campaign during 1940–41 that became known as the Blitz. Tens of thousands of civilians were killed and many more injured. Millions of houses were damaged or destroyed.

Plans were made for temporary alternative places for the House of Commons and House of Lords to sit, including possible wholesale evacuation from London, but ultimately – like the king and queen down the road at Buckingham Palace – it was thought important for national morale that Parliament remained in the capital. The Houses sat a few times nearby in Church House in times of emergency, but the MPs and peers preferred to remain in the Palace and risk the bombing, with extensive air-raid precautions.[1]

The Palace of Westminster suffered twelve direct hits from bombing plus further damage caused by explosions nearby. There were 1,224 alerts totalling 2,198 hours; three people were killed and fifteen injured.[2] Worst of all was the night of 10–11 May 1941, when the skies were clear with a full moon to light the Luftwaffe's way. The House of Commons chamber and Westminster Hall both sustained direct hits. It was not possible to save both, but Colonel Walter Elliot MP took charge and had no hesitation in instructing the fire brigade to 'Save the Hall'. The medieval Hall with its magnificent hammer beam roof was protected at the expense of the post-1834 Commons chamber, which was reduced to a smoking ruin. The Commons sat afterwards in the Lords chamber, while the Lords decamped to the Robing Room further down the Palace.

Without a huge number of volunteers, it would not have been possible to save the Hall or to defend the vast, distinctive and emblematic Victorian Palace from an unstinting and unpredictable threat of destruction. Overall, it is estimated that 1,168 people took part in this essential work, 788 of these for more than six months. As well as the Red Cross nurses, they included Home

Guard volunteers, custodians, police, fire guards and Air Raid Precautions (ARP) firemen.

Women played a full and significant part in Parliament's war effort. A snapshot of those deemed essential for the work of both Houses can be found in a 'Nominal Roll of Staff', compiled in November 1942 for evacuation purposes when it was envisaged that Parliament could be relocated to a secret location code-named HK. This was in fact Stratford-upon-Avon, where both Houses were to share the Royal Shakespeare Theatre and the staff were to be billeted in hotels and private houses in the town.

The Commons list comprises 378 staff, of whom forty-six (12 per cent) were women.[3] Most of the people itemised – including sixty-two police officers and ninety-four journalists in the Press Gallery – were not directly employed by the Commons. Of the forty-six women, twenty-one served the Commons in the Serjeant at Arms Department, Committee and Private Bill Office, and Refreshment Department. The rest worked for third parties including HMSO (as typists in the Official Report and as teleprinting operators), the Empire Parliamentary Association, the Post and Telegraph Office, and the Whips' Office. And there was one woman journalist, Ellen Baylis.[4]

A similar snapshot list of Lords staff to be evacuated shows seventy-eight in total including sixteen women (20.5 per cent). The sixteen women were employed across the Lord Chancellor's Office and Parliament Office (including Miss Court and her team), with two typists in the Lords Official Report and two typists working for Gurneys.[5] All this demonstrates that women formed a significant minority of essential workers in Parliament – a large pool that could also be drawn upon for war defence work. These were just the staff deemed necessary for Parliament to operate in Stratford-upon-Avon.

ESSENTIAL WOMEN AT WESTMINSTER

On 20 August 1943, a comprehensive list of everyone who worked in the Palace of Westminster was compiled for the purposes of fire prevention duty. It includes large numbers of staff who were there to support the building and therefore not on the earlier evacuation lists, including Works, Estates, Supplies and Stone Restoration teams. Overall, 554 were men and 101 were women (18.2 per cent), although many teams including the police, ARP firemen and custodians (Lords staff performing a security role) had no female workers at all. Others had only small numbers, such as Mrs Wheeler, seamstress, the sole woman alongside twenty-nine men in the

Supplies Department. Female workers were concentrated in the Commons Refreshment Department, with nineteen, followed by twelve women counter clerks and telephonists in the Post Office, and eleven women staff in the Lords Refreshment Department.[6]

Although there had been a reduction in numbers of residents since the previous war, a significant number of women also still lived in the Palace. In a national register taken in September 1939, there were thirty-four residents of whom twenty-four were women, including the House of Lords Housekeeper, Catherine Bell, still living in after all these years; the House of Lords Catering Manageress Elsie Hoath and her assistant Marie Preece; and eight barmaids and waitresses in the House of Commons Refreshment Department. Among various family members and domestic servants in the official residences was Nancy Fitzroy, the 45-year-old daughter of Speaker Fitzroy (the Speaker himself and the bulk of his household were elsewhere as Parliament was in recess). Nancy, who loved camping and other outdoor pursuits, was listed with no paid occupation but was a volunteer member of the Red Cross and Voluntary Aid Detachment.

Many residents of the Palace vacated their homes once the bombing started, but others stayed; the parliamentary village was alive and well throughout the war. A.P. Herbert MP described it as a grim place to work: dark, the windows all blown out, cardboard and sandbags, with pictures and tapestries removed and replaced by camp beds and anti-gas refuges, and the Smoking Room closing early to allow the staff to get home.[7] How much worse must it have been for those who had to be present all the time, night and day.

MRS ALAN THOMSON, BRITISH RED CROSS COMMANDANT

The first new arrivals on the scene in September 1939 were the Red Cross nurses. To the consternation of the authorities, it quickly became apparent that as full-time civilian nurse reservists, they ought to be paid; however, there was no budget for this. The Lord Great Chamberlain's office explained to the Treasury that their presence was necessary 'because of the inability to provide any female First Aid Workers … You will readily recognise the difficulties we have here in the insufficiency of staff – especially female staff – in the two Houses of Parliament.'[8]

The clear implication was that, if only there were more female staff in Parliament, they would roll up their sleeves and become first aiders. The

Treasury explained in turn that in government departments the arrangements were for first aid to be administered by trained volunteers (male and female) from the office staff, as, 'trained hospital nurses are worth their weight in gold at the present time'.[9]

The British Red Cross nurses were managed by their on-site Commandant, Edythe Mary Thomson, 61 years old at the outbreak of war. Thomson was undoubtedly a redoubtable woman from a redoubtable family with many international, military and parliamentary links. She was born in 1878 in Rio de Janeiro, Brazil. Her father, John Owen Unwin, was described on successive censuses as a 'Brazilian merchant' but, as he was born in Coggeshall, Essex, it seems he was a merchant operating in Brazil rather than a Brazilian national. Edythe's husband was Brigadier Alan Fortescue Thomson, who was born in Nelson, New Zealand, and was an officer in the Royal Artillery. They had three children. Their elder daughter Clare married Anthony Crommelin Crossley, a writer who was elected a Conservative MP in 1931. Sadly, he died aged 36 in an air crash in August 1939, just a couple of weeks before his mother-in-law arrived to run first aid services in Parliament.

Colonel J.D. Waters was tasked with liaising with the Commandant, or 'Mrs Alan Thomson', as she was invariably known. John Dallas Waters had been awarded the DSO for conspicuous gallantry and devotion to duty in the First World War, but he must have still found it challenging to deal with this woman, who wrote to him every couple of days – as well as telephoning and insisting on meeting him in person. She initially used the general headed paper of the Red Cross Westminster Division but, as she settled in, she began to add, 'First Aid Post, Palace of Westminster'. By December, she was well and truly established with her own official printed 'Palace of Westminster First Aid Post' headed paper. Thomson wrote to Waters about provision of gas masks and gas protection clothing for her team; requirements for crockery, cutlery, waste paper baskets, food and refreshment areas; queries about which refuges needed to be staffed, on which days, and how long before and after the sittings of the Houses; cleaning of the refuges and rest rooms; installation of 'Elsan Closet' lavatories in the refuges; and the need for a direct-line telephone to be installed in her bedroom. On the last, she wrote, 'It would be a great help to me in my work here and I would gladly bear the expense entirely myself and the expense of its removal later on.'[10]

The most significant challenge of all was around payment. The Commandant did not want a salary herself, but her Assistant Commandant and many of the other nurses merited a wage of £2 a week and 1s 6d meal allowance, the rate set by the government for full-time nursing reservists.

Thomson had arrived with fifteen full-time and nineteen part-time nurses, the part-timers being mostly business girls who came in on night shifts and sometimes on Sundays to relieve the full-timers.[11] The requirement was quickly reduced to ten nurses, but even this necessitated a significant amount of money. Waters applied to the Ministry of Health, the House of Lords Offices Committee and the Treasury but met reluctance and refusal. Thomson was in a difficult position, writing to Waters:

> The last thing the British Red Cross want in any way to be is mercenary. It is entirely contrary to their history and teaching, in fact to the spirit of the whole affair. Their desire is to help and serve in every possible way they can. With regard to my present staff here – the ten working on shifts of eight hours, as we arranged, night and day – most of them with the best will in the world cannot afford to give voluntary service, and it is my duty to try and look after their interests.[12]

The state-registered nurses were withdrawn, and Thomson managed to raise a staff of five nurses willing to operate, like herself, on a voluntary basis. The work was made possible by reducing the numbers of refuges and the hours required, together with an assurance from Westminster Hospital that they would support Parliament at the first sign of an emergency. The Treasury was pleased and agreed to top up with paid nurses if insufficient volunteers were available, the official remarking that 'it would be desirable to avoid mingling paid nurses with unpaid nurses lest the ardour of the latter be damped by the fact that some of their colleagues are in receipt of pay'.[13]

Commandant Edythe Thomson continued to lead her small band of volunteers in Parliament throughout the war. Seven of her team served for more than three years, and although four of these were younger women in their thirties, others were veterans of nursing during the First World War. The most decorated was Emily Margaret Vivian Berry (known as Meg), born in Edinburgh in 1890, who had served in western France between 1915 and 1919. In addition to the campaign medals – the 1914–15 Star, British War Medal and Victory Medal for service overseas[14] – she was awarded the Royal Red Cross Medal, 2nd class, by the king at Buckingham Palace in 1919. She worked at the Palace of Westminster between May 1941 and April 1945 and died in Stirling in 1985.

Edythe Thomson's younger daughter Priscilla, Lady Grant of Monymusk, lost her first husband, Sir Arthur Grant, to the war when he was killed in action in 1944. But Priscilla would carry on the parliamentary family connection, as she went on to become one of the rare women MPs – and then an early life peer. After an unsuccessful attempt to stand in the general election of 1945, she was elected Conservative MP for Aberdeen South in 1946 and held the seat until 1966. She married her second husband John Buchan (son of the novelist), 1st Baron Tweedsmuir, in 1948. Her parents were strong supporters of hers, and it was reported in 1959 that the strain of a general election caused her elderly mother to collapse in a shop in Aberdeen. A friend said, 'I think it may just be exhaustion … Mrs Thomson attended most of Lady Tweedsmuir's meetings, sometimes two in an evening.'[15]

In 1970, Lady Tweedsmuir was made a life peer, becoming Baroness Tweedsmuir of Belhelvie, able to sit alongside her husband in the House of Lords in her own right. She was a minister in the House of Lords until 1974, then Chairman of the Select Committee on the European Communities until her untimely death from cancer in 1978. Her mother, Edythe Thomson, out-lived her by several months, dying at the ripe old age of 100, having seen her daughter succeed politically beyond her wildest dreams during her days in her old first aid stamping ground.

FIRE WATCHING

Fire watching was a way in which many women in Britain were drawn into home defence – including in Parliament. Following the Blitz in autumn 1940, fire watching began to be organised and many women participated voluntarily. Earl Winterton wrote of the Palace of Westminster fire watchers as 'a happy, friendly body in which all social distinctions were ignored',[16] apparently blissfully unaware that there were not enough volunteers to cover the whole site at the time of the May 1941 bombing. A report by the Home Office only a few days before declared, 'I think the present figures are appalling.' Victor Goodman, the Palace ARP Officer (who later rose to be Clerk of the Parliaments), explained that there was sufficient cover during the week, including from MPs, but the difficulty was:

> There is a deliberate and open refusal by the majority of staff … to cooperate or volunteer in any kind of way. Their grievances, as far as I can gather, are that Members will never do duty at weekends or in recesses.[17]

Although Goodman did not add his voice in support of those grievances, he did not deny the truth of them either.

To cover the gap, the role was supplemented by police and the London Fire Brigade – stepping into the breach in the same way that the Red Cross had done for nursing provision. Goodman specifically requested fire-watching cover from the Metropolitan Police for the fateful weekend of 9, 10 and 11 May 1941.[18] The result of that was that Gordon Farrant and Arthur Ernest Stead, war reserve constables from the Metropolitan Police aged 29 and 33, died while fire watching from a turret above the Royal Gallery in the House of Lords during the bombing of 11 May. A contemporary account relates that as people were evacuated from the Lords' end of the building, one man and one woman, a doctor and a nurse – presumably one of Mrs Thomson's team – bravely remained behind to operate on a wounded man who, sadly, died less than an hour later.[19] This must have been the House of Lords Resident Superintendent, Edward Laurence Heywood Elliott, who lost his life in that air raid; he left a wife and two daughters, the younger only 16 years old.

From 30 May 1941, fire watching became compulsory for men aged 16–60 who worked in the Palace.[20] A Parliamentary Fire Committee was set up and began to create lists of eligible people. Women also volunteered at this point, including the 60-year-old House of Lords Accountant May Court, who was already a Reserve Fire Spotter near her home in Chelsea but expressed willingness to participate at Westminster instead.[21] Given that three people had been killed on site only a few weeks before, there can have been no illusions about how dangerous the task could be. By October, there were 140 civilians and 160 Home Guard personnel on fire-watching duty in Parliament, supplemented by firemen from the National Fire Service and from July 1942 a dedicated body of thirty full-time paid firemen.[22]

From May 1942, it became compulsory for women to do fire watching in work premises where there were insufficient numbers of men. The participation of women in fire watching nationally was controversial, due to concerns not just about placing women in the line of fire but also about exposing them to immorality while working during hours of darkness. Female MPs, including Mavis Tate, fought hard for women to have equal compensation with men for war injuries. Tate and Edith Summerskill spoke with passion on this subject during a House of Commons debate in 1942:

Think of a woman fire-spotter, a spinster of 40, with dependent relatives, working side by side with a bachelor of 20, living at home with his mother and father. They are both permanently injured by the same bomb ... the spinster of 40 would get 28s. and the bachelor of 20 would get 35s ... Is it fair? There is only one answer. Let me remind the House of the woman ambulance driver or nurse in a blitz. If she is permanently injured, she will get far less than a man in an underground shelter.[23]

Parity was eventually achieved following the report of the Select Committee on Equal Compensation in 1943.[24]

As pressure increased, the Fire Committee created its most comprehensive list of potential fire watchers in Parliament on 20 August 1943 – including 101 women. Some workers were deemed ineligible, such as the ten female secretarial employees of Ashworth's and Watney & Powell, presumably because they were not on Parliament's payroll. About fifty other women were exempt because they were over age (45), under age (20), or had family responsibilities. Others had exemptions also available to men: being deemed medically unfit; being involved with civil defence elsewhere; or for reasons of hardship agreed by a tribunal.[25]

THE PALACE OF WESTMINSTER HOME GUARD

Known initially as the Local Defence Volunteers, the national Home Guard was founded in May 1940 as a volunteer force of citizens set up to defend Britain in event of invasion. Over 100 volunteers were quickly recruited to the Palace of Westminster Home Guard, properly called the 'C' Company, 35th London (Civil Service) Battalion. They were mostly older men with previous war experience and included a number of MPs and peers. They took part in Palace fire-watching and sentry duties on the terrace in addition to manning a gun at the exit to Westminster Underground station and taking responsibility for anti-tank measures on Westminster Bridge. Churchill inspected the Palace of Westminster Home Guard on 12 May 1942, on the second anniversary of the national Home Guard.[26] This force took its duties very seriously. One of its members even gave his life: Patrick Munro, Conservative MP for Llandaff and Barry, died during a Home Guard exercise on 3 May 1942, aged 58, and is recorded on Parliament's war memorials.

It might seem surprising today that women were part of 'Dad's Army'.[27] It was controversial, with arguments made by opponents that women did not want to participate. It was alleged that providing uniforms for them would be too expensive, that they did not have the physique for such work and that they should not be exposed to danger. But Edith Summerskill MP was instrumental in campaigning for women to be brought into the Home Guard nationally. During a debate in the House of Commons, she spoke about how hundreds of women were keen to join, undeterred by any lack of uniform, and pointed out that women were operating in all industries and as land girls, doing hard work on farms. She likened it to the old arguments about the vote:

I realise that I am almost in the same position as were speakers 20 or 30 years ago when they asked for the franchise for women. I realise the tremendous prejudices which still exist in the male mind … Is it conceivable that if there was an invasion, the women of London, Liverpool or Coventry would immediately retire to their houses in order not to provoke the enemy? Is it not much more likely that the women would come out into the streets, bringing their household goods if necessary, and barricade fire streets?[28]

The government was not convinced, and Summerskill battled on for three years, even creating her own organisation, the Women's Home Defence force. These units sprang up across the country, receiving weapons training and working alongside the Home Guard wherever possible. Other supporters of Summerskill's campaign to include women in the Home Guard were Mavis Tate MP; Viola Apsley MP, who became the first woman wheelchair-using MP on her election in 1943; nurse and social reformer Rachel Crowdy; and Dame Helen Gwynne-Vaughan, leader of the Auxiliary Territorial Service (ATS), the women's branch of the British Army.[29] The government finally agreed to the formation of the Home Guard Women Auxiliaries in May 1943.

PARLIAMENT'S HOME GUARD WOMEN AUXILIARIES

Summerskill must have been pleased to see that eventually her arguments bore fruit in the heart of Parliament. Six women auxiliaries joined the Palace of Westminster Home Guard, neatly listed in parliamentary records separately from the Home Guard men. The women were Vera Michel, Vera Heslop, Pauline Bebbington, Pamela Matthew, Barbara Shuttleworth and Pamela Ward. Photographs show four of them (Bebbington, Matthew, Shuttleworth and Ward) lining up for inspection by the Lord Chancellor, Lord Simon and the Speaker, Colonel Clifton Brown, in Speaker's Court on 30 October 1944 (Figures 15 and 16). The women stood alongside the men, although not in uniform; the government refused to allow uniforms for women in the Home Guard, citing shortages of clothing material and a fear of similar demands from other civilian organisations.[30] It is likely that the Palace of Westminster women auxiliaries wore their own clothes but chose to adopt a dress code: white blouses underneath dark coats with Portcullis brooches on the lapels (men wore these as cap badges), plus hats and dark shoes. They carried handbags which can be seen clamped under their arms.

Figure 15: Palace of Westminster Home Guard lining up for inspection by the Speaker, Douglas Clifton Brown, and the Lord Chancellor, Lord Simon, October 1944.

Figure 16: Palace of Westminster Home Guard, October 1944. Left to right: Corporal Harry Charleton (MP for Leeds South), Pamela Ward, Pauline Bebbington, Barbara Shuttleworth and Pamela Matthew.

The role played by the women is described in the caption of one photograph: 'There are also a few women auxiliaries who work on communications and are expert shots.'[31] This indicates that the Westminster Home Guard women were involved in weapons training, which was particularly controversial. There was strong public opinion that it was not proper for women to engage in combat, even when serving in the armed forces; women in the WRNS, WAAF and WAAC had non-combatant status (even when they did in fact engage in combat), which kept them in separate organisations from the men and on inferior terms and conditions until the 1990s. The government did not support weapons training for women in the Home Guard, but the local and voluntary character of the Home Guard lent itself to relative autonomy for commanding officers, who allowed women to participate to varying degrees.[32]

Who were the women auxiliaries? Of the six, Vera Michel was Welfare Officer for the Westminster Munitions Unit, of which more below. From a professional point of view, perhaps the most unusual was Vera Heslop, who worked for Watney & Powell, a political consultancy firm which also provided secretarial services. Its female staff based in the Palace of Westminster, including Heslop, provided a wide range of services to MPs including drafting parliamentary questions and handling constituency correspondence.[33]

Heslop was born Vera Sherman in Hackney in 1916 and married chartered accountant Peter G. Heslop in 1941. Describing herself in 1939 as a 'foreign correspondent secretary', she wrote an article for *International Woman Suffrage News* in 1942 about the qualifications required to work for an MP: 'She must be a sort of family lawyer, matrimonial causes bureau, financial genius and constituent-soother.' The examples given provide a great insight into the work of Watney & Powell's services, as well as that of Members' staff generally, and prefigures the role of constituency staff today:

> It is quite astonishing to see what people write to their M.P.s about. I can recall letters from soldiers abroad who are worried about their wives' conduct, letters from wives afraid of jealous husbands, puzzles about allowances, pensions, wages, missing relatives. Constituents may turn up at the House, and you may find yourself left to deal with a deputation complaining about the price of tomatoes.[34]

The workload may have been inflated by war issues, but Watney & Powell was operating well before the war and there clearly was demand for such services from at least some MPs. Heslop described drafting parliamentary questions, judging which issues should be followed up and which not, maintaining social networks, writing letters in her MP's style and to the party line, and ended with the wry observation, 'In fact if she is really a good secretary and can do all these things, she is perhaps ready to be a member herself.'[35] Sadly Heslop did not go on to become an MP herself. In 1946, she married again, to Czechoslovak RAF officer Vaclav Kaspar, had two children and lived in Czechoslovakia for a few years. In a letter to *The Times* in 1961 she wrote, 'I lived under a totalitarian regime for only a very short time, would shoot my son rather than let him suffer it.'[36] After returning to the UK, she continued to work for MPs while bringing up her children, and died in Bromley, Kent, in 1987.

The other four auxiliaries – Ward, Bebbington, Shuttleworth and Matthew – were all secretarial staff employed by the House of Commons. Three of them had conventional careers, appointed as very young single women, who enjoyed a small amount of progression within the secretarial hierarchy but eventually left Parliament for new lives as married women. Pauline Margaret Bebbington was appointed as a Typist in the Committee Office in January 1940, aged 20, Pamela Charlotte Ward as a Temporary Typist to the Clerk of the House in November 1940, aged 18, and Pamela Matthew as a Typist in the Committee Office in January 1941, also aged 18.

Ward was the first to marry, to Alistair R.S. Tweddle in 1943. She continued to work until after the war, resigning in 1946. She died in 1987 in Sutton, Surrey. Bebbington and Matthew were both appointed to the established staff in 1945 and later promoted to Personal Assistants. Bebbington resigned on her marriage to John C. Stone in 1949 and died in 2001 in north Dorset; Matthew resigned on her marriage to John Fraser McLauchlan in 1956 and died in 1999 in Tunbridge Wells.

THE MURDER-SUICIDE: BARBARA SHUTTLEWORTH

The fourth secretary – Shuttleworth – had a similar start but a very different fate. Born in Knaresborough, Yorkshire, in September 1922, Barbara Sylvia Shuttleworth was appointed Temporary Typist in the Committee Office in April 1942, aged 19. She was put on the established staff in 1946 and became a Personal Assistant in the research section of the House of Commons Library in 1947. Like so many other female staff in Parliament, she had a parliamentary family connection: her mother, Gwendoline Cardew Shuttleworth, was the daughter of Sir Rowland Hirst Barran (1858–1949), a wholesale clothing manufacturer and Liberal MP for North Leeds 1902–18. Her father, John Ughtred Thornton Shuttleworth, was a stockbroker from a family of several generations of Shuttleworths who were British Army officers based in India, and he served in the Indian Army during the Second World War.[37]

On 30 July 1948, Barbara Shuttleworth's life was cut abruptly short at the age of just 25. She was shot twice by Felic Jan Kurt Sterba, aged 52, a former colonel in the Polish RAF, at his flat in Bayswater. Sterba then tried to shoot himself without success and so threw himself out of the seventh-floor window. Both died later in hospital. The Coroner's inquest found that Sterba murdered Shuttleworth and then killed himself while the balance of his mind was disturbed.

Nine days earlier, on 21 July, Barbara's engagement had been announced in *The Times*, the *Manchester Guardian* and the *Yorkshire Post* to Thomas Michael Lupton, a 28-year-old architecture student, with whom she had been in a relationship for two years. Shuttleworth would have been familiar with the Lupton family from her youth. Her MP grandfather Rowland Barran lived at the Beechwood Estate in Roundhay, Leeds, which belonged to his friend and fellow local Liberal politician and woollen cloth manufacturer, Francis (Frank) Martineau Lupton, Tom's great-uncle. It is easy to imagine Barbara Shuttleworth and Tom Lupton meeting on some Liberal–Leeds political or family occasion, being thrown together as they were much the same age, and a relationship developing; their mothers would surely have been delighted to see the two families coming together. They had bought their first home, a flat in Highgate. The night before she died, the happy couple had dined together and he had given her keys to the flat.[38]

But Sterba intervened. He had first met Shuttleworth in June 1943, and they had struck up a relationship in bombed-out London. We cannot know for sure if it was friendship or more at this time. Although he was easily old enough to be her father, and with a wife and child back in Poland, he was a decorated air force officer stranded in the UK who may have seemed a romantic and interesting liaison for a 21-year-old typist who was also fire watching and drilling with the Palace of Westminster Home Guard.

Both would have assumed that Sterba would return to Poland as soon as the war was over, but Poland ended up on the wrong side of the Iron Curtain in 1945 and he remained stuck in London. Shuttleworth moved on with her post-war life, was promoted to a new role in the House of Commons Library and began a new relationship with Tom Lupton. Her co-worker and fellow former Home Guard Auxiliary Pauline Bebbington said in evidence at the inquest that she thought Shuttleworth's friendship with a Polish officer had ended eighteen months earlier, and perhaps that was how Shuttleworth viewed it too.

On the day of her death, Shuttleworth had been going to have lunch with Bebbington and several others, prior to the summer recess, but Bebbington reported:

> At 12.45 I was in a ground floor passage of the House of Commons when Miss Shuttleworth passed. She was hurrying out of the building and I called after her to ask about lunch. She replied, 'I'm lunching out' and she appeared to have forgotten she was lunching with me.[39]

Shuttleworth was going to tell Sterba about her engagement; she had also arranged to meet her mother at 4.30 p.m. to see the new flat.

But she wasn't telling Sterba her news because they were friends, she was telling Sterba because he was obsessed with her. His diary records him phoning her, night after night, and her not answering; sending letters and gifts to her at work; standing underneath her window, waiting for her. The numerous press reports of the murder-suicide hinted at the salacious nature of their relationship, her presence in his diary and letters, as do contemporary interpretations of it as a 'death pact'.[40] All the evidence shows that, if it was a pact, it was only so in Sterba's head. The investigating officer, Detective Inspector Shelley Symes, was clear in his report that 'this double tragedy was not a suicide pact', and the Divisional Detective agreed: 'This was a straightforward case of murder and suicide – to which the woman was not a consenting party.'[41] Had this happened today, it is very likely that his behaviour would be characterised as stalking and that Shuttleworth would consequently have sought a restraining order – which may or may not have saved her.

Sterba's farewell letter to his son in Poland is a masterpiece in making excuses for his own bad behaviour and victim-blaming a woman young enough to be his daughter:

> I don't blame anybody, and I myself am not to be blamed ... I was a weak man and broken through hard fate. She is a bad woman, Barbara, she influenced me to my divorce ... She is very bad, but I love her, therefore I take her with me. Pray for my poor soul.[42]

Undoubtedly his life was hard and lonely, and the war had dealt him a poor hand. None of that is any excuse for murdering Barbara Shuttleworth, whose death raises problematic questions that are still facing us today.

THE WESTMINSTER MUNITIONS UNIT

As the Palace of Westminster Home Guard drilled in the courtyards, another wartime activity was taking place beneath their feet. Between December 1943 and December 1945, the Westminster Munitions Unit operated underneath Central Lobby at the very centre of Parliament.

The unit originated in June and July 1942. In response to offers of voluntary labour from the Members, officials and staff of the Palace, evening munitions training and work was organised for them at the London County Council Westminster Technical Institute nearby. Nearly seventy people participated in simple metalwork tasks, including cutting copper driving blanks for shells, roughing-out gear blanks and turning rollers for hangar pulleys and nuts for aircraft wireless equipment. Female participants included Thelma Cazalet MP, who wrote afterwards, 'I must say I thoroughly enjoyed doing the munitions.'[43] Other women who volunteered included staff from the Committee Office,[44] the Refreshment Department, the Government Whips' Office and one of the typists from the Official Report. There were also women from Parliament's First Aid Post – plus residents of the Palace and assorted friends or relatives. One such was Miriam Howard, 65, whose family background may well have encouraged her towards munitions work. Her husband was Brigadier Sir Charles Howard, appointed Serjeant at Arms in 1935, who had extensive previous armed service experience in the Boer War and First World War. Her father was army officer Lieutenant Colonel Edward Mashiter Dansey and one of her brothers was Claude Dansey, an army officer who became a senior officer in MI6.

After only two months, however, London County Council reclaimed the space and the munitions work stopped, to the dismay of various volunteers including women, one of whom wrote:

> I was lucky enough to go on two occasions to the technical school and like everyone else I am very sorry the work there has ceased ... I am tremendously keen to continue if it can be arranged. I am naturally good with machines of all kinds, and I have had a small amount of experience of factory work.[45]

It was then proposed to have a munitions workshop on site in the Palace to tap into such enthusiasm. Space beneath the Central Lobby was identified as suitable, and after many months of negotiations led by Strathearn Gordon and Thomas George Barnett Cocks, senior clerks in the House of Commons, the Westminster Munitions Unit (WMU) started production

in December 1943. It would run for two years, its success undoubtedly due
to its overall management by engineer Colin Donaldson.[46] Understandably
– given the location in the heart of the Palace of Westminster – there was no
work with explosives, only with non-flammable metals, although there must
have still been risk. The main product of the factory was a torque amplifier
which was part of a predictor unit for mobile and stationary anti-aircraft
guns. Work was also undertaken in the assembly, rather than the manufac-
ture, of detonator holders and priming fuses, which were then dispatched
to the filling factories. Over 2 million shell fuse parts were checked for the
Woolwich Arsenal Inspection Department and 95,000 special packing-case
fittings were made as a sideline.

Given the long gap since the early munitions work, the WMU was set
up from scratch with a small staff of full-time workers along with more
than 100 new part-time volunteers. They were recruited from among the
Members, officials and staff of both Houses, from other people working
in the Palace, such as police, firemen, postmen and civil servants, and from
assorted relatives and friends. There was no problem in finding volunteers
for the WMU and a high proportion were women. As well as machine
operators, there were women clerical and stores staff, and an all-female
catering team led by the cook, Mrs Trollope, which served 150 meals a day.
Mrs Trollope continued to run the catering despite suffering bomb damage
to her home in Victoria in May 1944, which meant that she had to live a considerable distance away.[47]

The munitions workers included women who were also cleaners,
secretaries, telephone engineers, civil servants, wives of MPs and even a musi-
cian.[48] Most were enormously enthusiastic about the work. Some presumably
needed the money, too, while others chose to give their munitions wages to
an Amenities Fund. MPs were not paid because this was forbidden as an office
of profit under the Crown; however, after a query from Marigold Sinclair,
wife of Archibald Sinclair, Secretary of State for Air, it was agreed that their
wives could be paid for their work. Lady Sinclair wrote about her work in the
WMU in a newspaper article, careful not to give away its location:

> My factory is underground. It is very like the cave of the Seven Dwarfs …
> My machine is comforting because it is so impersonal and straightforward,
> and I have to concentrate on it. I can't argue with it and if anything goes
> wrong the odds are it is my own fault. It is beautiful too, but I don't get
> sentimental about it. I just use it is as carefully and well as I can, and feel
> the comfort which comes from the thought that – in however small and
> insignificant a way – I am fighting a little bit too.[49]

Figure 17: Mrs Hodges at the capstan lathe, Westminster Munitions Unit, 1945.

The participation of women in the WMU appears to have been uncontroversial and in line with the national picture. Unlike many other factory situations, the WMU provided a rare opportunity for women of all ages and from a wide variety of backgrounds to work together on a common project in their spare time. This was because of its unique location, which required above all that its workers had access to the Palace of Westminster. Women occupying significant roles in the workshop included Mrs Hodges (Figure 17), a skilled capstan lathe operator – a machine tool worker – who lived in Whiteley Road in Upper Norwood. Although she cannot be identified for certain, a plausible candidate is Lilian May Vinall, born in 1884. She married Ernest James Hodges of Whiteley Road in 1905 at the age of 21 and brought up at least six children over the next twenty years. Her husband, a printing machine minder, died on New Year's Eve 1943 at the time the unit was established; if she was not already working in a similarly industrial job, then her sad loss may have provided the impetus for her to join the war effort.

A female chartered accountant managed the finances for the unit for a salary of 12 guineas a month, Mrs D.M. Pyke, or 'D.M. Vaughan' as her company name was given on its headed notepaper. Dorothea Mina Vaughan was born in Mansfield in 1907, married food scientist (later a famously eccentric TV science presenter) Magnus Pyke in 1937, had two children, and died in 1986.[50] Women were only able to become chartered accountants

after the Sex Disqualification (Removal) Act 1919 and remained very small
in numbers for many years, so Mrs Pyke was something of a pioneer (House
of Lords Accountant Miss Court was not a chartered accountant). Pyke
was one of just eighty-four female members of the Institute of Chartered
Accountants of England and Wales in 1940.[51]

However, the most senior woman was the Welfare Officer. During initial
discussions about setting up the WMU, Miriam Howard had been invited
to take on this role. She consented to act temporarily and remained on
the organising committee representing welfare issues. But the unit clearly
needed a full-time personnel manager and Vera Michel was appointed to the
role in May 1943. Born Vera Louise Simonis in 1915 in Hampstead, and a
welfare worker, she married David O. Michel in 1942. At the WMU, she was
responsible for managing the female staff and volunteers, recruiting workers
and overseeing the canteen, air-raid precautions, first aid and welfare. For all
this she received considerable acclaim. At the unit's Christmas dinner in 1944,
Austin Hopkinson MP, Chair of the Unit, proudly declared her a 'dragon':

> She has done a vast amount of work for us and work which I think
> Mr Donaldson would be the first to admit he could not have undertaken.
> Female labour is a problem, and I don't mean domestic labour. The best
> system I know we have in my works. My manager said when I came to the
> question of female labour that I had better have what I call dragons, who
> were put in charge of bodies of young women and we have had no trouble
> at all.[52]

After the war, Michel worked as a welfare officer in the Home Office. She
married again later in life and died as Vera Downes, a retired jeweller, in East
Sussex in 2012.

'THANKS FOR HIS VALUABLE SERVICES'

As the war drew to a close, thoughts turned to how to acknowledge and
reward civilian war service. The Defence Medal was instituted in May
1945 and was awarded to people with three years' service in the UK in the
Home Guard, First Aid and other approved services, as well as to military
personnel with shorter periods of non-operational service at home and
overseas. Although the WMU had not been established for long enough for
this honour, many staff serving in the civil defence of Parliament had been
involved for more than three years and were eligible, including those doing

first aid and fire watching. A procedure was set up for people in Parliament to apply, and bids came in from Commandant Mrs Alan Thomson and seven of her nursing staff; Hoath and Preece in the Lords Refreshment Department; Lilian Maud Mitchell from the Telephone Exchange; and Bebbington, Shuttleworth, Matthew and Ward from the Commons Committee Office. Each application was checked to ensure it met the qualifying length of service and was then stamped and approved.[53]

The Fire Committee also created certificates especially for service in the Palace of Westminster, signed by the Speaker and with a Portcullis emblem at the top.[54] These certificates were awarded to all those who took part in the defence of the Palace of Westminster, including the women in the Home Guard and the WMU. On 8 June 1945, a final party was held by the Speaker, Douglas Clifton Brown, and everyone received their certificates. Victory in Europe had been declared a month before, although the war in Japan was still continuing and the WMU remained operational. The celebration could not have waited any longer, however, as Parliament was about to be dissolved for the 1945 general election. Unfortunately, one nurse, Emily Low, was unable to attend the party and never received her certificate; it remains in the Parliamentary Archives.

The women present at the party would have undoubtedly been pleased and proud for their involvement to be recognised. At the front of the queue to receive her certificate was Miss D.J. Davson, Clerk in the House of Commons.[55] However, she could not have helped but notice that her certificate thanked her for 'his' valuable services to Civil Defence in the Palace of Westminster (Figure 18). This mistake was not made on all the women's certificates – Emily Low's was correct – but Miss Davson was unlucky, and her contribution was blurred in this formal and final record.

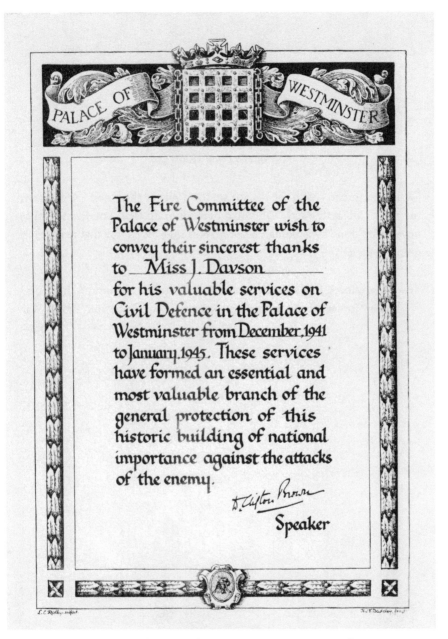

Figure 18: Josephine Davson's Palace of Westminster war service certificate, 1945.

In Her Own Words

'When it came to laying the Report on the Table of the house – you know, my male colleagues said "Oh you'd better not do that, you know, it has never been done by a woman before!" So I said "Well, for that reason I'm going to do it!"'

Kay Midwinter, first woman Clerk in the House of Commons, in an oral history interview describing her experiences in the Second World War

13

'GIRL CLERK IN COMMONS'!

GIRL CLERK IN COMMONS. Parliamentary history was made yesterday by a girl. Miss K Midwinter, dark, slim, businesslike, who served the League of Nations for nine years, has been appointed a temporary clerk of the House of Commons. She is the first woman to hold such a post.[1]

Thus was Kay Midwinter's appointment reported in the press in May 1940. Recruited specifically to free up a man for war service, the 'Girl Clerk' (age 32) was the first of three female clerks who worked for the House of Commons National Expenditure Committee during the Second World War. Highly praised by her managers and by Irene Ward and Joan Davidson, the female MPs on the Committee, Midwinter made a substantial contribution to the work of the Select Committee and worked closely with Ward and Davidson on two reports, on the women's armed services and women factory workers. Midwinter was followed by two other temporary women clerks: Josephine Davson, whose promising career in the House of Commons was curtailed by the marriage bar, and Monica Felton, who became infamous for entirely different reasons.

CLERKS IN PARLIAMENT

In the outside world, a clerk might reasonably be assumed to be an office worker performing duties such as answering the phone and filing paperwork:

a middle-class and respectable position, but probably rather lowly. However, in the House of Commons and House of Lords, this was not at all the case. Clerks were and are the top rung of staff in the parliamentary administrations. Clerks are expected to be constitutional experts, giving MPs and peers impartial advice on issues such as parliamentary privilege and procedure. Inside the chambers, senior clerks sit in dark outfits at the Table, providing advice to the Speaker and recording decisions of the House. Beyond the chambers, clerks advise on bills and petitions, conduct divisions and manage and deliver the work of Select Committees.

The First World War had left the numbers and individuals in such senior and specialist positions untouched, and while Walter Erskine had to individually justify every male attendant, messenger, porter, cleaner and nightwatchman exempted from conscription, the clerks were largely left alone. But by the advent of the Second World War, things had started to change. Although the Commons would not have taken much notice of May Court's reign as Accountant over in the Lords, women were significantly more visible in the Commons, employed directly in secretarial and administrative roles, not just via Ashworth's. The most senior government ministers were also now likely to employ women as their own staff, who could be found pressing their business justification to be admitted to dining rooms, galleries and offices.[2]

Furthermore, from the moment Nancy Astor became the first woman to take her seat at Westminster on 1 December 1919, women had been participating in parliamentary proceedings as MPs, in the chamber, in committee rooms, paltry in numbers[3] but present and visible nonetheless. From 1939, perhaps most publicly visible was the work of the dozen women MPs in support of the war effort, including Nancy Astor, Eleanor Rathbone, Irene Ward and Mavis Tate on the Woman Power Committee, and particularly Ellen Wilkinson as the one female MP who was a government minister during the war. As a junior minister in the Home Office from October 1940, Wilkinson was responsible for home defence, including the distribution of air-raid shelters, and could be seen touring bombed cities to raise morale.

It must have been helpful for the self-esteem of women workers in Parliament to see such progress, and male managers must have mused that, if a woman could be nationally responsible for home defence, it was hard to justify a role such as a clerk being reserved for a man. Thus, when a clerk position became vacant in 1941, the decision was made to free up a man for war service by employing a woman instead. Midwinter applied, and her previous experience with committee work was the deciding factor over other candidates.

The novelty of this can hardly be overstated. The *Yorkshire Evening Post* reported on the reactions of MPs:

> Considerable surprise was caused at question time in the House of Commons yesterday when a dark-haired young woman who had never been seen there before walked into the chamber and calmly stood among MPs looking around with interest at them.[4]

Meanwhile, Midwinter's new work colleagues looked on aghast. One of her fellow clerks, Basil Drennan, wrote to his parents that it had created 'a sensation in the Committee Office, a woman amongst all these men and for the first time in history ... Another sanctuary gone, I feel.'[5]

Kay Midwinter must have been confident and self-assured to take on such a pioneering and visible role in the heart of the wartime House of Commons. As it happened, she brought some life experience with her which evidently stood her in good stead: ten years living independently in Geneva and essential work experience at the League of Nations.

MIDWINTER AT THE LEAGUE OF NATIONS

Kathleen Margaret Midwinter (known as Kay) was born on 6 March 1909 in Wednesbury, Staffordshire. She was the daughter of Ethel and Stanley Midwinter, an electrical engineer. Sadly, her mother died in 1917 during childbirth, leaving Stanley a widower with two children – Kay, aged 8, and her younger brother Derrick, 6. Stanley remarried two years later, settled in Eastbourne, where he worked for the electricity works, and had another daughter. The family may have scattered somewhat; at least, in 1921 Kay was living with her maternal grandmother in Beckenham, Kent.

Kay Midwinter initially worked in London as a shorthand typist between 1926 and 1930, and began studying for the Chartered Institute of Secretaries examination. However, her life took a different turn when she successfully competed in an open competition to work at the League of Nations Secretariat in Geneva, Switzerland. She was fluent in French (it is not clear how), which would have been an advantage, although many years later she remembered, 'Looks, that helped – I was rather good looking.' She was initially offered a temporary contract, which she turned down, and was then offered a permanent contract, which she accepted, aged 21.

The League of Nations had been formed in the aftermath of the First World War in 1919. Its aim was to promote international cooperation and to achieve peace and security.[6] At the time Midwinter joined the League on 3 November 1930, it had enjoyed some successes resolving international disagreements during the 1920s and she reflected, 'This promised a life career in a worthwhile cause, that of helping to preserve peace in the world.'

Many League staff would have shared such idealism, but this may not have been borne out through their own situation. Although the League promised equal pay and opportunities in theory, that was not the case in practice. The only woman to lead a section, Rachel Crowdy, head of the Social Section between 1922 and 1930, was sacked and replaced by a man at higher rank and salary. Female employees of the League Secretariat were placed in the Second Division for clerical workers almost by default, with few appointed to the higher administrative First Division, regardless of their aptitude, qualifications or level of work performed. Midwinter would have been one of a large 'cohort of British secretaries, précis-writers, translators and typists', many of whom were over-performing for their grade.[7] Her employment card shows that she was based in the shorthand typist pool at first, then in the Financial Section for two years, then following another spell in the pool, moved to the Administrative Board of the Staff Pensions Fund. Her own recollection is of a much wider range of duties than this might imply, including research, statistical work, minute-writing, committee procedure and summarising speeches delivered in English and French.

Midwinter found living in Geneva fascinating, and enjoyed mountain climbing, skiing, show-jumping and amateur theatricals. In 1936, she spent a week travelling alone on horseback from Geneva to Berne and back, writing to *The Times*:

> Last summer I set off with a young thoroughbred and rode from Geneva to Berne and then back ... a distance of about 200 miles, in six days ... Everywhere I was greeted with much kindness ... There is no more agreeable and intimate way of getting to know a country and its people than on horseback, and there is no better way of becoming friends with your horse than by sharing with him long hours and difficult moments on the road.[8]

Unfortunately, the 1930s were not so good for the League of Nations, which found itself increasingly unable to prevent international conflict. Japan invaded Manchuria in 1931; Italy invaded Abyssinia (now Ethiopia) in 1935; and Hitler's Germany invaded Austria in 1938. The League continued to do useful work in other areas such as health and social affairs, transport and communications, and economics and finance. It hosted conferences, intergovernmental committees and meetings of experts which Midwinter and her colleagues worked to support, but ultimately it could not prevent the Second World War.

In April 1940, League of Nations' staff contracts were suspended indefinitely and Midwinter went on holiday to the UK. The League had clearly become irrelevant and Midwinter must have thought she was unlikely to return. While in London she had a job interview for Clerk in the House of Commons, the first time a woman had been considered for such a post. The *Western Morning News* was proud to report the appointment of a 'Torquay Girl', but in fact Midwinter's only connection with Torquay was that her father Stanley was living there, running a private hotel. She was at home with him when she received the job offer from the House of Commons by telephone.

THE NATIONAL EXPENDITURE COMMITTEE

The House of Commons Select Committee on National Expenditure, also called the National Expenditure Committee or NEC, was a huge committee set up to scrutinise public expenditure during the Second World War and suggest economies. Chaired by Conservative MP Sir John Wardlaw-Milne, the Committee initially had twenty-eight members, later increased to thirty-two. The NEC selected topics for investigation, made visits, took evidence from witnesses and submitted reports to the House of Commons. It was also granted special powers to submit memoranda directly to the prime minister when considerations of national security precluded publishing the material in a report. The Committee did much of its work through sub-committees on specific subjects, appointing a total of twenty-six different sub-committees over the six years it was in existence. The sub-committees were reorganised almost every session, to investigate different aspects of national expenditure.

Midwinter was appointed on 29 April 1940 and initially acted as Personal Assistant to Captain Cyril Diver, the Clerk of the NEC. Although her initial duties were undoubtedly largely secretarial, it is likely that the traditional boundary for women between administrative and executive work which she had encountered at the League of Nations could more easily be surmounted in wartime. It soon became clear that she had the ability to clerk a committee herself, and when a vacancy arose, she became Clerk to the Sub-Committee on Transport in April 1941, then Clerk to the Works (A) Sub-Committee in 1942, both under the chairmanship of Conservative MP and engineer Sir Arnold Gridley. In 1942, a 'small ad hoc' informal Sub-Committee on Women's Medical Services was set up, also clerked by Midwinter, undoubtably selected because she was a woman. This Sub-Committee consisted of the two women MPs on the NEC, Viscountess Davidson and Irene Ward (chairman), to take evidence on the medical services of the Women's Royal Naval Service (WRNS), Auxiliary Territorial Service (ATS) and Women's Auxiliary Air Force (WAAF). It was later tasked with examining welfare and medical arrangements available for women in factories.

Midwinter's clerkly duties were described by herself as follows:

> To conduct the correspondence of the committee generally; to call wit-nesses; to arrange visits and tours and accompany the sub-committee on such visits; to draw up plans of enquiry for the Chairman and advise on Parliamentary procedure; to make contact with Government depart-ments through liaison officers; to amplify and check information and facts received in evidence; to write the draft report if the Chairman so wishes, or at any rate to assist largely in its preparation; to watch the draft report through its various committee stages, and draft the Final Report which had to be laid on the table of the Clerk of the House in session.[9]

For the Women's Medical Services Sub-Committee, it was considered unde-sirable to have a male note-taker present at some meetings, giving Midwinter the additional burden of having to take a running note. She was well regarded and highly praised for all her work by Diver and O.C. (Orlo) Williams, Clerk of Committees. Diver particularly noted that among her achievements was a report on coal: 'From the unsatisfactory and limited material to which she was confined she showed considerable ability in producing on this thorny subject a useful document which was not substantially amended' – praise indeed, from a senior male clerk! Coal production was, of course, an enor-mously important subject at that time and essential to the war effort.

Midwinter then moved straight on to the Sub-Committee on Women's Medical Services. Its first report was entirely drafted by her and passed with hardly any amendment, only five weeks after the coal report. Diver consid-ered its success was 'largely attributable to Miss Midwinter's tactful handling of an inquiry which provided considerable Departmental opposition, to her continuous hard work and to her ability to take a good draft'. Williams con-sidered, 'It is not too much to say that she is very largely responsible for the valuable work of the Sub-Committee on Women's Services; and her zeal is such that I am often anxious if she can endure the strain.'[10]

A tiny flavour of Midwinter's wartime life can be gained from the cor-respondence of fellow Committee Clerk Basil Drennan, who overcame his initial qualms to accept Midwinter as a colleague. In April 1941, a joint visit by his Navy and her Transport Sub-Committees to shipyards on the Clyde was mooted, the first time he had to work with her:

> I have to make the arrangements in collaboration with Kay Midwinter, who is taking over the Transport Committee, and have told her that she & Lady D. [Viscountess Davidson MP] will be in competition for the title of Queen of the May.

A few weeks later he noted, 'Kay Midwinter took her Committee off to Glasgow today and she has a very sore throat and feels rotten.' They later seem to have become friends. In May 1942 they went to a show together (*Fine and Dandy* – 'Leslie Henson in great form') and a month later Drennan refers to 'a little party Kay Midwinter hopes to get up'.[11] It was a long way from horse riding from Geneva to Berne, and set against the background of the Blitz, but perhaps Midwinter found some pleasure in the social life of Commons clerks.

'INADEQUATELY PAID'

Midwinter remembered her experiences in wartime Parliament as breaking new ground, even by something as simple as standing on the floor of the House of Commons:

> During the war I was standing behind the Speaker's Chair about 5 or 6 yards from Churchill while he made all his famous war speeches. He used to glare at me as much to say 'What's this woman doing?' but he never challenged me. I was expecting to be ordered to be removed from the Chamber, but it was great fun and then when it came to laying the Report on the table of the house – you know, my male colleagues said 'Oh you'd better not do that, you know, it has never been done by a woman before!' So I said 'Well, for that reason I'm going to do it!' So there we are. But really one was up against male prejudice throughout. Absolutely. There was never any question of promotion.[12]

It was not just promotion but also pay. Despite being so well regarded, Midwinter was paid far less than male colleagues doing exactly the same job. She had initially accepted a poor rate of pay (£260 a year) as she was anxious to get on with useful war work and ignorant of the cost of living in London. When she took over a committee in 1941 she was put on a salary scale of

£350–£480 – a big improvement and yet, as Diver observed, 'Her burdens have been considerably greater than, and have been as efficiently carried as, those of other sub-committee clerks whose emoluments are more than twice what she is receiving'.[13] Her friend Basil Drennan, for example, was earning £850 in this period.

Midwinter did have allies among the MPs, however. In July 1942, O.C. Williams wrote to Sir Gilbert Campion, Clerk of the House of Commons, that Irene Ward and Lady Davidson had 'expressed directly to Captain Diver and myself their conviction that Miss Midwinter is inadequately paid, and their intention of taking the matter up directly with Mr Speaker'. Their investigations into women's welfare had led them to ask her what salary she was receiving, although Williams hastened to add, 'I have an assurance that Miss Midwinter herself made no solicitations or suggestions to these ladies regarding her personal affairs'.[14] There was no suggestion by anyone that she deserved equal pay with the men – this was a post-war battle to be fought by others – just that she was inadequately paid.

The involvement of MPs lobbying the Speaker forced the Treasury into agreeing Midwinter might be granted some increase, on the grounds of more than two years' service.[15] Years later, Irene Ward remembered her actions:

> It is not of course considered good form for a Member to raise questions of the staff salaries and is frowned upon, but that doesn't worry me. I had to fight during the War for the clerks on the National Expenditure Committee which included some unpleasant raspberries from the Speaker of the House, but I won and I didn't lose a minute's sleep either.[16]

Although Ward remembered winning, in fact, Midwinter's salary was upped merely to a range of £480–£650, 'being the women's equivalent of £600–£800', as officially stated in the House of Commons salary book.[17] By the time Midwinter left the House of Commons in 1943 she was earning £530 – still well below the *minimum* scale of her male colleagues.

THE FOREIGN OFFICE AND THE UNITED NATIONS

Midwinter was transferred 'rather reluctantly' to the Foreign Office on 14 October 1943, on the initiative of Ward and Davidson, who wanted to see the Foreign Office open its ranks to women – the last department in Whitehall to do so. She found life there very difficult until the appointment of Philip Noel-Baker as Minister of State in 1945, whom she knew through his League of Nations work as well as via the House of Commons. She remembered, 'The Foreign Office being what it was, rather a snobbish closed environment, it was sufficient for word to get around that I knew the new Minister of State for the whole atmosphere to change.'[18]

At the Foreign Office, Midwinter worked on winding up the League of Nations and planning its replacement after the war. She had a special assignment as adviser to the UK delegation to the Preparatory Commission for the United Nations, where she was one of just fourteen women present (ten delegates, three advisers and Eleanor Roosevelt). Midwinter subsequently advised Mrs Roosevelt about refugee questions while working at the United Nations, remembering, 'It was a great privilege to work with this lady whom I admired tremendously and she remained throughout her period of office always interested in the status of women'.[19]

In 1946, Midwinter was invited to join the United Nations secretariat, and she worked there based in New York between 1946 and 1953, organising many events and travelling across the world. The Lebanese government awarded her the Medal of Merit of the Cedars, the first to be given to a woman. She transferred to the UN in Geneva in 1954 and must have been pleased to return to the city she had been so happy living in before the war. There she organised some forty seminars, twenty-two study groups and fifteen expert groups in seventeen countries with over 3,000 participants, over many years until her retirement in 1969. On 11 July 1968, Midwinter married Lieutenant Colonel Arthur Herbert Vergin OBE in Midhurst, west Sussex, and took the surname Midwinter-Vergin. She was 59 years old and he was 76. He died in 1978 and she died in 1995, in Geneva.

CAUGHT BY THE MARRIAGE BAR: MISS D.J. DAVSON

Midwinter paved the way for two other temporary women clerks in the House of Commons during the war. The first of these was Dorothy Josephine Davson, known as Josephine but always referred to in parliamentary records as Miss D.J. Davson. Born on 23 December 1919 in Newton Abbot, one of twins, her father George served in the Royal Engineers during the First World War and was employed in the 1920s by the Crown Agents (a body providing services for the Colonial Office), based over the road from Parliament, in 4 Millbank. Her grandfather was Sir Charles Davson, a colonial judge who rose to become Chief Justice of Fiji and Chief Judicial Commissioner for the West Pacific before the First World War. Such connections may have helped Josephine Davson to come to work as a Typist in the Committee Office in 1938, one of number of female secretarial staff at that time.

Davson was appointed a Temporary Clerk in the Committee and Private Bill Office on 1 April 1941, taking over Midwinter's role as assistant to Captain Diver, and on the same low starting salary as Midwinter, £260 a year. During discussions on pay, Davson was praised almost as highly by her managers as Midwinter. Diver said, 'She acts as what can only be described as the general secretary to the whole NEC organization.'[20] All most secret and confidential material passed through her hands. O.C. Williams hoped to retain Davson after the war and noted, 'She is most certainly underpaid at present rates; and I have no doubt whatever that were she in any other Department, five minutes' talk with the Treasury would secure her an adequate scale of salary.'[21] The Treasury decided she should be put on a salary range up to £320 – not a huge increase.[22] However, Davson had independent means, so may have worked for spending money rather than as a necessity.

Williams must have been pleased that Davson did indeed stay throughout the war, and she was rewarded by being put on the established staff on 5 July 1946 – giving her a permanent and pensionable job for the first time. It might have been the start of a long and successful career as a House of Commons Clerk. However, it was short-lived, as she married Geoffrey M. Wolfe later that year, on 8 October. They met after the war, playing tennis. Geoffrey Wolfe was an engineer and meteorologist who helped plan the D-Day landings while in the Royal Navy, advising Eisenhower on which would be the most promising day.

Josephine Wolfe was removed from the established staff on her marriage and retained in an unestablished capacity as a shorthand typist, and thus ended the Commons wartime experiment with female clerks. On 15 October 1946, just one week after her marriage, the marriage bar was abolished in the Civil Service, a decision that would have filtered down to Parliament. She was extremely unlucky to be caught by the bar. After all her wartime responsibilities managing the NEC, it is hard to imagine today that she appreciated being put right back where she had started. However, her family think that she had traditional attitudes and was probably happy to return to home life on her marriage.

The Wolfes had three sons and nine grandchildren. Geoffrey died in 2007; Josephine's twin brother Noel lived until 2017; and incredibly, Josephine herself lived until January 2021, reaching the ripe old age of 101. She is remembered by her descendants as kind and generous, always calm, wearing floral dresses and pearls, with exquisite manners, terrible driving skills and a wicked sense of humour.

'A SORT OF ECONOMIC ADVISER': DR MONICA FELTON

In June 1942, Basil Drennan wrote to his parents with news of another woman clerk, a 'new temporary colleague to act as a sort of economic adviser, who has been pushed on to us at the instance of the chairman of the Production & Supply sub-committee'. This was Labour MP Lewis Silkin. Drennan added, 'She is a red-haired lame woman who is a member of the LCC and who has been working in the Ministry of Supply. She rather gives me the horrors.'[23]

This was Dr Monica Felton, an elected Labour member of London County Council (LCC), who was employed as a Temporary Clerk in the House of Commons between May 1942 and December 1943. Parliamentary staff must be politically impartial, so it was most unusual for a clerk to have such an obvious political party affiliation: Silkin must have been very insistent. Silkin had also been a member of the LCC, elected in 1925, before becoming a Labour MP in 1936. He and Felton had a strong shared interest in town planning.

In 1951, Felton became the subject of a debate in the House of Commons. Conservative MP Charles Taylor remarked:

I understand that there was a time during the war when, on the recommendation of Mr. Silkin, now Lord Silkin, she was employed in a secretarial capacity on the Select Committee on National Expenditure of this House.[24]

Taylor's understanding was correct insofar that Silkin recommended her, but incorrect in that Felton was definitely not employed in a secretarial capacity. Unlike Midwinter and Davson, and so many other women on their arrival in Parliament, Felton had no background in shorthand typing or secretarial work at all: she was an economist. She was appointed on a starting salary of £600 – way above the rate for any secretary and much closer to the men's rate than Midwinter or Davson ever got. Felton had a PhD and previous government service at the Board of Trade and Ministry of Supply, hence the better salary, although it was still less than she had been earning in her previous role.

However, by 1951 Felton had become famous for altogether different reasons. A certain amount of distancing was going on, and it is not surprising that any MP might have wanted to play down Felton's employment in the House of Commons.

THE STALIN PEACE PRIZE

Monica Glory Page was born on 23 September 1906, daughter of a Primitive Methodist minister. She attended Southampton Girls' Grammar School and then University College Southampton, achieving a BSc (Econ). She obtained a Studentship for Women at the LSE on the recommendation of R.H. Tawney in 1929. Her doctoral thesis title was originally 'The Industrial Revolution and the emancipation of women' but became 'A study of emigration from Great Britain 1802–1860'.[25] In 1931, she was awarded a PhD in Economic History from the LSE and the same year she married Berwyn Idris Felton, also an LSE student.

The composer Michael Tippett recalled in his autobiography that he applied to join the Communist Party in 1935 at the same time as 'a man known as Tank and his wife Monica Felton'.[26] It is not clear if Tank and Monica actually joined the Communists, or where Tank's nickname came from, and their marriage does not appear to have lasted very long,[27] but certainly Monica Felton went on to pursue left-wing politics. She became a lecturer for the Workers' Educational Association where Ernest Millington, later an MP, remembered being taught by Monica, 'whose leadership suited me as she was a Marxist'.[28] For a period, she was organising secretary of the Labour Book Service, catering for the literary needs of Labour Party members and Trade Unions.[29] Felton was elected to the LCC as a Labour member for St Pancras South West in 1937, along with Maurice Orbach, later an MP. However, Felton clearly felt some disillusionment with party politics and attitudes to women, critiquing later:

> The dreary grind of the Labour Party machine – the committee meetings, the selection conferences at which candidates were chosen, canvassing, street corner meetings and loudspeaker vans, the members of the women's section addressing envelopes and taking it in turns to bring the tea.[30]

At the LCC, she was Chairman of the Supplies Committee between 1939 and 1941, and then served in the Ministry of Supply before coming to work for the House of Commons. With her connection to Silkin and party politics, it is unlikely she fitted in very well to the working environment of committee clerks under Captain Diver and O.C. Williams; it is also hard to imagine her going to shows and parties with Basil Drennan and colleagues. She resigned with permission from the House of Commons on 31 December 1943, by which time she was earning £640.[31]

After the war, Silkin became Minister for Town and Country Planning in the Attlee government and he appointed Felton to be chairman of first Peterlee and then Stevenage New Town Development Corporations between 1949 and 1951.[32] However, she was fired from Stevenage by Hugh Dalton after going on an unauthorised trip to North Korea for the left-wing Women's International Democratic Federation in 1951. It was a very controversial visit and Dalton came under much pressure to dismiss her.[33] On her return, she accused American, South Korean and even British troops of involvement in massacres of the Korean population and other atrocities, on Radio Moscow and in the *Daily Worker*, and was awarded the Stalin Peace Prize. For this, she was accused in Parliament and in the popular press of being a Communist and even of treason.

The Public Prosecutor's opinion was there was no evidence for a charge of treason, sedition or anything else.[34] But the episode made her infamous and ruined her career in the UK: Labour MP Willie Hamilton referred to her as 'a sinister and repulsive kind of figure' in the House of Commons a few years later.[35] Unapologetic and unrepentant, Monica Felton wrote a book about her experiences in North Korea, then made a new life for herself in India, where she died in 1970.

Overall, Midwinter, Davson and Felton came to the House of Commons from very different backgrounds and life experiences, and left for very different future paths across the world. They are united in being parliamentary pioneers, the first women in roles previously only ever held by men. Midwinter, in particular, felt the significance of her success, and wrote that her career was made possible 'mainly because during the war many opportunities in a variety of fields were opened up to women for the first time in which they found themselves competing on an equal footing with men'. Although of course this is true, she got her League of Nations job without any such opportunity, aged just 21 in a foreign country. She faced up to inequality in the House of Commons and hostility in the Foreign Office, and successfully held her various jobs by virtue of her skills and experience. Davson and Felton likewise would never have been appointed without proven aptitude.

Sadly, these first three women clerks were almost forgotten in the House of Commons within a generation.

In Her Own Words

'You said that in every Government Dept where women perform the same work as men, they receive the same salary. I am anxious to know whether this covers my appointment on the Official Report.'

Jean Winder, first woman Hansard reporter, writing to
Hugh Gaitskell, Chancellor of the Exchequer, on equal pay, 1951

14

HANSARD AND THE BATTLE FOR EQUAL PAY

In 1951, Irene Ward MP stood up in the House of Commons to advocate for equal pay for a woman employed by the House of Commons. As published in Hansard, the official report of parliamentary debates, Ward declared:

> The House of Commons is run on the basis of equal pay ... but there is one woman on the HANSARD staff in the Gallery, Mrs. Winder, who has not got equal pay ... I have got Mrs. Winder's permission to draw the attention of the House to what I consider is an intolerable constitutional position, in which we have servants of the House who have no protection whatever refused a salary which has been specifically recommended by Mr. Speaker.[1]

The irony of a Hansard reporter's situation being reported in Hansard cannot have been lost on anyone present, least of all Mrs Winder herself. Winder had been fighting a long, drawn-out battle with the Treasury about her pay for many years by this point. Her very employment as a woman reporting on debates in Parliament was itself unique and groundbreaking.

SEGREGATION IN THE CHAMBER

To understand just how revolutionary was the idea of a woman Hansard reporter, it must first be realised that for centuries it had been regarded as against parliamentary privilege for anyone to report on parliamentary proceedings (although various reports did of course creep out and speeches were published unofficially). The first parliamentary reporters were journalists employed by newspapers, allowed to report on Parliament from 1803, with debates collected and published by private presses such as that of T.C. Hansard; his name is used as a title for parliamentary debates to this day. After the 1834 fire and the rebuilding of the Commons chamber by Charles Barry, provision was made for journalists in the House of Commons to sit separately from the public, in a press gallery above the Speaker's Chair. Access was granted to individual journalists by the Serjeant at Arms. They then banded together to form a select Parliamentary Press Gallery group. Its members were, of course, all men and the atmosphere very clubby, working in close and cramped quarters, with their own refreshment rooms.

One reason for this gendered approach was the location of the work. Women were segregated from men in the House of Commons debating chamber. As already noted, women visitors watching debates had to sit in a separate gallery from men, the Ladies' Gallery, situated above the Press Gallery, from which it was notoriously difficult to see and hear. The first request for an official female parliamentary reporter, from the *Women's Penny Paper*, was refused in 1890 when the Serjeant declared, 'The consequences were too difficult to conceive.' A further request from the *Women's Tribune* was turned down in 1906, by which time militant suffrage activity had reached the Ladies' Gallery, so the Serjeant may have been especially cautious.[2]

In 1909, the Commons and Lords began to employ staff to record and publish edited verbatim debates. A Department of the Official Report was established in each House and Hansard reporters sat in each of the press galleries to listen to the debates, take shorthand notes and prepare them for publication. All were men. Women could be trusted only with the mechanical task of subsequently typing up the debates, not with the actual reporting.

THE EARLY FEMALE HANSARD REPORTERS

Things began to change in 1917, when women visitors were first allowed to sit in the Strangers' Gallery alongside men and the grille was removed from the windows of the Ladies' Gallery. The first evidence of women being employed by Hansard as reporters on a temporary basis comes from 1919, when full verbatim reporting was extended to the work of Standing Committees (who consider the detail of bills). There was consequent pressure on staffing: the Editor of Debates (the head of office), W. Turner Perkins, told a Select Committee that he would need eight temporary staff on top of his twelve permanent reporters to cover the additional work, who could be men or women. He compared women 'very favourably' to men and the questioning makes clear that he was already employing women on a temporary basis:

Perkins: For instance, in addition to the four ladies who are covering the Acquisition of Land Bill this afternoon, I have just engaged a lady in the last ten minutes to assist in the Transport Committee.

Mr MacVeagh: The Speaker was wrong, then, when he said the ladies were not born who could do that work?

Perkins: I have known lady reporters who do their work remarkably well … Good stenographers and intelligent women.[3]

Nevertheless, these first women Hansard reporters were temporary or casual workers. Perkins was speaking directly after the First World War when the memory of women working in roles usually held by men was still recent, and indeed it was likely there were still shortages of male labour in certain areas. With the return of the men to their previous civilian work, it was unlikely for such an attitude to persevere long into the 1920s. Perhaps just as importantly, Standing Committee debates did not usually take place on the floor of the House of Commons but in a committee room. A committee room might be a very grand and intimidating space, but it was very different from the green benches of the Commons chamber. There were no galleries; MPs sat and debated around a horseshoe shape, with staff and the public watching from the end or the side of the room.

Women were not permitted to report on Select Committee proceedings, which also took place in committee rooms but were written up by the ancient company of Gurneys. Since the eighteenth century, the senior partner in the firm W.B. Gurney & Sons enjoyed the title Official Shorthand Writer to Parliament. As well as reporting the proceedings of Select Committees, this company had also covered occasions such as state trials in Westminster Hall. Gurneys refused point blank to employ female shorthand writers before the Second World War, with the Official Shorthand Writer, Herbert Arthur Stevens, declaring in 1932 that 'I have never thought that a woman was physically capable of doing it'.[4] This might reflect broader prejudice against women as shorthand writers in a court setting; the first woman was not admitted as a member of the Institute of Shorthand Writers Practising in the Supreme Court of Judicature until 1954.[5]

Meanwhile, the Press Gallery similarly remained an all-male preserve. A change in official parliamentary policy was marked in 1919, as the Serjeant at Arms, influenced perhaps by Parliament's passage of the Sex Disqualification (Removal) Act 1919 as well as the election of Nancy Astor as the first woman MP to take her seat, stated that 'in future no distinction of sex could be made in regard to admission'.[6] Two women reporters were duly allowed into the Press Gallery to report on Astor taking her seat in the Commons in December 1919. They were issued with special pink tickets (pink indicating their access was temporary rather than being a marker of gender) and the male journalists clustered around them to hear their opinion on Astor's outfit and hat.

But this was a one-off and did not mark a sea-change in access to the Press Gallery. A request from *Women's News and Views* in 1922–23 was refused, and only a few temporary exceptions followed. Most notable perhaps was Ellen Wilkinson, who worked as a journalist in between serving as MP for Middlesbrough East until 1931 and Jarrow from 1935. It would have been a brave Serjeant at Arms to deny 'Red' Ellen Wilkinson, the 'Mighty Atom', a ticket to the Press Gallery! But it took the Second World War to bring permanent change.

THE PRESS GALLERY 'HAREEM'

As with women clerks, shortages of men due to wartime conscription brought opportunities for women – in this case, to report on parliamentary proceedings for the first time. The first breakthrough was not in Hansard, but in the wider Parliamentary Press Gallery.

Ellen Baylis, known as 'Bay', had a First World War background in common with the Girl Porters, having joined Reuters Telegram Company in 1916 as a 14-year-old messenger girl, with long curls and a large pink ribbon bow. She was appointed to Reuters' parliamentary staff in 1927 and, despite marrying Tom Harris in 1932, kept her job. As a private company, Reuters would not have been subject to the same pressure to enforce the marriage bar as schools and Civil Service departments were in this period. Bay's situation had perhaps more in common with a few exceptional early women at the BBC who were also allowed to work after marriage.[7] Bay continued to use her maiden name in the office, thus blurring the issue.

As Reuters' male staff went off to fight in the war, Bay became the first woman to hold a personal permanent ticket to the Parliamentary Press

Gallery in November 1941. The Reuters chief of parliamentary news, Valentine Harvey, penned a rather ill-judged and facetious missive to the chairman of the Press Gallery, Stanley Robinson from *The Times*, to explain this development:

> I beg to inform you that from next Tuesday I am starting a hareem in the Gallery in the person of Miss Ellen Baylis who has been in the Reuter service for more years than she likes me to recall, has acted as controller of my office end and is now to help me in our room. She will be subbing for me and generally holding the fort ... She is a very quiet and unassuming person, well used to men. She is married.

The analogy with a harem, the living quarters of women in a Muslim household, jokingly drew on sexualised stereotypes to make light of Bay's presence and to imply that she would be under strict male control. Robinson's reply was similarly tongue-in-cheek but with a clear message:

> You were the last man I imagined would install a hareem in these hallowed precincts. I cannot but regard it as letting the Gallery down. In spite of all your encomiums of the lady – which I fully accept – I feel that this step cannot be too strongly deprecated. Apart from the effect on the Gallery generally, this foreign body must have a restrictive effect on the explosive relief which a harassed hon. Sec. frequently gives to his feelings, within earshot of the proposed hareem.[8]

The Parliamentary Press Gallery was a large and important part of the 'Westminster Village' and the presence of Bay must have made quite a splash, despite Harvey's clumsy efforts to allay fears. Although other women were subsequently given Press Gallery tickets during the war years, Bay clearly held a significant role and was the only woman among ninety-four journalists listed in an inventory of staff for evacuation planning purposes in November 1942. Bay remembered pressure to be quiet and unassuming, recalling later in life, 'I was told never to intrude upon any group of men even if one of the group should be a Reuter colleague', and that she should never wear bright clothing that might attract attention. Despite these efforts, she caused a scandal walking into the House of Lords without a hat, leading to discussion over difficulties over clothing coupons and shortage of clothes. As a result, women were subsequently allowed into the Lords without hats.[9]

'LOADED WITH GOLD, SILVER AND BRONZE MEDALS': JEAN WINDER

Three years after the Press Gallery had paved the way, with the war still continuing, Hansard finally cracked and appointed its first female reporter in January 1944: Mrs Jean Winder.

Florence May Hayward (known always as Jean) was born in 1907 in Stockwell, London. Her parents managed pubs, although her father died when she was 6. She trained as a secretary at Hettie Craig-Kelly's secretarial training college and copying office in Moorgate. Her reporting career started back in 1926 at the time of the General Strike, when she was a secretarial student seeking to test her shorthand skills. She took down the news from the crystal set and read it back to her family at a fee of 6*d* a head. As she remembered, 'I've caught something that but for me would have vanished. Now it's down in black and white, for ever.'[10]

Her career took her as far as the Caribbean, when she and Craig-Kelly were official verbatim reporters to the Royal Commission on the West Indies (the Moyne Commission) in 1938–39, reported in the press as 'Women Secretaries 12,000 Mile Trip: They Are Taking 80 Notebooks'.[11] The Commission, which included two women members (medical doctor Mary Blacklock and social reformer Rachel Crowdy, formerly of the League of Nations secretariat), investigated living conditions in Britain's Caribbean colonies following civil unrest in the region. It was a huge inquiry, with formal evidence taken in twenty-six centres from 370 witnesses or groups of witnesses over more than six months. Seven hundred and eighty-nine memoranda of evidence were received, and 300 other communications. Hayward and Craig-Kelly are thanked in the acknowledgements of the Commission's report – written in 1939 although not published until 1945 due to the controversial nature of the findings – as reporters 'who carried out their duties under most difficult conditions'.[12]

In October 1940, Jean Hayward married naval officer Ralph Spearing Winder. He was made OBE and became commanding officer on HMS *Visenda* a few months later. Under his command the *Visenda* destroyed German U-Boat U-551 in March 1941, for which he was awarded the DSC posthumously. He had been killed in a separate incident on active service on 22 June 1941.

Winder may never have stopped working, of course, but at any rate childless widows were conscripted for war service when Parliament passed the National Service (No. 2) Act in December 1941. She once referred to working with 'about 50 women in one room in the factory, all doing clerical work', which may have referred to war work before she came to the House of Commons. By the time that Winder arrived at the Commons in 1944 she had twenty years' experience of verbatim reporting and was described as 'loaded with gold, silver and bronze medals for writing shorthand at incredible speeds'.[13]

WINDER'S APPOINTMENT: PRESERVING THE PRINCIPLE OF SEX DIFFERENTIATION

On her appointment at the House of Commons in 1944, Jean Winder was put on a one-year contract at a salary of £400, plus a war bonus and additional fees for any standing committee work. The Editor of the Official Report, Mr P.F. Cole, wrote to Ralph Verney, Secretary to the Speaker, making it clear that:

> The only reason why I thought of appointing a woman was that I was unable to find a man for the job ... the Hansard staff has lost four good men to the services and it was absolutely necessary to take steps to secure further assistance.[14]

The salary of £400 was the same as the minimum rate of pay for a male reporter and there was dispute about this even at this early point, with Cole explaining that he had no idea that the different rates of pay between men and women in the Civil Service would apply to his staff. He did not think he could have secured her employment for less, and also, 'the existing staff would strongly object to being undercut by a woman'. Verney duly wrote to the Treasury to say the Speaker regarded her appointment at this rate as 'essential and necessary', given the impossibility of recruiting men for this specialised work. A Treasury note concludes, 'This is obviously a special case and I do not think it will embarrass us to pass it.'[15] Embarrassment, rather than any point of principle or indeed financial calculation, appears to have been the dominant consideration.

Later that year, fees for standing committee work were incorporated into the basic salaries of male reporters. As an exception, Winder continued to be employed on the previous basis and was still entitled to the additional fees. The Treasury agreed this, having been assured by the House of Commons Accountant that Winder would only be called on for Standing Committee work when no outsiders or regular male reporters were available. Then in October 1945, on the retirement of a man, Cole wrote to Verney to request that Winder be made permanent. He spoke very highly of her, and requested equal pay:

> I now respectfully ask that Mr Speaker should recommend Mrs Winder's appointment to the regular Hansard staff at the full rate for a man, both in salary and in bonus … Unless we can offer her the full rate I fear that she will not agree to remain on the staff, nor should I wish her to remain at an under-cutting salary. At the same time I am very anxious to retain her services. She has helped us in a time of great difficulty and shortage, has proved a capable and efficient reporter, and has learned our ways and formulas. Indeed the commendations of her work from individual Members of the House have exceeded those obtained for the work of any other member of the staff.[16]

Verney duly wrote to this effect to the Treasury. The Treasury had no problem with making Winder permanent, but equal pay was another issue altogether. Its officials were keen to 'preserve the principle of sex differentiation', even if

Figure 19: *The Staff of the Official Report*, 1947. Includes Jean Winder (standing, centre, behind Editor of Debates Percy Cole and his wife Clara).

that meant losing her services. The women's equivalent scale was £450–600, and they suggested that she enter it at £470. Cole and Verney pushed back, Verney involving the Speaker personally. The Treasury file grumbled, 'The Editor seems to adopt gangster methods in trying to solve his difficulties.' Eventually, a compromise was reached: Winder was put on the women's scale rather than the men's scale, but starting at a higher point of £560. This solved the problem in the short term.

It was later alleged that Winder had been promised on her appointment that she would have equal pay. She had indeed received such an undertaking from the House of Commons on her temporary appointment in 1944, but this was not renewed when she was made permanent the following year – certainly not by the Treasury. Her appointment letter referred simply to her higher starting point without specifying that this was on a different pay scale, so it may well have appeared to her that the original undertaking would stand. It also appears that in 1945 all parties thought that this was an interim solution 'pending the abandonment of sex differentiation'. Sex differentiation did not end, however, and a few years later the situation came to a head when Winder reached the top of the women's pay band.

'WOMAN WHO HEARS ALL IS PAID LESS'

Equal pay, an object of feminist campaigning since the nineteenth century, came to the fore after the Second World War. Following the triumph of the Equal Compensation Select Committee, which successfully argued for equal compensation for men and women civilians wounded in the war, the Equal Pay Campaign Committee, a campaigning group, was set up in 1944 by Conservative MP Mavis Tate. A long-term advocate of equal pay, Tate was greatly affected by her visit to Buchenwald concentration camp in 1945. She lost her seat later the same year, sadly dying by suicide in 1947.

However, her fellow Conservative MP Irene Ward, a great champion of equal rights for women, was there to take up the cudgels as she had done for Kay Midwinter some years earlier. In November 1950, Ward put down a written parliamentary question to the Chancellor of the Exchequer, asking 'if he will give the names of those women in the Civil Service in receipt of equal pay for equal work'. Hugh Gaitskell, the Chancellor, did not give names but he did say that there were between 500 and 600 women in the Civil Service who were paid the same as men.[17]

Of course, Jean Winder saw the answer recorded in Hansard. She wrote to Gaitskell in January 1951 on House of Commons headed notepaper to enquire if this applied to her post. The Treasury replied that she had misinterpreted the Chancellor's reply, and in any case it did not apply to her post as she was not a civil servant. This last point was actually a tricky one for the Treasury to navigate, as it was endeavouring to set House of Commons salaries by analogy to Civil Service grades. It held the purse strings but did not employ the staff.

Winder was not to be deterred, and the Treasury was next approached by A.J. Moyes, the House of Commons Accountant, who set out several arguments on behalf of Winder. One of these was that female reporters in the Press Gallery were paid the same as the men – one can imagine Winder chatting to Bay from Reuters and what Bay might have said! Moyes also stated that the Editor of the Official Report 'affirms that she does exactly the same duty and has the same responsibilities as her male colleagues, and that she is highly efficient'. Although such arguments may seem reasonable today, they held no sway with the Treasury in 1951.

Winder had friends in high places, and on 30 May the Speaker, Douglas Clifton Brown, wrote personally to Gaitskell, saying, 'I feel strongly that Mrs Winder's claim to be so treated is really unanswerable'. The Speaker may have thought it unanswerable, but the Treasury certainly did not! 'Here is Mrs Winder back again,' the file note sighs. Gaitskell's reply stated that the equal pay issue did not apply to the Civil Service grade most like Winder's. Gaitskell also declared that there could be no analogy with Dame Evelyn Sharp. Evelyn Sharp was a pioneering senior civil servant, one of the first women to successfully enter the highest administrative grade in 1926, who would later become the first female Permanent Secretary. Sharp had become Deputy Secretary in the Ministry of Town and Local Government in 1946, receiving the men's rate.

'This is a dreadful equal pay case which has been dragging on for years,' exclaims the next note in the Treasury file, by Mary Loughnane, a Treasury official. Ward then brought the case into the public domain by raising Winder's case in the Commons in August 1951, which was reported under the headline, 'Woman Who Hears All Is Paid Less'.[18] The publicity was in vain; nothing happened.

THE INTEGRITY OF IRENE WARD

Many MPs might well have felt at this point that they had done all they could for Jean Winder. Ward had campaigned on equal pay as an issue, raised the Civil Service situation as a parliamentary question and received a partially helpful answer from Gaitskell, lobbied the Treasury privately on behalf of Winder, and then raised the case in public, having it recorded in the very pages of Hansard. All to no avail.

But Ward did not give in, and after her party, the Conservatives, regained power in the general election of October 1951 she could now draw on political allies to further the case as well as opposition support. The wider issue of equal pay in the Civil Service was raised again in Parliament in May 1952 when two Labour MPs, Elaine Burton and Charles Pannell, referred to unequal pay in Hansard. Pannell said:

> There are 18 HANSARD reporters who do their very best to make our speeches read more intelligently than they sometimes sound. There are 17 who receive the rate for the job. There is one of them, a woman doing exactly the same work, who does not receive the rate for the job.[19]

In July 1952, Ward wrote to John Boyd-Carpenter MP, Financial Secretary to the Treasury, complaining that he had not raised Winder's claim for equal pay as she had asked him to. She made it both personal and political in a way she could not have done with an opposition politician:

> I am fed up to the teeth with our Party saying one thing in opposition and something else in power. There are some things which are difficult to accomplish but there are some things which are not.[20]

She also remarked, 'If Ruffside [Speaker Clifton Brown, now Viscount Ruffside] had had a little more guts ... this rank injustice would have been settled long ago.'

By this point, the Treasury clearly felt that it could not back down in this matter without great loss of face, and effort was now put into discovering whether there had been a pledge of equal pay to Winder in the past, and if so, who had made it and when. Ward was pleased at this change of tone: 'I am glad we have got down to brass tacks and are no longer exchanging Treasury letters!!! I feel a bit better.' She explained that Winder had received nothing in writing, but the Editor of Debates (Vincent Hamson, who served from 1951 to 1954) had substantiated it, telling her that he had been let down. The Speaker had recommended equal pay, and his word was never questioned in the House ('only by the Treasury'), and Winder would have liked to have raised it through her union, but the Speaker had not permitted it. Ward ended on a note of empathy for Winder's position:

When I told Mrs Winder that I had let you know that she got men's rate on night shift, she said that had been kept very quiet in case it was taken away!! What a ghastly feeling to have to hug.

Treasury officials were not sympathetic about Ward 'continuing to pester' Boyd-Carpenter, and tried to deflect the matter away from the role of the Treasury towards the Speaker and Commons officials, but Ward was not having it. The correspondence rolled on for another year until eventually, in late 1953, the Treasury was finally worn down. Its officials agreed that the maximum of Winder's pay scale should be raised to the same level as the men's, and importantly, would rise with theirs. This was equal pay in all but name.

Jean Winder's battle for equal pay had run for nine years. Without Ward championing her, it is unlikely that she would have won against the might of the Treasury, whose officials had resisted throughout. This was despite support for Winder from all the key people at the House of Commons: the Speaker, the Accountant, the Editor of Debates. Above all, Winder was grateful to Ward, saying years later:

> Of them all, I shall remember Irene Ward – she has such integrity. When she went into politics someone told her 'you must never break a promise' – and she never has.[21]

Ward continued to fight for the principle of equal pay both inside and outside Parliament. The Equal Pay Campaign Committee started a petition in 1952 asking for 'equal pay for equal work between men and women in the public services', which was signed by more than 80,000 people. It was presented to Parliament on 9 March 1954 amid great publicity by a cross-party group of four women MPs: Irene Ward, Edith Summerskill, Barbara Castle and Patricia Ford. They arrived in horse-drawn carriages decorated in purple, green and white rosettes and streamers, evoking suffragette actions of the past.

Two years after Winder's victory, and following a huge public petition, equal pay was finally agreed in the public sector in 1955 and implemented in stages, including in Parliament, up to 1961. In practice, of course, it took many years to filter through. Private employers were not included; this had to wait until another high-profile and lengthy battle for equal pay – the Dagenham Ford workers' strike in 1968. That was the impetus for Barbara Castle's Equal Pay Act 1970, which came into force in 1975.

WINDER'S FINAL YEARS: ROMANCE IN THE PRESS GALLERY

Mrs Winder resigned from the House of Commons in April 1960, still the sole woman Hansard reporter. She claimed in public that she now wanted to be a freelancer, reporting on meetings and conferences. However, a month later she married Jack Hawke, parliamentary correspondent for the *Daily Telegraph*, a former chairman of the Parliamentary Press Gallery and a widower. By now the marriage bar had been abolished but perhaps Winder still felt pressure to resign on marriage, or wanted to stop working anyway. The gratuity women staff were entitled to be paid on marriage may also have been an incentive. Or maybe it would have been just too awkward a situation to have a Hansard reporter married to a journalist sitting next to her up in the Press Gallery.

The couple moved to Devon on Hawke's retirement in 1969, and Jean Winder died in 2005, having lived to the ripe old age of 98. Her obituary in *The Times* praised her proficiency and professionalism, and acknowledged her battle for equal pay:

> She could cope with any regional accent and every style of oratory, from Churchill to Bevan, and she worked without recorders or stenographic machines. Nor were concessions made to her because she was a woman. She worked the same gruelling hours as her male colleagues. If there was any early resentment, she saw it off by the unflagging courtesy that eventually won her equal pay.[22]

'MUCH UNDERRATED': WINDER ON WOMEN MPS

Reflecting on her time in Parliament in 1960, Winder vividly evoked the atmosphere:

> It has been said that Parliament is the heart of the nation, and that is true. In times of crisis, you can practically hear it beating. The joy, the relief of victory, the utter sadness and dejection during Suez – the feeling within the House was so concentrated as to be practically unbearable.

She also remembered individuals:

There's the sheer humanity of Parliament. For instance, I remember the day when Jimmy Maxton, the fiery Clydeside member, returned after one of his long illnesses, and Churchill walked over to him, quietly putting an arm around his shoulders. Or red-headed Ellen Wilkinson presiding over a Standing Committee which was talking about supplies to kindergarten classes – I shall never forget the gravity they brought to the subject of nappies and safety-pins.[23]

Women MPs, Winder averred, were much underrated. As well as Irene Ward, she mentioned Edith Summerskill, Margaret Herbison, Eirene White, Pat Hornsby-Smith and Edith Pitt as 'knowledgeable, efficient and modest'. Winder would have particularly known Eirene White, political correspondent for the *Manchester Evening News*, who became the first female provincial journalist to be admitted to the parliamentary lobby. White was elected as a Labour MP in 1950 and later became a government minister.

Of the 1959 intake, elected only six months before Winder's retirement, she opined, 'I'm greatly struck by the new young women, Margaret Thatcher, Judith Hart and Harvie Anderson – they're most capable and fluent.' This was a prescient selection by Winder. Judith Hart was to become only the fifth ever woman Cabinet Minister in 1968; Betty Harvie Anderson would be the first woman to sit in the Speaker's Chair as Deputy Speaker from 1970; and Margaret Thatcher, of course, would become the first female prime minister in 1979.

As a female first in Parliament herself, Winder would have appreciated such achievements. She may have been sad to leave Hansard in 1960 to see it become an all-male bastion, again. The next woman Hansard reporter was not appointed until 1968.

In Her Own Words

'So we sat and knitted and read because there were no committees to work for … and then a job came up in the Serjeant at Arms office. And that was because the shorthand typist in the Serjeant at Arms office turned up one day with nail varnish.'

Mary Frampton remembering how a job opportunity in
the House of Commons arose, 1950

15

THE STRAIN OF CARRYING LADDERS: THE LIBRARY AND ARCHIVES

In 1955, Miss J.M. Maton from the Council of Women Civil Servants wrote to complain to Strathearn Gordon, the House of Commons Librarian. She had seen an advertisement for a job which was restricted to men only. Gordon replied that this was 'with the greatest regret' as 12ft ladders were required to be carried along passages, 'and we find the girls cannot stand the resulting strain and tension'. Night work was also required, which was not desirable for women.[1]

Maton subsequently had a meeting with Gordon, where he advanced additional arguments including that if MPs saw a woman trying to move a ladder they would offer to help. His case against women doing night work was 'based almost entirely on natural instincts strengthened by unfortunate experience in the past'. Maton later reflected ruefully, 'My interview with the chief Librarian was most unsuccessful, although I demonstrated – I hope effectively – that I could carry one of his longest ladders!'[2] The ladder-carrying controversy, subsequently taken up by Irene Ward MP, shines a light on female staff in the Commons Library, one of the few places in Parliament which did in fact employ women in greater numbers and in professional positions immediately after 1945.

The House of Commons Library set up a research section in 1945 to provide more detailed assistance to MPs and this led to an influx of new staff. Some were there to provide secretarial and administrative support, such as the Home Guard veterans Pauline Bebbington and Barbara Shuttleworth who came across from the Committee Office to the Library. Others came into research, information and librarianship roles. Meanwhile, in the House of Lords, the library remained all-male but a woman archivist was appointed to the Record Office in 1950. Research and information services were therefore at the forefront of women's progression in Parliament immediately after the Second World War.

LADDERS IN THE LIBRARY

In 1945, the House of Commons Library had just seven staff, all men. The Librarian, John Vivian Kitto, and the Assistant Librarian, Hilary St George Saunders, operated a traditional service in the comfortable book-lined rooms. Saunders took over as Librarian in February 1946 and, following recommendations of a Select Committee and pressure from an influx of new MPs, started to transform the library into a modern, professional institution with a reference and research service. By 1947, staff numbers had more than doubled to nineteen; by 1962 there were thirty-two.[3] And they began to include women. In the wider world, librarianship had long been considered an occupation suitable for women, as an expansion of their roles within the home, family and in education. Female workers began to dominate numerically in the sector in England from the 1930s, although underrepresented in senior posts and in academic services and seen as better-suited to roles such as children's librarianship and cataloguing.

Although Parliament had so far been immune to female librarians, the expansion of posts brought new opportunities. The first women in professional library roles were Ann Salter and Caireen Fawcett Thompson, recruited as short-term temporary cataloguers from March 1946. Thompson was the daughter of author Charles J.S. Thompson, who had been medical librarian at the Wellcome Institute for the History of Medicine.[4] The first permanent appointment was Dorothy Elizabeth Dusart, known as Betty, a statistician, who came into the role of Junior Library Clerk on 15 October 1946, aged 21.

Dusart was born in Lewes, Sussex, in 1925. Her father was a wholesaler in toilet goods and hairdressers' sundries, with First World War service in the Royal Marines. Employed on a salary scale starting at £240, by 1949 Dusart was being paid £408, nearly the top of the scale and well above the female secretarial staff in the library. She married Stanley Hacking in 1951 and resigned from the Commons in October 1952 after six years' service. The marriage bar was no longer formally in operation by this time so Dusart may have been following social norms of the time or have been influenced by the gratuity paid to women leaving on marriage, which was still an incentive to resign.

At the same time Dusart arrived, so too did Roseanne O'Reilly, a fascinating woman who enjoyed a much longer career in the Commons. O'Reilly was newly demobilised from the WRNS and, according to her obituary in the *Daily Telegraph*, had served at Bletchley Park. Women made up two-thirds of staff at Bletchley, home of the Second World War codebreakers including many members of the WRNS, so O'Reilly may well have played her part there. Her father had served in both world wars and died on active service in 1944. Parliamentary family connections were still in operation: the Librarian, Saunders, was her godfather and also a distant cousin.[5]

O'Reilly was employed initially as a temporary shorthand typist from 14 October 1946, one of a number of women in such roles across the House of Commons; she learned shorthand in a fortnight beforehand. However, she was placed on the established staff on 1 January 1947, became Personal Assistant to the Librarian in 1949, progressed to a professional role as Information Service Clerk in 1958, and went on to have a long, successful career in the library over forty years. She worked in the Reference Room throughout, at a time well before computers when it was difficult to get simple information. She started the 'Responsiones', a card index to elusive information, and other tools such as a non-parliamentary speech collection. Her career path was restricted as she did not have a degree, and she watched graduates with less knowledge come in over her with some resentment. However, she also said that she 'laughed for 40 years', had lots of friends including MPs, and enjoyed every minute despite the hard work.[6]

The murder of Barbara Shuttleworth took place in 1948 while Dusart and O'Reilly were employed in the library. Mary Frampton, another post-war secretary, remembered this tragic event as providing her employment opportunity; 'It was possible there was a vacancy because [of] one of the girls in the Library, her Polish lover had shot her during summer recess.'[7] O'Reilly retired in 1986 and her reminiscences in the library newsletter show that the murder was still not quite forgotten:

> I could tell you about all the changes I have seen … About a funny friend of R A B Butler's who joined the staff for a short time and who wasn't paid, and who called all the Members by their pet names … About the present Librarian's arrival as a new boy and how I thought that he thought he had come to a madhouse. About how one of the secretaries was shot during her lunch hour.[8]

Saunders resigned as Librarian in 1950 due to ill health and died the following year. He was replaced by Strathearn 'Strathie' Gordon, a former clerk who had been one of the driving forces behind the Westminster Munitions Unit. Gordon later promoted O'Reilly from a back-room role to the front face of the Members' Library, but otherwise he appears not to have been so open to women staff as Saunders had been – as exemplified by the ladder-carrying controversy in 1955. The case was taken up by Irene Ward MP, who had done so much to help first Kay Midwinter and then Jean Winder. As remembered by Jill Knight MP some years afterwards:

> Dame Irene Ward was incensed to see in the columns of *The Times* an advertisement for a librarian in the House of Commons which stated that men only need apply … she received an unsatisfactory answer to the effect that … a librarian in the House of Commons Library would be expected to carry heavy ladders to get books down from the upper shelves. Dame Irene threw down her Order Paper in anger, stalked out of the Chamber, went along to the Library, picked up a ladder, put it over her shoulder and came back into the Chamber, or tried to do so … Dame Irene stood at the Bar of the House with the ladder across her shoulders … it occasioned considerable trouble, because as she turned from side to side many hon. Members were in constant danger of decapitation. She shouted 'I have the ladder, and it is not too heavy.'[9]

This incident may be parliamentary myth, for as Ward wrote to Miss Maton at the Council of Women Civil Servants at the time, 'I have had a lot of fun telling the Authorities that I would be seen appearing with a ladder penetrating into the Chamber. I think this put the wind up everybody.'[10] Nevertheless, it forced Gordon to defend his position. As well as the physical aspect, he also argued that the sheer numbers of female librarians wishing to work in the Commons was a problem: 'When recruitment to posts for Assistant Librarian were opened to women, several hundred applied whereas the number of men who applied was very much smaller.'[11] This demonstrates the wider demographic of librarianship as a female-dominated profession at a time when the war may have caused shortages of male candidates. Women able to take advantage of educational opportunities to qualify as librarians were keen to enter the workforce; they were also cheaper labour, particularly before equal pay began to be introduced from the 1950s. Ward won the day, obtaining an agreement by the Civil Service Commission to use the same method of appointment for Commons Library clerkships as for other staff, as a guarantee that appointments would go to most suitable candidate.

Roseanne O'Reilly has been described as the first woman executive servant of the Commons Library,[12] although that distinction belongs properly to Dusart, who had the title of Junior Library Clerk on her appointment and a salary to match. O'Reilly herself regarded the first woman Library Clerk as having been Jane Fiddick, née Hodlin, who was from the next generation of women library staff, appointed in 1963.[13] Jane Fiddick had not only the job title but the distinction of being the first woman Officer of the House of Commons, another point which rankled with O'Reilly, who was never awarded this status. The officer/non-officer distinction seems to have increased in importance for parliamentary staff in the post-war period, presumably as a result of such distinctions being made in the armed forces during the war. Officers had access privileges previously only given to male clerks, so a female officer was a significant development. Fiddick later remembered, 'The police and attendants, let alone Members, weren't warned and when I ventured into the Chamber or the Tea Room or other areas forbidden to ordinary mortals, I was constantly and embarrassingly challenged.'[14]

LIFE IN THE POST-WAR PALACE

O'Reilly was one of three women staff in the Commons in the late 1940s and early 1950s who later recorded oral histories, the others being her friends Mary Frampton and Pat Brandt. Mary Frampton was employed as a shorthand typist from November 1948, aged 20, initially in the Committee Office. No committees were set up in 1950 because of the two general elections, so Frampton occupied herself by knitting until a job opportunity arose in the Serjeant at Arms Department. The previous typist there was moved to another job, having arrived at work one day wearing nail varnish which was unacceptable to the Serjeant. Appointed in her place, Frampton worked there for five successive Serjeants over many years, was made MBE in 1967 and eventually rose to become Clerk in Charge of the Serjeant at Arms Office. Occupying the most senior non-officer post in the department, her responsibilities included serving warrants on behalf of Select Committees. She applied 'rather tongue-in-cheek' for the position of Assistant Serjeant, an officer role, near the end of her career, but without success.

Pat Brandt came to work as Secretary to the Clerk Assistant Edward Fellowes from 1951, and then as his Personal Assistant after he became Clerk of the House. As well as performing administrative work, she developed procedural knowledge over time, especially after her promotion, and worked with many MPs. She was awarded an MBE on the recommendation of Fellowes but resigned in 1963 because she did not get on with his successor. Although she wed later on – becoming Pat Lugard-Brayne, and having a family

– she remembered ruefully that the circumstances of her departure from the Commons meant that she had missed out on the customary marriage gratuity.

The recollections of the three collectively provide an evocative flavour of parliamentary working lives in the immediate post-war period when many of the male staff still wore military uniforms. MPs were still sitting in the Lords chamber while the Commons was rebuilt after the bombing. O'Reilly remembered how empty the Palace was: she would drive in and park right outside in New Palace Yard. The library was, she said, manned by 'about eight old, old men'. Frampton recalled that there were more people repairing the building than running it and it was very quiet apart from hammers and drills. Initially, she worked in a particular committee room because it was the only undamaged space available, and she didn't see Westminster Hall for a couple of years because a hardboard tunnel screened vital repair work. Security was minimal and the police officers simply recognised everyone.

Although fifteen women MPs were elected in the 1945 general election, they were too few in number to make much impact across the building. O'Reilly recalled one or two, including Bessie Braddock, but they didn't come into the library. The women MPs made little difference to Frampton's work either. Some departments still had no female staff: the Speaker's Office never typed anything because they had no typists, and letters would be returned to Brandt with handwritten responses. Nothing was ever filed either. The pioneering wartime women clerks had largely been forgotten, with Brandt remarking, 'One wondered whether there ever would be girl clerks ... it was just beginning ... I don't think the clerks ever interviewed a girl, not that I remember, not in my day.' Clearly, she felt that women were up to the job as she added, 'I felt on quite a par with the junior clerks ... one could have done a lot of their work.'

All three women were appointed thanks to an initial personal connections, and all remembered recommending family and friends for jobs too. They worked hard with long hours while the House was sitting, felt they were well paid and enjoyed plenty of time off during recesses. They appreciated opportunities to travel abroad to provide administrative support for the Parliamentary Assembly of Council of Europe. (The Council of Europe is a human rights organisation initially founded by the UK and nine other European countries in 1949, and its Parliamentary Assembly was mostly staffed by British and French clerks.) Frampton and Brandt recalled a great divide between House staff and Members' staff. There was no secretarial allowance for MPs in those days, not until 1969 (MPs' salaries had only been introduced in 1911), and working conditions were poor. Frampton, who had some responsibility for allocating accommodation, recalled how one secretary would be shared by a dozen MPs, eight or nine secretaries used one telephone, and forty-one of them were housed in the telephone exchange space with two filing cabinet drawers each.

One such secretary was the redoubtable Jean Armour Brown. Born in 1894 and having served in the Women's Army Auxiliary Corps (WAAC) in the First World War, she married, had a family and then came to work in the House of Commons for Eleanor Rathbone MP in 1944. She took on many other MPs and peers over the years, Conservative and Labour, and was awarded an MBE in 1975 at the age of 81, as the longest-serving secretary in the House.[15] She died in 1990.

As for Roseanne O'Reilly, she was awarded an MBE in 1978 and retired from the library in 1986. Remarkably, this was not the end of her career in Parliament. She returned to work for the Speaker when Betty Boothroyd became Speaker of the House of Commons in 1992. O'Reilly's recollection was that following a chance meeting she was mentioned to Boothroyd and invited to come and cook, and the Speaker would not take no for an answer: 'After a month I said I couldn't cope with it and she said you'll get used to it and I did.'[16]

Boothroyd's memories on taking her Speakership were: 'I inherited a daytime domestic help and a batman-chauffeur who made me a cup of tea at 4.30 p.m.' – a far cry from the extensive households of her predecessors. 'My independence was fully restored only when Roseanne O'Reilly was persuaded to come out of retirement to be my housekeeper.' And so O'Reilly's job title in the Speaker's House was Housekeeper – an incredible late twentieth-century throwback to the long history of redoubtable housekeepers in households across Parliament. O'Reilly lived in a flat in Pimlico while keeping house for Boothroyd, including assisting with Boothroyd's official social occasions and accompanying her on work trips abroad as well as behind-the-scenes support. When Mo Mowlam MP was being treated for cancer, Boothroyd invited her to rest in Speaker's House whenever she wanted, and remembered, 'Roseanne was wonderful. She prepared the bedroom and when Mo woke up after her rest there would be a cup of tea and some Marmite on toast.'[17] A few weeks after Boothroyd's retirement in 2000, O'Reilly too retired for a second and final time; she died in 2010 aged 84.

'RECORDS GIRL': THE HOUSE OF LORDS RECORD OFFICE

Over in the House of Lords, there had been no trailblazing Second World War appointments of female clerks or Hansard reporters. By 1945, there had been women MPs for twenty-five years in the Commons, but women were still banned from sitting as Members of the House of Lords, and the scanty female staffing levels reflected that. A small enclave of women origi-nally employed in the days of Miss Court maintained their positions in what was now the Copying Department – Rosalys Joan Griffith, Rosalind Clara Evernden and Joan Parnell Culverwell – holding middle-ranking roles such as Executive Officer and Examiner of Local Acts. However, deprived of its accountancy function, the Copying Department was now a typing pool, and other women continued to occupy low-status and low-paid roles such as housemaids and waitresses as they always had done. The Lords' Library was tiny compared to the Commons', with only four staff as late as 1960 and only six by 1970, and no women. Only the Refreshment Department continued to be led by women, Elsie Hoath and her successors, through to 1981.

However, one lone pioneering woman was appointed to a professional information position. Elisabeth Ross Poyser MA became Assistant Clerk of the Records in the House of Lords Record Office in July 1950, second-in-command to Maurice Bond, Clerk of the Records.[18] The Record Office looked after the millions of unique historical records of both Houses of Parliament, held in the Victoria Tower. Although the records dated back to 1497, the office was only set up in 1946 so Poyser was one of the earliest archivists employed by Parliament.

Poyser was born in 1923 in Wisbech, Cambridgeshire. Her father was a printer, stationer and bookseller, and her mother was a schoolteacher. Educated at St Paul's Girls' School, but with her schooling interrupted by evacuation at the start of the Second World War, she was a history research student at Newnham College, Cambridge, before coming to the Lords. She does not seem to have arrived with any particular knowledge or expertise in parliamentary history. Her postgraduate study was on Anglo-Tuscan trade through the port of Leghorn, *c.* 1560–1740, and her only work experience was as a Temporary Assistant Principal at the Ministry of Works between 1944 and 1945.[19] Her recruitment to the Lords was sufficiently notable to make the press with the headline 'Records Girl' (Figure 20). Another piece in the *Evening News* noted that her job required her to climb 250 steps inside the Victoria Tower, but 'fortunately she is young and active, spends much of her leisure time walking with her father, who lives at Clapham, or playing squash and tennis'.[20]

Notably, the reason for having a Records Girl was that Maurice Bond set out to recruit a woman. He wanted a woman graduate in History or Classics, with an archives diploma or research degree and palaeography and Latin skills, so he wrote to the Public Record Office and the Institute of Historical

RECORDS GIRL

Pictured here is the new assistant to the Clerk of the Records of the House of Lords —Miss Elizabeth Ross Poyser, 26. Her work will be among the half-million documents in the Victoria Tower of the Palace of Westminster.

Figure 20: 'Records Girl', press cutting, August 1950.

Research to ask if they could recommend female candidates. Names were supplied, Bond interviewed six women and Poyser got the job. The role was to run the public search room, prepare records for microfilming, list Acts of Parliament, box and index the Parchment Collection, undertake research and writing for publications and continue the calendar (a detailed chronological list) of House of Lords manuscripts. It was set at the same grade as for Assistant Keeper of the Records at the Public Record Office, but of course paid at the – lower – female equivalent rate.[21]

Although Bond regarded the post as particularly suited to a woman, he did not explain why. There is no evidence that he was motivated by reasons of gender equality or balance across the office, and testimony by colleagues who knew him well is that he would have been looking at the requirements of the post, relevant skills and knowledge, and potential of the applicant, as well as seeking comparability between his staff hierarchy and the clerks.[22] Bond did have to argue hard for increased staffing and may have suggested a woman in part because she would be cheaper to employ. Additionally, he would have expected a reasonable pool of candidates. As with librarianship, women entered archives as a profession in greater numbers after the war, and women were also being recruited to do historical work for projects such as the Victoria County History.[23]

When Bond next came to recruit an archivist in 1953, he specified that he wanted a male graduate. Harry Cobb was appointed to support renovation work in the Victoria Tower, including supervising moves of records and the work of contractors. It appears that Bond was again matching the job to what he consciously or unconsciously assumed to be appropriate gender attributes. Bond warned that 'the Tower is a horrid place now and the candidate should be tough psychologically as well as physically', although the candidate was also supposed to come with history, Latin and palaeography skills.[24]

There was a delay in formal approval for Poyser's appointment in 1950 and Bond wrote apologising for not keeping her informed, 'a mixture of muddle-headedness and rush on my part'. Once a start date was agreed, he wrote, 'I look forward to plunging with you into Commercial Treaties and Dunkirk Evacuation and Destruction (1714 vintage) on Monday!' He may have been a little taken aback by her reply – she had been reading his calendars of House of Lords manuscripts and was not enthused:

> When I arrive I hope to have mastered your methods of calendaring. To tell the truth, on glancing through it, I find some things don't much appeal to my interests, but no doubt I shall extend my range in due course – 'the archivist should be all things to his archive' etc.[25]

Poyser arrived to be given a memorandum about her work, including an enormous reading list which included procedural monsters such as the *Standing Orders of the House of Lords* and *Erskine May's Parliamentary Practice* (and a suggestion at the end that she could herself write a history of the Parliament Office, as there wasn't one); advice that she could buy herself a map of the Palace for 1*d*; and Miss Griffith in the Copying Department would give her 'further help about canteens etc.'.[26] It cannot have been a welcoming environment and the officer/non-officer distinction was just as strong in the Lords as in the Commons. The clerks lunched with library staff, but not with Record Office staff. A few days after she started work, the Secretary to the Lord Great Chamberlain wrote stiffly to Bond to state that Poyser was an official rather than an officer of the House, and thus not entitled to the access privileges enjoyed by officers.[27]

One such privilege should have been use of the libraries, but the House of Lords Librarian, Charles Clay, did not want women in his library. In 1952, Bond managed to obtain agreement with the Deputy Librarian, Christopher Dobson, that Poyser could use the library during mornings only, providing she only sat in one of the end rooms and not the main room, and she could get books herself from the main room in the morning but library staff would get books for her after 1 p.m. – the clear implication was that Clay must not see her.[28] It was not plain sailing and Poyser apparently found the Commons Library down the corridor, with its handful of female staff, more accommodating. Following an encounter in 1953 where Poyser was accused of doing personal rather than work research, Dobson wrote to Bond:

> Just after I telephoned to you this morning, I saw Miss Poyser. Her cool countenance and penetrating eyes told me I was very much in her bad books. And I fear I am in yours too. If so, I am sorry ... I realise now that it was not my place to suggest to Miss Poyser that it was not her job to carry out lengthy researches in Printed Journals; and I should have known that she was only doing the work of your office for which you are responsible.[29]

Although Bond and Poyser did not have a particularly good working relationship, Bond took steps to try to rectify this discrimination when he could. In 1958, a major piece of House of Lords reform took place with the passage of the Life Peerages Act. This created a new category of peers who were appointed for life only (rather than passing the honour down to their children), and opened up membership of the House of Lords to women for the first time. Four women took their seats in the House of Lords in October 1958. The wind of change blew through the Lords until it reached

the library, assisted by Clay's retirement in 1956. In March 1959, Bond wrote
to the Secretary to the Lord Great Chamberlain explaining:

> Now there are Lady peers, Chr. Dobson has withdrawn all restrictions
> on Miss P's use of the Library. Could we therefore agree that both she
> and Cobb may have the right to do whatever other officers of the House
> may do?[30]

No reply is recorded and one can only hope that life was made a little easier
for Poyser and Cobb from that point on.

Harry Cobb, who went on to succeed Bond as Clerk of the Records in
1981, later reflected that he considered leaving the Lords in the early 1960s
because Poyser was senior to him and would have been promoted to the
top job ahead of him. However, this orderly succession never happened
as in 1965 Poyser departed Parliament for a new job at the Westminster
Archdiocesan Archives, another pioneering role as she was the first lay-
woman to work for the Westminster Archdiocese. No further female
archivists were appointed in the Lords for many years, with women working
only in lower-graded and specialist roles such as document repair and micro-
film photography. Cobb thought that women would not like the labour of
pushing trolleys of documents around, while acknowledging that things did
later change.[31]

One curious footnote is that although Maurice Bond never appointed
any other female archivists he did marry one, Shelagh Mary Lewis, in 1954.
Lewis had been a contemporary of Poyser at Newnham before studying
for the archives diploma at University College London and working in
Northamptonshire Record Office. She had been one of the names recommended for interview by UCL for Poyser's post, although Bond did not in
fact consider her for that. Shelagh left paid work on marriage but continued to research and publish on historical and archival subjects, notably at
St George's Chapel, Windsor. The Bonds enjoyed a happy marriage, even
keeping a joint diary, until Shelagh's tragically early death in 1973. Poyser
wrote Shelagh's obituary for the Society of Archivists.[32] Poyser remained as
Diocesan Archivist until her retirement in 1989.

Like Roseanne O'Reilly, Poyser died in 2010. Unlike O'Reilly, Poyser
left no oral history and the memory of being among this first generation of
women information professionals in Parliament died with her.

EPILOGUE

THE PULL OF THE PAST

Although at first sight the world of our necessary women may seem long gone, in many ways it still survives today. Most of the places where they worked, lived, triumphed – and in all too many instances suffered – have been lost without trace. Almost all of the chaotic and vibrant old Palace has disappeared altogether. Only Westminster Hall where Mrs Furlong sold her fruit and the crypt chapel next to where Emily Wilding Davison so bravely hid are still recognisably the same. While parts of the beautiful Tudor cloister through which Ellen Manners Sutton grandly swept are still there, this is deserted and marginalised space. And for all its robust construction, the new Palace that replaced the old is now, in its turn, in peril, its labyrinth of wires and pipes posing a fire hazard and its beautiful surface stonework dangerously crumbling away in places.

Inside, though, Parliament's grand state rooms, the chambers and committee rooms, the libraries and refreshment rooms remain well-preserved and finely presented masterpieces of Victorian art and design. Even the Commons chamber, reconstructed after the Second World War bombing to reflect its lost predecessor, elegantly reinterprets Charles Barry's original scheme through a mid-twentieth-century aesthetic prism – although fortunately omitting the Ladies' Gallery. Jane Julia Bennett would today have no difficulty in finding her way through from the royal Robing Room and into the Lords chamber, and then onwards through Central Lobby to the Commons chamber – and, apart from some technological innovations, would probably not be greatly surprised by what she saw. Perhaps some of her keys would still fit in the door locks.

Yet most of the rest of the vast interior of the Victorian palace has since 1900 been gradually but completely repurposed – and has changed beyond recognition. The bedroom where Eliza Arscot went mad is now an office for Parliamentary Archives staff, while the cramped accommodation where Charlotte Bladon was beaten and abused by her husband forms part of a modern kitchen serving the famous Commons Tea Room. The prime minister's parliamentary office is in the former drawing room of the Clerk of the House, where the Palgrave family perhaps entertained the elderly Anne Rickman, and will certainly have celebrated her life and work. The area below Central Lobby where – remarkably and dangerously – Mrs Hodges toiled in the wartime munitions factory is now a much-prized storage space. Hidden away in its obscure corner near the west front, less obvious even than the stone memorial to staff lost in the First World War in the courtyard nearby, Miss Bell's front doorbell serves today as a poignant and tangible reminder of all the women who once laboured and lived in the Palace of Westminster.

But many things have barely changed. Parliament continues with its unending cycle of making laws and holding the executive to account, in debating chambers still reflecting the layout of the medieval chapel of St Stephen and with many of its practices and procedures unvaried over many centuries. And just as crucial to its work as they ever were are the catering and cleaning staff. Returning after two centuries, our irrepressible catering manager and cook 'Jane' would surely be delighted to discover a modern-day Bellamy's Café, named in tribute to its long-lost predecessor, in a building in Parliament Street, dispensing fast and nutritious food to the parliamentary community. As in Jane's day, Parliament's catering outlets are served by both women and men, with women in the majority.

The kindly, matronly Lords Housekeeper Amelia de Laney would also find the gender balance of the cleaning and maintenance teams in both Houses broadly unchanged since her time a century ago. Today the distinctions between roles are more blurred: in the Lords the housemaids are now known as housekeepers and these posts are open to men. De Laney would doubtless warmly welcome the improved working conditions for the staff and the provision of cleaning equipment – and, given her long struggle for a bath to be installed in her rooms, the availability of showers for all to use.

THE SHOCK OF THE NEW

As the twentieth century began, the pace of change was not fast enough for some. Mary Jane Anderson scrawled her discontent at being 'Housekeeper Cook General Servant Mother payment for which is no wages no Vote' across her census form. Meanwhile, new opportunities for women to become secretaries and typists, including her daughter, had arrived in the Palace of Westminster. Bedrooms and drawing rooms were turned into offices with dictation cubicles for the remarkable and entrepreneurial May Ashworth and her young female workforce. And then the necessities of war and the early stages of female emancipation gave women the chance to start to break the mould in a variety of jobs, fuelled by ability, resilience, determination and, in many cases, family connections. Many contemporaries inside and outside Parliament found some of these new appointments deeply shocking – all were groundbreaking.

The First World War saw the innovation of four girls appointed to porter parcels and packages around the House of Commons, despite enormous initial reluctance by the Serjeant at Arms. The tragic death of the youngest, Mabel Clark, from influenza in 1918 echoes the experiences of the wider population facing global pandemic – as does the fact that their jobs went back to men after the conflict ended. But over in the Lords, May Court built on her wartime opportunity to reign from 1926 to 1944 as head of office and Accountant, supported for years by a team of women. This 'monstrous regiment', as it was dubbed by the press and probably reflecting the views of insiders, was a rare female-run enclave in the interwar period. Far less prominent outside, but equally successful, was the redoubtable Elsie Hoath, Catering Manager in the Lords. Appointed in 1939 to a role that no one else would tackle, she was the first person to crack the parliamentary catering conundrum for more than a century, balancing the books by providing peers with simple but tasty meals rather than fine dining.

The Second World War put the Palace under siege and provided many opportunities for Parliament's female workers to volunteer as much-needed nurses, fire watchers and Home Guard Auxiliaries, or to serve in the Westminster Munitions Unit. As bombs rained down across London and the Commons chamber burned, their dedication and contributions were exemplary, on a par with women outside. Much more exceptional was when, in 1941, pioneering and self-confident Kay Midwinter was appointed a clerk in the Commons to provide expert advice and support to Select Committees. As she stepped on to the floor of the House of Commons to lay her first report, to the shock and horror of her male colleagues and under the glare of Winston Churchill, another male bastion crumbled – but only up to a point. Midwinter and the two other women clerks who followed her were paid far less than the men, and none outlasted the war.

Another groundbreaking wartime appointee would last far longer: Jean Winder, the first female Hansard reporter. But once again this was on a far lower rate of pay than her male colleagues. Winder listened from the Press Gallery, took note of what the Chancellor of the Exchequer said on equal pay and began her battle. It took a high-profile war of attrition lasting almost a decade for this to be rectified. Dame Irene Ward MP fought for Midwinter and Winder, and also for the right of women to compete for professional posts in the Commons Library on equal terms with men – in 1955 even threatening to brandish a heavy ladder in the chamber to demonstrate her point. Over in the Lords, undeterred by the hundreds of steps in the Victoria Tower, Elisabeth Poyser researched and listed the historical records of Parliament, helping to ensure the stories in this book could be preserved and uncovered for audiences today.

By now the trailblazing and newsworthy appointments of women to professional roles had come to an end, for the time being. As Midwinter and Winder moved on from Parliament, they must have been sorely disappointed to see that they had no immediate successors. Their doughty champion, Irene Ward, would doubtless have been equally mortified. It was not until the last decades of the twentieth century that such recruitments started again in both Houses in any numbers, and women began to be appointed into the most senior posts.

But that is a story for others to tell.

THANKS AND ACKNOWLEDGEMENTS

We are grateful to many archivists, librarians and curators for providing advice on and access to our source material, including staff at The National Archives, the Women's Library at LSE, Bodleian Library, British Library, London Metropolitan Archives, Newnham College Cambridge, Westminster City Archives, Westminster Diocesan Archives and elsewhere. Malcolm Cooper was most helpful in making the Metropolitan and City Police Orphanage archives available. Above all we are grateful to all the wonderful staff at the UK Parliamentary Archives – in particular, Stephen Ellison, Caroline Shenton and Adrian Brown, successive Directors of the Parliamentary Archives; David Prior, Head of Public Services and Outreach; Claire Batley; Annie Pinder; and the late Simon Gough.

Many staff in Parliament, past and present, have been supportive of our project including: Philippa Tudor who supported Mari's PhD into women and Parliament as an approved course when head of House of Lords Human Resources; Mark Collins, Parliamentary Estates Historian and Archivist; Jackie Storer, David Clark, Emily Bourne and other staff of the Speaker's Office; Jacqy Sharpe, Colin Lee, Sir David Natzler, Lord Lisvane (Sir Robert Rogers), Sir David Beamish, Sir John Sainty and other clerks in the House of Commons and House of Lords; Oonagh Gay, Isobel White, Dora Clark and Corie Chambers from the Commons Library; Robin Fell, former Principal Doorkeeper; Portia Dadley, Diane Buck, Cara Clark, Stephen Farrell and all in the Commons Hansard Writing Team; John Vice in Lords Hansard; Gemma Webb; and last but by no means least, Malcolm Hay, Melissa

Hamnett and everyone in Parliament's Heritage Collections team, past and present. A very special mention to Melanie Unwin, former Deputy Curator of Works of Art, who was unfailing in all her efforts to promote women in Parliament's works of art collection.

Many current and former Members of both Houses have led and inspired research into the history of women in Parliament in which we have both been involved for many years. We would like in particular to acknowledge and thank Helene, Baroness Hayman; Frances, Baroness de Souza; Rachel Reeves MP; Maria Miller MP; Anita, Baroness Gale; Anne, Baroness Jenkin; and Jacqui Smith. We are very grateful to the members of the Vote 100 Exhibition Advisory Group in 2018 – Alison McGovern MP, Nicky Morgan MP, Alison Thewliss MP, the late Diana, Baroness Maddock and the late Patricia, Baroness Hollis.

We also pay tribute to the Workplace Equalities Network ParliGENDER, for its excellent work in identifying and challenging inequality and discrimination in order to improve and promote gender equality at every level and in every part of Parliament.

We are grateful to many historians and others for discussions and information on women at work and women in Parliament over the years including: Sally Alexander, Helen Antrobus, Diane Atkinson, Rosemary Auchmuty, Ros Ball, Paula Bartley, Frances Bedford, Laura Beers, Lisa Berry-Waite, Clarisse Berthèzene, Elizabeth Biggs, Lucy Bland, Mineke Bosch, Judith Bourne, Kate Bradley, Mary Branson, Katie Carpenter, Richard Carr, Chloe Challender, Elaine Chalus, Elizabeth Chapman, Red Chidgey, Sarah Childs, Susan Cohen, Beverley Cook, John Cooper, Krista Cowman, Elizabeth Crawford, Emma Crewe, Sharon Crozier-De Rosa, Jennifer Davey, Dana Denis-Smith, Caroline Derry, Claire Eustance, Amy Galvin, Helen Glew, Jacqueline Glomski, Julie Gottlieb, Daniel J.R. Grey, Amy Griggs-Kliger, Kourtney Harper, Melinda Haunton, Alexandra Hughes-Johnson, Richard Huzzey, Vicky Iglikowski-Broad, Lyndsey Jenkins, Angela V. John, Helen Langley, Cristina Leston-Bandeira, Jill Liddington, Anne Logan, Helene Martin Gee, Helen McCarthy, Alexandra Meakin, Henry Miller, Sumita Mukherjee, Gillian Murphy, Kate Murphy, Rick Nimmo, Helen Pankhurst, Naomi Paxton, Jill Pay, June Purvis, Nirmal Puwar, Erika Rackley, Louise Raw, Sarah Richardson, Charlotte Lydia Riley, Jane Robinson, Kevin Schurer, Laura Schwartz, Elizabeth Shepherd, Angela K. Smith, Matthew Smith, Adrian Steel, Anne Summers, Duncan Sutherland, Pat Thane, Richard Toye, Murray Tremellen, Jacqui Turner, Lesley Urbach, Elizabeth Wells, Kirsty Wright. In particular, Paul Seaward, Robin Eagles, Paul Hunneyball, Emma Peplow, Kathryn Rix, Philip Salmon, Martin Spychal and all at the History of Parliament Trust have always been a great source of knowledge, advice and expertise. Members of the Women's History Network and the Friends of the Women's Library have also been helpful and supportive over many years.

We thank our agent, Clare Grist Taylor, for helping us shape our ambitious and sprawling research into stories for this book. We thank people who gave us opportunities to research and publish our earlier work on women staff, including Mark Curthoys from the *Oxford Dictionary of National Biography*. Mari would especially like to thank her postdoc writing group who have been waiting a long time for her to produce a book: Kathleen Sherit, Christopher Knowles, Claire Hilton, Matthew Passmore and Mary Salinsky. Especial thanks to Claire Hilton for comments on Eliza Arscot.

We are indebted to family members of women staff in Parliament who have been so generous in sharing recollections, information and pictures of their ancestors. They include the Furlong family for Mary Furlong; Helena Coney for the Bladons; Charlie Rogers for the Jewill-Rogers family; Charles ('Chuck') Court for May Court; the Wolfe family for Josephine Davson. We would be delighted to hear from descendants of any other of our featured women staff. We are grateful to the researchers of the History of the Royal Masonic School for Girls for background on Amelia de Laney, and to Clarissa Reilly for early discussions on May Ashworth.

We are also grateful to the Parliamentary Archives, Parliament's Heritage Collections, the Yeoman Usher in the House of Lords, the Women's Library at the London School of Economics, Charles ('Chuck') Court, the West London NHS Trust and the Wolfe family for their kind permission to reproduce images. All reasonable efforts have been made to contact the copyright holders of figures 15–17 and 19–20 to establish permissions. If you have any details on this issue, please contact the publisher.

Finally, we would like to express our utmost thanks to all our friends and families. In particular, Mari would like to thank Sam Morgan and Robby Durrant for unending love and support, and Emma Taverner and Anna Towlson for solidarity. Liz likewise to Tim Smith, Emily, James, Elliot and Sam Hallam Jones, Judy Hallam and Ian Biggerstaff, and Cathy and Richard Holmes.

SOURCES AND FURTHER READING

GENERAL

This book draws on a wide range of unpublished primary sources, particularly from the Parliamentary Archives (PA), The National Archives (TNA), British Library (BL), Westminster City Archives, London Metropolitan Archives (LMA) and the Women's Library at LSE.

Key online resources and databases include: Ancestry, Findmypast, FamilySearch, British Newspaper Archive, Times Digital Archive, *London Gazette*, Historic Hansard, UK Parliamentary Papers, *Oxford Dictionary of National Biography*, Hathi Trust, Virtual St Stephen's, History of Parliament, Museum of London, London Picture Archive, Yale Center for British Art and the Commonwealth War Graves Commission.

Other published primary sources, factbooks and biographical lists include: the Journals of the House of Commons and House of Lords, *Dod's Parliamentary Companion*, *Imperial Kalendar*, W.R. McKay, 'Clerks in the House of Commons, 1363–1989: a biographical list' (London, 1989); J.C. Sainty, 'The Parliament Office in the nineteenth and early twentieth centuries: biographical notes on clerks in the House of Lords, 1800 to 1939' (London, 1990).

Architectural histories utilised include the *History of the King's Works*; M.H. Port, ed., *The Houses of Parliament* (New Haven and London, 1976);

R. Cooke, *The Palace of Westminster* (London, 1987); D. Cannadine, ed., *The Houses of Parliament: History, Art, Architecture* (2000).

CHAPTER 1: THE CHAOTIC WORLD OF THE OLD PALACE OF WESTMINSTER: MEET THE WOMEN

There is much invaluable background material for the pre-fire era on the History of Parliament blog, available via its website, as are also the essential biographies of MPs. A. Wright and P. Smith, *Parliament Past and Present* (London [1902], available on the Internet Archive), is a copious bran tub of lively anecdotes, colourful legends and useful – if not always entirely accurate – information for this chapter and Chapter 5.

On the role of women, see M. Takayanagi, M. Unwin and P. Seaward, eds., *Voice and Vote: Celebrating 100 Years of Votes for Women* (London, 2018) with associated resources on the UK Parliament website. For the old Palace, see the architectural histories noted above – and for the fire of 1834 and much else of great value, C. Shenton, *The Day Parliament Burned Down* (Oxford, 2012). For more on the Speaker's House, see E. Hallam Smith, 'The "gothic slum", MPs and Stephen's cloister, 1548–2017', *Parliamentary History*, 41:1 (2022), pp. 279–302 at pp. 282–85. Research for that article, and for other projects on the buildings and history of the old and new Palaces, has been supported by the Houses of Parliament, the University of York and the Leverhulme Trust through an Emeritus Research Fellowship grant.

The Rickman papers are today dispersed. Some of the originals, including paintings and important letters, may be found in the Parliamentary Archives and Art Collection and in the Westminster City Archives. See the editions by Williams and Hill, and on John Rickman, O. Williams, *The Clerical Organisation of the House of Commons, 1661–1850* (Oxford, 1954), esp. pp. 93–98.

For broader context see, as well as works cited in the notes, L. Davidoff and C. Hall, *Family Fortunes*, rev. edition (London, 2002), and for example, J. McDermid, *The Schooling of Girls in Britain and Ireland* (Abingdon, 2012). For women and politics, in addition to the works cited see: K. Gleadle and S. Richardson, eds., *Women in British Politics: The Power of the Petticoat* (Basingstoke, 2000); K. Gleadle, *Borderline Citizens: Women, Gender and Political Culture in Britain, 1815–1867* (Oxford, 2009); S. Richardson, *The Political Worlds of Women: Gender and Politics in Nineteenth-century Britain* (Abingdon, 2013), pp. 130–35; and A. Galvin, 'Painting a political identity, women and the House of Commons, *c.* 1818–1834', Chapter 7 in C. Wiley and L.E. Rose, eds., *Women's Suffrage in Word, Image, Music, Stage and Screen*: *The Making of a Movement* (London, 2021).

CHAPTER 2: ELLEN MANNERS SUTTON: SCANDAL AT THE SPEAKER'S HOUSE

Lady Blessington's life, career and publications have – with good reason – attracted many biographers and some appear in the notes. For a good recent account of her salon, see S. Schmid, *British Literary Salons of the Late Eighteenth and Early Nineteenth Centuries* (London, 2013). Ellen's life is helpfully covered by Madden, but otherwise she plays a tangential part in these studies. Despite her high profile in her own day, today she is far less well known than Marguerite. Our account of Ellen's life and career has been fashioned from published and unpublished diaries, letters and memoirs, from a wealth of newspaper reports and a variety of archival and family history sources, many cited in the notes.

CHAPTER 3: WOMAN IN CHARGE: JANE JULIA BENNETT, HOUSE OF LORDS HOUSEKEEPER

Most of the evidence for this chapter derives from the *Royal Kalendars*, Parliamentary Papers, civil registration records, census returns and other archival sources. The most important, providing a wealth of interest, are Parliamentary Archives LGC/2/4 and LGC/5/3-LGC/5/8. Our material about life in the Palace during its reconstruction has been drawn together primarily from records and plans at TNA, in the series WORK 11 and WORK 29. J.C. Sainty, 'The Office of Housekeeper of the House of Lords', *Parliamentary History*, 27:2 (2008), pp. 256–60, is an important starting place. On the causes and progress of the 1834 fire, see Shenton, *The Day Parliament Burned Down*.

For context, see P. Harling, *The Modern British State: An Historical Introduction* (Oxford, 2001), pp. 53–57 and *The Waning of 'Old Corruption': The Politics of Economical Reform in Britain, 1779–1846* (Oxford, 1996) – although the parts played by women and children were of far greater interest to the radicals of their day than they have been to subsequent historians. On housekeepers in the world outside, M. Higgs, *Servants' Stories: Life Below Stairs in their Own Words* (Barnsley, 2015) has some interesting examples. For background on the sad case of Mrs Moyes: B. Weiss, *The Hell of the English: Bankruptcy and the Victorian Novel* (London, 1986) and V.M. Lester, *Victorian Insolvency: Bankruptcy, Imprisonment for Debt, and Company Winding-up in Nineteenth-Century England* (Oxford, 1995).

CHAPTER 4: CATERING FOR THE MEMBERS: JANE, GODDESS OF BELLAMY'S

There is a rich array of hitherto largely untapped sources for this chapter, some cited in the notes: archival (in the Parliamentary Archives and TNA), parliamentary papers and newspaper articles. On Bellamy's kitchen, P. Seaward's blog on the History of Parliament website is a key starting point and there is essential background in P. Salmon, 'The House of Commons, 1801–1911', pp. 249–70 in C. Jones, ed., *A Short History of Parliament* (Woodbridge, 2009), and in J.C. Sainty, 'The subordinate staff of the Serjeant at Arms, 1660–1850', pp. 395–400 in *Parliamentary History*, 25 (2006). There is also much valuable material in O. Williams, *The Clerical Organisation of the House of Commons, 1661–1850* (Oxford, 1954) and *The Officials of the House of Commons* (London, 1909). For the work and goals of the Kitchen Committee, see M.H. Port, '"The Best Club in the World"? The House of Commons, *c.*1860–1915', pp. 166–99 in *Parliamentary History*, 21 (2008).

On the complexities of nineteenth-century divorce law and separation, see M. Takayanagi, 'Jane Campbell, parliamentary divorce pioneer', History of Parliament blog (2016); plus the sources cited and the classic L. Stone, *Road to Divorce, England, 1530–1887* (Oxford, 1990). *Voice and Vote* is a valuable introduction to female suffrage, and also, from a host of recent publications, J. Robinson, *Hearts and Minds: The Untold Story of the Great Pilgrimage and How Women Won the Vote* (London, 2018).

CHAPTER 5: THE ADMIRABLE MRS GULLY AND HER GALLERY

This chapter is focused mainly on the press – and its main source is the wealth of material to be found in the newspapers, supplemented with public records: census returns, legal proceedings including divorce papers and a wide range of plans and files in WORK 11 and WORK 29. For the Victorian Speaker's House, see also Cannadine, ed., *The Houses of Parliament*, pp. 202–7. On the Ladies' Gallery see the highly informative works of Sarah Richardson, Kathryn Gleadle and Amy Galvin as noted above, Chapter 1.

CHAPTER 6: 'LOSING THEIR REASON': ELIZA ARSCOT AND HER FELLOW HOUSEKEEPERS

The stories of the House of Lords Housekeepers and housemaids can be found scattered across the enormously rich records of the Lord Great

Chamberlain at the Parliamentary Archives, supplemented by House of Lords Offices Committee reports and other material in UK Parliamentary Papers, and family history sources. Eliza Arscot's case notes are among the Hanwell Asylum records at London Metropolitan Archives. Details of Amelia de Laney's life are supplemented by research for the History of the Royal Masonic School for Girls.

The history of women and madness has been the subject of much scholarship since the pioneering feminist work of P. Chesler, *Women and Madness* (1974) and E. Showalter, *The Female Malady: Women, Madness and English Culture 1830–1980* (1985). An excellent summary of the field and how it has evolved can be found in A. Milne-Smith, 'Gender and madness in nineteenth-century Britain', *History Compass* (2022). For facts and figures on asylum admissions and details of admission to and life in lunatic asylums, L. Hide, *Gender and Class in English Asylums, 1890–1914* (2014).

CHAPTER 7: THE EVER-YOUTHFUL MISS ASHWORTH: TYPING COMES TO PARLIAMENT

The story of Miss Ashworth and her business has been painstakingly pieced together from many sources in the Parliamentary Archives, UK Parliamentary Papers, the trade press, newspapers and family history sources. Also see: M. Takayanagi, 'Ashworth, Mary Howard [May], (1863–1928)', *Oxford Dictionary of National Biography* online (Oxford, 2014). Miss Ashworth and many other women featured from this point on were initially researched for M. Takayanagi, 'Parliament and Women *c.* 1900–1945', PhD thesis (King's College London, 2012), Chapter 7, although a wealth of new material has been found since then.

For the broader context of women as typists, shorthand writers and in secretarial roles in this period: M. Zimmeck, 'Jobs for the girls: The expansion of clerical work for women, 1850–1914', in A.V. John, ed., *Unequal Opportunities: Women's Employment in England 1800–1918* (Oxford, 1986); G. Anderson, ed., *The White-Blouse Revolution: Female Office Workers Since 1870* (Manchester, 1988); R. Guerriero-Wilson, 'Women's work in offices and the preservation of men's "breadwinning" jobs in early twentieth-century Glasgow', pp. 463–82 in *Women's History Review*, 10:3 (2001); T. Davy, '"A Cissy Job for Men, a Nice Job for Girls": women shorthand typists in London 1900–1939', pp. 124–44 in L. Davidoff and B. Westover, eds., *Our Work, Our Lives, Our Words: Women's History and Women's Work* (Basingstoke, 1986).

CHAPTER 8: FOR ONE NIGHT ONLY? EMILY WILDING DAVISON IN THE CUPBOARD

This chapter draws extensively on the reports relating to Emily Wilding Davison in the Parliamentary Archives' excellent 'Police and Suffragettes' Serjeant at Arms file (HC/SA/SJ/10/12), although there is sadly no report on census night in this file. Fortunately, similar reports were made to the Office of Works, now held at TNA, including one on census night. Davison's accounts are conveniently collected in C.P. Collette, *In the Thick of the Fight: The Writing of Emily Wilding Davison, Militant Suffragette* (Ann Arbor, 2013). For the Grille Incident: C. Eustance, 'Protests from behind the grille: gender and the transformation of parliament, 1867–1918', pp. 107–26 in *Parliamentary History*, 16 (1997). Amy Galvin has contextualised the actions of Davison and the suffragettes in the Palace of Westminster as part of a wider study of women in Parliament's physical spaces, from the Ventilator attic through the Ladies' Gallery and then across the estate: A. Galvin, 'From Suffragette to citizen: Female experience of parliamentary spaces in long-nineteenth century Britain' (unpublished PhD thesis, University of Warwick, 2020). The Anderson 1911 census form was a fantastic new research discovery by Mari, building on assiduous research by Liz tracing all the employees of Ashworth's in 1921; we are grateful to Elizabeth Crawford for advice on its significance. The Anderson family history has been painstakingly pieced together using Findmypast for the British side and FamilySearch for the American side.

The suffrage literature is far too vast to adequately summarise here. Always useful is E. Crawford, *The Women's Suffrage Movement: A Reference Guide 1866–1928* (1999). For suffrage campaigners and the census, J. Liddington, *Vanishing for the Vote* (Manchester, 2014). For the Pankhursts, J. Purvis, *Emmeline Pankhurst: A Biography* (2002) and *Christabel Pankhurst: A Biography* (2018), and R. Holmes, *Sylvia Pankhurst: Natural Born Rebel* (2020). For the militant suffragettes, D. Atkinson, *Rise Up Women! The Remarkable Lives of the Suffragettes* (London, 2018). For the non-militant suffragists, J. Robinson, *Hearts and Minds*, as for Chapter 4 above. A useful introduction to the US story is: 2020 Women's Vote Centennial Initiative and St James's House, *A Vote for Women: Celebrating the Women's Suffrage Movement and the 19th Amendment* (2021).

CHAPTER 9: A WARTIME INNOVATION: THE GIRL PORTERS

The story of the Girl Porters is told in one file in the Parliamentary Archives (HC/SA/SJ/9/13/15), without which there would be no knowledge that these four young women held these wartime roles. The individuals have been traced through family history sources and the Clark family additionally through the Metropolitan and City Police Orphanage archives, still held by the charity in Putney, London.

The wider role of girl messengers in the Civil Service is referred to in contemporary accounts such as: H. Martindale, *Women Servants of the State 1870–1938: A History of Women in the Civil Service* (London, 1938); D. Evans, *Women and the Civil Service* (London, 1934). For women workers more generally: D. Thom, *Nice Girls and Rude Girls: Women Workers in World War I* (London, 1998).

CHAPTER 10: THE MONSTROUS REGIMENT: WOMEN MANAGERS IN THE LORDS

References to the Lords' managers in this chapter are scattered across various files in the Parliamentary Archives and TNA. House of Lords Offices Committee reports (published in UK Parliamentary Papers and sometimes also in Hansard) are particularly valuable in tracing employment of Lords staff including in the Accounting Department and the Refreshment Department. This has been supplemented by family history sources, newspaper articles and First World War records at TNA and the Commonwealth War Graves Commission website. Also see: M. Takayanagi, 'Court, Hannah Frances Mary [May] (1880–1945), accountant and parliamentary official', *Oxford Dictionary of National Biography* online (2018). For Elsie Bowerman: E. Crawford, 'Bowerman, Elsie Edith (1889–1973), suffragette and lawyer', *Oxford Dictionary of National Biography* online (2004).

On women in accountancy, see S.P. Walker, 'Professions and patriarchy revisited: Accountancy in England and Wales, 1887–1914', pp. 185–225 in *Accounting History Review* 21:2 (2011); J. Berney, *Celebrating 100 Years of Women in Chartered Accountancy*, 2019 [accessed via: icaew.com/100years]. For the impact of the Sex Disqualification (Removal) Act 1919 on women in professions generally, especially law, see: 'Special issue: Challenging Women', J. Bourne and C. Morris, eds., *Women's History Review*, 9:4 (2020); E. Rackley and R. Auchmuty, eds., *Women's Legal Landmarks* (London, 2018). For women in the Civil Service: M. Zimmeck, 'Strategies and stratagems for the employment of women in the British Civil Service, 1919–1939', pp. 901–24 in *Historical Journal*, 27 (1984). More generally on working women in this period: S. Todd, *Young Women, Work and Family 1918–1959* (Oxford, 2005); H. McCarthy, *Double Lives: A History of Working Motherhood* (London, 2020). On the Scottish Women's Hospitals: L. Leneman, 'Medical women at war, 1914–1918', pp. 160–77 in *Medical History*, 38:2 (1994).

CHAPTER 11: MISS BELL AND HER BELL: THE LATER HOUSEKEEPERS

As with the earlier House of Lords housekeepers and housemaids, records on Rogers and Bell can be found in the records of the Lord Great Chamberlain at the Parliamentary Archives, supplemented by House of Lords Offices Committee reports and other material in UK Parliamentary Papers, and family history sources. A stray Lords' pensions book (HL/PO/AC/6/7) was also helpful for employment details, particularly of the housemaids. The records of the House of Commons housemaids and sessional cleaners are pieced together from the correspondence of the Serjeant at Arms in the Parliamentary Archives and family history sources.

For domestic service and women workers in this period, see: L. Delap, *Knowing Their Place: Domestic Service in Twentieth-century Britain* (2011); and S. Todd, *Young Women, Work and Family 1918–1959* (2005).

CHAPTER 12: EXPERT SHOTS AND DRAGONS: PARLIAMENT AT WAR

The civil defence of the Palace of Westminster during the Second World War could be a whole book in itself. A general overview is: J. Tanfield, *In Parliament 1939–50: The Effect of War on the Palace of Westminster* (London, 1991). Also see: M. Christensen, 'The Westminster Munitions Unit', *Archive*, 79 (2013); M. Takayanagi, 'The Home Front in the "Westminster Village": women staff in Parliament during the Second World War', *Women's History Review* (2016). This chapter uses rich sources at the Parliamentary Archives including from the offices of the Lord Great Chamberlain, the Parliament Office, the Clerk of the House and the Serjeant at Arms. Individuals have been traced through family history sources including the 1939 Register via Findmypast – similar to a census, this survey was taken by the government on 29 September 1939 to ascertain the size and nature of the civilian population for the war effort.

The murder of Barbara Shuttleworth draws on the police file at TNA. For a broader contemporary narrative across Westminster: W. Sansom, *The Blitz: Westminster at War* (1947). For women and home defence: P. Summerfield and C. Peniston-Bird, *Contesting Home Defence: Men, Women and the Home Guard in the Second World War* (Manchester, 2007); C. Peniston-Bird, 'Of hockey sticks and Sten guns: British Auxiliaries and their weapons in the Second World War', *Women's History Magazine*, 76 (2014); S.R. Grayzel, *At Home and Under Fire: Air Raids and Culture in Britain from the Great War to the Blitz* (Cambridge,

2012). For women in the armed forces and the later path to combatant status: K. Sherit, *Women on the Front Line* (Stroud, 2020).

CHAPTER 13: 'GIRL CLERK IN COMMONS'!

Kay Midwinter's career through the League of Nations, Foreign Office and United Nations is described in her own words in her oral history for the UN Career Records Project at the Bodleian Library. Also see: M. Takayanagi, 'Midwinter, Kathleen Margaret [Kay] (1909–1995)', *Oxford Dictionary of National Biography* online (2014). A whole biography could be written about Monica Felton, but the only study to date focuses on her role as a town planner: M. Clapson, 'The rise and fall of Monica Felton, British town planner and peace activist, 1930s to 1950s', pp. 211–29 in *Planning Perspectives*, 30:2 (2014). Otherwise, the careers of the early women clerks have mainly been traced through Fees Office and Clerk of the House records in the Parliamentary Archives, along with family history sources and information from the family of Josephine Davson.

For women workers in the Second World War more generally: P. Summerfield, *Women Workers in the Second World War: Production and Patriarchy in Conflict* (London, 1989); P. Summerfield, *Reconstructing Women's Wartime Lives: Discourse and Subjectivity in Oral Histories of the Second World War* (Manchester, 1998); G. Braybon and P. Summerfield, *Out of the Cage: Women's Experiences in Two World Wars* (London, 1987). For women working in foreign affairs and diplomacy; H. McCarthy, *Women of the World: The Rise of the Female Diplomat* (London, 2014).

CHAPTER 14: HANSARD AND THE BATTLE FOR EQUAL PAY

The full story of Jean Winder's epic battle for equal pay is told in a voluminous Treasury file at TNA (T 221/258), supplemented by material in the Parliamentary Archives and family history sources. Portia Dadley and the House of Commons Hansard Writing Team have been tireless in their further research into and promotion of Jean Winder, and of Hansard in the Second World War more generally. You can read their work in their blogposts on the Commons Hansard blog and the Parliamentary Archives blog.

For Hansard more broadly: J. Vice and S. Farrell, *The History of Hansard* (House of Lords, 2017); W. Law, *Our Hansard or the True Mirror of Parliament* (1950). For the Parliamentary Press Gallery: A. Sparrow, *Obscure Scribblers:*

A History of Parliamentary Journalism (London, 2003). For more on issues such as the marriage bar and equal pay: H. Jones, *Women in British Public Life, 1914–50: Gender, Power and Social Policy* (Harlow, 2000); H. Glew, *Gender, Rhetoric and Regulation: Women's Work in the Civil Service and the London County Council, 1900–55* (Manchester, 2016).

CHAPTER 15: THE STRAIN OF CARRYING LADDERS: THE LIBRARY AND ARCHIVES

Roseanne O'Reilly, Mary Frampton and Pat Lugard-Brayne (née Brandt) are the three women among eighteen oral histories of House of Commons staff recorded by Gloria Tyler and now in the British Library. On the Commons Library: D. Menhennet, *The House of Commons Library: A History*, House of Commons Library Document no. 21 (2nd edition, 2000); O. Gay, 'Slumber and Success: The House of Commons Library after May', pp. 33–44 in P. Evans, ed., *Essays on the History of Parliamentary Procedure in Honour of Thomas Erskine May* (London, 2017). Early Commons staff employment details come from the Parliamentary Archives Fees Office file, HC/FA/FO/1/171. For women and librarianship, see: E. Kerslake, 'A history of women workers in English libraries, 1871–1974' (PhD thesis, Loughborough University, 1999). On payment of MPs: R. Kelly, 'Members pay and allowances: A brief history', House of Commons Library Standard Note SN/PC/05075 (2009).

The work and staff of the House of Lords Record Office, now the Parliamentary Archives, can best be traced through its published annual reports. Information on Poyser's life beyond Parliament is kindly supplied by Newnham College Archives and Westminster Diocesan Archives. On women peers: see D. Sutherland, 'Peeresses, parliament, and prejudice: the admission of women to the House of Lords, 1918–1963', *Parliaments, Estates and Representation*, 20 (2000). For the development of the archival profession and the role of women: E. Shepherd, *Archives and Archivists in 20th-century England* (London, 2009); E. Shepherd, 'Hidden voices in the archives: pioneering women archivists in 20th-century England', pp. 83–104 in E. Foscarini, H. MacNeil, B. Mak and G. Oliver, eds., *Engaging with Records and Archives: Histories and Theories* (London, 2016).

NOTES

CHAPTER 1: THE CHAOTIC WORLD OF THE OLD PALACE OF WESTMINSTER: MEET THE WOMEN

1. J. Pearson, *Pearson's Political Dictionary* (London, 1792), pp. 15, 25, 37–38.
2. The National Archives (hereafter TNA), PROB 18/102/44; PROB 11/1446/54.
3. T. Allen, *The History and Antiquities of London, Southwark, etc.*, vol. 4 (London, 1829), pp. 202–03.
4. *Pearson's Political Dictionary*, pp. 6, 19, 31; *Gentleman's Magazine*, 59/1 (1789), p. 279.
5. TNA, AO 1/2468/208, AO 1/2470/215; Parliamentary Archives (hereafter PA), HL/PO/CO/1/12; HL/PO/JO/10/5/86.
6. PA, LGC/5/5, no. 38, return of persons resident in the House of Lords, 1832; TNA, WORK 11/26/5, claims for compensation after the fire of 1834.
7. O. Williams, *Lamb's Friend the Census Taker: Life and Letters of John Rickman* (London, 1912), pp. 77, 116.
8. C. Hill, *Good Company in Old Westminster and the Temple* (London, 1925), pp. 22–23.
9. Williams, *Lamb's Friend the Census Taker*, pp. 121–22.
10. M.E. Palgrave, 'The Ladies' gallery of the old House of Commons', *The Leisure Hour*, 48 (June 1899), pp. 491–95 at p. 495.
11. Hill, *Good Company in Old Westminster and the Temple*, pp. 88–99.
12. S.D. Smith, *Slavery, Family and Gentry Capitalism in the British Atlantic: The World of the Lascelles, 1648–1834* (Cambridge, 2006), pp. 271–75; and University College London, British Slave-Owners' Database online, under Gibbes.
13. M. Tremellen, '"A palace within a Palace": The Speaker's House at Westminster, 1794–1834', PhD dissertation, University of York (forthcoming) citing William Wilberforce's diary.
14. Hill, *Good Company in Old Westminster and the Temple*, pp. 7–8.
15. Ibid., pp. 8–9.

16. E. Hallam Smith, 'Ventilating the Commons, Heating the Lords', *Parliamentary History*, 38:1 (2019), pp. 74–102 at pp. 93–94.
17. J. Grant, *Random Recollections of the House of Commons* (London, 1836), pp. 17–18.
18. S. Richardson, 'Parliament as viewed through a woman's eyes: gender and space in the 19th-century Commons', *Parliamentary History*, 38:1 (2019), pp. 119–34 at pp. 120–25.
19. PA, RIC/1, printed in C. Shenton, *The Day Parliament Burned Down* (Oxford, 2012), pp. 208–11.
20. Williams, *Lamb's Friend the Census Taker*, p. 312; PA, HL/PO/LB/1/2/1.
21. PA, RIC/3.

CHAPTER 2: ELLEN MANNERS SUTTON: SCANDAL AT THE SPEAKER'S HOUSE

1. Quoted by M. Sadleir, *Blessington-d'Orsay, a Masquerade* (London, 1933), pp. 136–37. In fact, Manners Sutton had only one daughter at this time, Charlotte (born in 1815).
2. R. Madden, *The Literary Life and Correspondence of the Countess of Blessington*, 3 vols (London, 1855), i, p. 377.
3. P.W. Wilson, ed., *The Greville Diary*, i (London, 1927), pp. 486–87.
4. C. Dickens, ed., *The Life of Charles James Mathews; Chiefly Autobiographical, with Selections from his Correspondence and Speeches*, i (London, 1879), pp. 80–81, 86; Balliol College Oxford Archives, box 22, VB1, letters from Charles Manners Sutton to the Rev Henry Jenkyns, 27 September and 4 October 1824.
5. Madden, *Literary Life*, i, p. 379.
6. TNA, FO 5/206, f. 175.
7. TNA, LC 11/38, ff. 52d–53.
8. E.B. Chancellor, ed., *The Diary of Philipp von Neumann*, i (London, 1928), pp. 194–95.
9. Lord John Russell, ed., *The Memoirs, Journals and Correspondence of Thomas Moore*, vi (London, 1854), pp. 13, 23.
10. F. Bamford and the Duke of Wellington, ed., *The Journal of Mrs Arbuthnot, 1820–1832*, ii (London, 1950), p. 306.
11. *The Greville Diary*, i, pp. 486–87.
12. Quoted by W.H. Scheuerle, 'Gardiner, Marguerite, Countess of Blessington (1789–1849)', *Oxford Dictionary of National Biography* online, 2004.
13. Bell's *New Weekly Messenger*, 25 August 1833, p. 14.
14. *Evening Mail*, 26 July 1830, p. 2.
15. *Morning Post*, 27 February 1833, p. 3.
16. Quoted by D.R. Fisher, ed., 'Manners Sutton, Charles (1780–1845)', *The History of Parliament: House of Commons 1820–1832* online, 2009.
17. PA, HO/SO/1/6.
18. *The News* (London), 26 October 1834, p. 2; *The Globe*, 30 October 1834, p. 4.
19. Bell's *New Weekly Messenger*, 26 October 1834, p. 5.
20. PA, RIC/3.
21. *London Evening Standard*, 14 November 1834, p. 3.
22. *Leeds Times*, 14 February 1835, p. 2.
23. *Tipperary Free Press*, 15 April 1835, p. 3.
24. E.g. *Perthshire Constitutional & Journal*, 31 July 1835, p. 1.
25. *Morning Post*, 29 August 1835, p. 3.

26. TNA, PROB 37/1350, 31 October and 28 December 1842.
27. Madden, *Literary Life*, i, p. 235.
28. Ibid., ii, p. 115.

CHAPTER 3: WOMAN IN CHARGE: JANE JULIA BENNETT, HOUSE OF LORDS HOUSEKEEPER

1. W.D. Rubinstein, 'The End of "Old Corruption" in Britain, 1780–1860', *Past and Present*, 101 (1983), pp. 55–86 at p. 61, n.8.
2. *Report of Select Committee on Establishment of the House of Commons*, HC 648 (1833), pp. 8–9.
3. Quoted by P. Harling, *The Waning of 'Old Corruption': The Politics of Economical Reform in Britain, 1779–1846* (Oxford, 1996), p. 114.
4. J. Wade, *The Extraordinary Black Book: An Exposition of Abuses in Church and State* (London, 1832), pp. 488–89.
5. *The Globe*, 25 April 1833, p. 2.
6. TNA, LC 3/68, p. 149.
7. Warwickshire County Record Office, CR114A/64, no. 14; CR114A/71, no. 20; G.E. Saville, ed., *Alcester: A History* (Studley, 1986), pp. 31, 49.
8. For a full list see J.C. Sainty, 'The Office of Housekeeper of the House of Lords', *Parliamentary History*, 27:2 (2008), pp. 256–60.
9. *Royal Kalendar*, 1818, p. 48; 1821, p. 46; 1822, p. 46 and civil registration records.
10. E.g., TNA, LC 11/26, quarter ending 5 January 1819; LC 11/33, no. 258, 1821; PA, LGC/2/4, pp. 293–97; PA, LGC/5/5, no. 38; Soane Museum, London, Private Correspondence XI.d.8, 21 February 1824.
11. *Oxford English Dictionary* online.
12. *Report of the Lords of the Council respecting the destruction by fire of the two Houses of Parliament*, HC 1 (1835), esp. pp. 29–32.
13. *Report ... Respecting the Destruction by Fire*, pp. 6, 10, 29–32.
14. TNA, WORK 11/26/5; WORK 1/21, pp. 298–300, 338–39.
15. *Report from the Select Committee on the Losses of the Late Speaker and Officers of the House by Fire*, HC 493 (1837), p. 20.
16. PA, LGC/5/4 no. 37.
17. *Morning Advertiser*, 24 April 1847, p. 1; *London Evening Standard*, 26 April 1847, p. 3.
18. PA, LGC/5/4, no. 37.
19. TNA, WORK 6/256.
20. TNA, WORK 6/280.
21. TNA, B 6/178, no. 1433; *Morning Post*, 11 December 1872, p. 7.
22. TNA, WORK 11/61, 5, 9 July 1873, 31 January 1878; PA, LGC/5/7, nos 9b, 10b, 22b.
23. PA, LGC/5/8, nos 96d, 128b, 130b-c; LGC/5/11/2, no. 176a; *Second Report from the Select Committee on the Office of the Clerk of the Parliaments*, HL 166 (1876), pp. 1–3.
24. *Third Report from the Select Committee on the Office of the Clerk of the Parliaments*, HL 191 (1877), p. 1.
25. *The Globe*, 8 February 1867, p. 3.
26. B. Hill, *Servants: English Domestics in the Eighteenth Century* (Oxford, 1996), pp. 41–42; P. Horn, *The Rise and Fall of the Victorian Servant* (Gloucester, 1986).
27. Served 1722–41: TNA AO 1/2451/157; AO 1/2457/176; see also J.C. Sainty, 'The subordinate staff of the Serjeant-at-Arms, 1660–1850', *Parliamentary History*, 25 (2006), pp. 395–400 at pp. 397–99.

CHAPTER 4: CATERING FOR THE MEMBERS: JANE, GODDESS OF BELLAMY'S

1. *Evening Chronicle*, 11 April 1835, p. 3; *Illustrated London News*, 13 August 1853, p. 2.
2. *Select Committee on Establishment of House of Commons*, HC 648 (1833), pp. 99, 245.
3. PA, HC/SA/SJ/3/18; TNA, PROB 10/7437/11, WORK 11/26/5; census returns 1841–61; *Select Committee on Establishment of House of Commons*, p. 187.
4. *Devizes and Wiltshire Gazette*, 17 February 1825, p. 4; and 26 March 1829, p. 4, citing the *New Monthly Magazine*.
5. Quoted by P. Seaward, 'Bellamy's', *Reformation to Referendum: Writing a New History of Parliament Project Blog*, History of Parliament online, 2020.
6. Bell's *New Weekly Messenger*, 2 November 1834, p. 4.
7. *Chartist Circular*, 6 June 1840, p. 3.
8. *The Globe*, 5 April 1850, p. 3.
9. PA, HC/CL/CO/EA/1/11, 17, 18 April, 2, 4, 19 May 1848.
10. PA, GRE/1/5, 1 June 1848.
11. TNA, WORK 11/17/13.
12. *Hereford Journal*, 14 March 1849, p. 5; *Clonmel Chronicle*, 24 August 1850, p. 4; Bell's *New Weekly Messenger*, 15 February 1852, p. 4; *Fourth Report from the Select Committee on the Kitchen and Refreshment Rooms (House of Commons)*, HC 448 (1863), p. iii.
13. TNA, WORK 11/9/7, 21 March 1851; *Illustrated London News*, 13 August 1853, p. 2; *Illustrated Times*, 17 July 1858, p. 14.
14. *Illustrated London News*, 4 February 1854, pp. 21, 27.
15. TNA, WORK 6/259, 265, 268, 274.
16. TNA, J 77/126/2494; H.R.B. Coney, *The Family of William and Hannah Bladon of Ingestre and Weston, Staffordshire* (Derbyshire, 2017), pp. 9–11.
17. R. Probert, *Divorced, Bigamist, Bereaved?* (Kenilworth, 2015), pp. 27–46, 80–81; O. Anderson, 'Civil society and separation in Victorian marriage', *Past and Present*, 163 (1999), pp. 161–201.
18. PA, LGC/5/7, no. 51b.
19. PA, LGC/5/11/1, no. 60.
20. *HC Debates*, 3rd series, vol. 121, cc. 432–4, 10 May 1852.
21. M. Takayanagi, M. Unwin and P. Seaward, eds., *Voice and Vote: Celebrating 100 Years of Votes for Women* (London, 2018), pp. 76–77.
22. A.B. Murphy and D. Raftery, eds., *Emily Davies: Collected Letters, 1861–75* (Charlottesville, 2004), p. xxxvi.
23. PA, LGC/5/7 nos 6d, 19c–f.
24. Information from the Furlong family.

CHAPTER 5: THE ADMIRABLE MRS GULLY AND HER GALLERY

1. *Westminster Gazette*, 15 November 1906, p. 9; *The Daily Telegraph*, 16 November 1906, p. 9.
2. PA, HC/SO/7/4.
3. *Sheffield Daily Telegraph*, 19 June 1895, p. 4; *Northern Guardian* (Hartlepool), 20 June 1895, p. 3; PA, HC/SO/7/6.
4. *Carlisle Journal*, 25 June 1895, p. 3.

5. *Edinburgh Evening News*, 11 April 1895, p. 2.
6. A. Kinnear, *Our House of Commons, its Realities and Romance* (London, 1901), pp. 207–08.
7. Ibid., p. 212.
8. Cambridge University Library, Add MS 8912/9; *Star of Gwent*, 9 May 1902, p. 5.
9. TNA, WORK 11/87.
10. *Dover Express*, 19 July 1895, p. 7.
11. Discussed and quoted by G. Sutherland, *In Search of the New Woman: Middle-Class Women and Work in Britain 1870–1914* (Cambridge, 2015), p. 1.
12. G. Anderson, ed., *The White-Blouse Revolution: Female Office Workers since 1870* (Manchester, 1988), pp. 20–21.
13. *Western Times*, 17 April 1899, p. 3.
14. *Dundee Evening Telegraph*, 18 May 1895, p. 2.
15. *Tablet*, 1 January 1859, p. 7; *Liverpool Mercury*, 29 March 1859, p. 7.
16. *London Evening Standard*, 21 July 1898, p. 3.
17. *Glasgow Herald*, 11 January 1899, p. 6.
18. M.E. Palgrave, 'The Ladies' Gallery of the old House of Commons', *The Leisure Hour*, 48 (June 1899), pp. 491–95 at p. 495 and 'The coronation of Queen Victoria', *The Girls' Own Paper*, 23 (1901–02), pp. 345–47 at p. 347.
19. *Daily News* (London), 17 October 1921, p. 4.
20. Ida B. Wells, *Crusade for Justice: The Autobiography of Ida B. Wells*, 2nd edition (Chicago, 2020), pp. 174–75.
21. *The Globe*, 24 March 1910, p. 1.
22. *Express* (London), 11 June 1868, p. 2.
23. *Huddersfield Daily Examiner*, 7 June 1888, p. 3.
24. *Coventry Evening Telegraph*, 2 May 1895, pp. 2, 4.
25. *North Devon Gazette*, 29 March 1898, p. 3.
26. R. Temple, *The House of Commons* (London, 1899), p. 21.
27. *The Queen*, 25 February 1893, p. 28; *Parliament Past and Present*, p. 92.
28. *London Evening Standard*, 25 January 1913, p. 11; TNA, WORK 11/176.
29. *The Times*, 16 November 1906, p. 8 and 21 November 1906, p. 4; *Daily Telegraph and Courier* (London), 1 July 1899, p. 6; Cambridge University Library, Add MS 8912/37-8, 42 (i)–(ii).
30. *Sheffield Independent*, 7 August 1878, p. 2; *Wells Journal*, 21 June 1900, p. 2; *Hampshire Telegraph*, 15 February 1882, p. 4.
31. *Parliament Past and Present*, pp. 61–62, 92–94.
32. TNA, J 77/892/7071, J 77/892/7086.
33. O. Salkeld, *Daisy's Diary: A Honeymoon Journey to the Far East*, ed. D. Mortimer (Kendal, 1993), pp. 7, 12, 105–06.
34. OPCS, *Marriage and Divorce Statistics* (London, 1990), p. 114.
35. *Oxfordshire Weekly News*, 4 March 1908, p. 2.
36. TNA, J 15/2797, no. 4542; J 15/2844, no. 2026.
37. *The Times*, 21 March 1908, p. 3.
38. TNA, J 77/961/9176.
39. *The Daily Telegraph*, 16 November 1906, p. 9; *The Times*, 21 November 1906, p. 4; *Birmingham Daily Gazette*, 16 November 1906, p. 4.
40. *Dublin Daily Express*, 8 November 1909, p. 10.
41. *Morning Post*, 11 November 1909, p. 7.

CHAPTER 6: 'LOSING THEIR REASON': ELIZA ARSCOT AND HER FELLOW HOUSEKEEPERS

1. London Metropolitan Archives (hereafter LMA), H11/HLL/B/19/072.
2. TNA, WORK 11/61.
3. *HC Debates*, 4th series, vol. 36, c. 598, 22 August 1895.
4. PA, LGC/5/9, nos 94a–b.
5. PA, LGC/5/9, no. 14.
6. LGC/5/11/1, no. 37b.
7. LGC/5/11/2, no. 258; LGC/5/14/2, no. 84; *Parliament Office 2nd Report*, HL 37 (1887), pp. 5–7.
8. LGC/5/13/3, no. 113.
9. *HL Debates*, 4th series, vol. 46, cc. 370–821, 5 February 1897; PA, LGC/5/15/1, nos 165–66.
10. *House of Lords Offices Committee 1st Report*, HL 9 (1896), p. 4.
11. TNA, WORK 11/61; PA, LGC/15/1.
12. TNA, WORK 11/61, letter dated 24 April 1896.
13. Her birthplace is variously recorded as Calstock and Gunnislake, only 2 miles apart in Cornwall, although her family mainly lived in Devon.
14. PA, LGC/15/1.
15. PA, LGC/2/17. Lady Hope is not further identified but may have been temperance advocate Elizabeth Cotton.
16. PA, LGC/15/1, LGC/15/2.
17. PA, LGC/16/2.
18. Ibid.
19. PA, LGC/2/17.
20. LMA, H11/HLL/B/05/021.
21. LMA, H11/HLL/B/19/50, H11/HLL/B/19/072.
22. LMA, H11/HLL/B/19/072.
23. TNA, WORK 11/61, note dated 14 March 1902.
24. *The New York Times*, 31 August 1902.
25. PA, HL/PO/AC/15/11.
26. PA, LGC/5/20/1.
27. TNA, WORK 11/61.
28. PA, LGC/2/19. Butler to the Lord Great Chamberlain, 29 November 1913.
29. Ibid., 11 December 1913.
30. PA, LGC/2/19. Lord Great Chamberlain to Wedgwood Benn, 12 January 1914.
31. Ibid., Butler to the Lord Great Chamberlain, 2 March 1914.
32. History of the Royal Masonic School for Girls blog (rmsghistoryextra.wordpress.com/tag/amelia-de-laney/).
33. PA, LGC/2/20. Butler to the Lord Great Chamberlain, 24 November 1919.
34. PA, LGC/2/18. Butler to the Lord Great Chamberlain, 18 March 1908.
35. *House of Lords Offices Committee 4th Report*, HL 150 (1919).

CHAPTER 7: THE EVER-YOUTHFUL MISS ASHWORTH: TYPING COMES TO PARLIAMENT

1. *Woman's Life*, quoted in G. Eley, *The Ruined Maid: Modes and Manners of Victorian Women* (Royston, 1970).

2. *Phonographer and Typist*, 7 April 1895, p. 83.
3. M. Zimmeck, 'Jobs for the girls: The expansion of clerical work for women, 1850–1918', pp. 153–77 in A.V. John, ed., *Unequal Opportunities: Women's Employment in England 1800–1914* (Oxford, 1986).
4. *The London Phonographer*, vol. 1, no. 4, September 1891.
5. *HC Debates*, 3rd series, vol. 303, c. 512 and c. 518, 11 March 1886.
6. *Select Committee on House of Commons (Accommodation)*, HC 268 (1894).
7. *HC Debates*, 4th series, vol. 32, c. 474, 29 March 1895.
8. *Phonographer and Typist*, April 1895, p. 83.
9. T. Davy, '"Cissy Job for Men, a Nice Job for Girls": women shorthand typists in London 1900–1939', pp. 124–44 in L. Davidoff and B. Westover, eds., *Our Work, Our Lives, Our Words: Women's History and Women's Work* (Basingstoke, 1986).
10. D.A. Green, 'The wonderful woman indexer of England: Nancy Bailey', *The Indexer*, 32:4 (2014), pp. 155–60.
11. M. Bateson, *Professional Women upon their Professions* (London, 1895).
12. *Phonographer and Typist*, May 1895, p. 85.
13. PA, HC/SA/SJ/1/2, p. 186, 2 September 1895.
14. *Woman's Life*, quoted in Eley, *The Ruined Maid*.
15. *Dundee Courier*, 11 April 1898.
16. *Wigton Advertiser*, 15 December 1900.
17. *Sixty-third Annual Report of the Registrar-General of Births, Deaths, and Marriages in England*, Cd. 761 (1901), p. xii. To be precise, the mean age for bachelors was 26.68 and 25.23 for spinsters.
18. Personal communication with family, 2016.
19. PA, HC/SA/SJ/1/2, 19 September 1904.
20. TNA, WO 339/75234.
21. PA, HC/SA/SJ/8/2, piece 33.
22. TNA, J 77/1555/8175.
23. TNA, J 77/1644/1084.
24. For more on the Andersons, see Chapter 8.
25. M. Heller, *London Clerical Workers, 1880–1914: Development of the Labour Market* (London, 2011).
26. The Past and Present of Croydon's London Road website (london-road-croydon.org/history/0163-zodiac-court-part-2.html).
27. V. Allen, *Hall Caine: Portrait of a Victorian Romancer* (Sheffield, 1997).
28. PA, HC/SJ/SA/8/3, piece 49.
29. Ibid., piece 65.
30. M. Roodhouse, 'The politics of business & the business of politics: Messrs Watney & Powell and the emergence of the consultant lobbyist in Britain, 1911–1993, Part I: OMNIACTIVE: Charles Watney and the St Stephen's Intelligence Bureau, 1911–1930', Parliamentary History seminar paper, January 2022.
31. LSE, Women's Library, 6/NCS/2/C/5.
32. LSE, Women's Library, 6/NCS/2/D/09/03.
33. W. Law, *Our Hansard or the True Mirror of Parliament* (London, 1950), p. 35.
34. Law, *Our Hansard*, pp. 3–4.
35. PA, HC/SO/2/16.
36. PA, HC/SA/SJ/13/9.
37. PA, HC/SA/SJ/9/31.

38. British Group of the Inter Parliamentary Union Executive Committee minutes, 10 July 1975, referring to accommodation arrangements for joint services of Parliament in 1965. Courtesy of Rick Nimmo.

CHAPTER 8: FOR ONE NIGHT ONLY? EMILY WILDING DAVISON IN THE CUPBOARD

1. *HC Debates*, 5th series, vol. 23, c. 1814, 3 April 1911.
2. TNA, RG 14/489.
3. A. Galvin, 'From suffragette to citizen: Female experience of Parliamentary spaces in long-nineteenth century Britain' (unpublished PhD thesis, University of Warwick, 2020).
4. PA, HC/SA/SJ/10/13/36.
5. PA, HC/SA/SJ/10/12/63.
6. *HC Debates*, 4th series, vol. 194, c. 243, 13 October 1908.
7. PA, HC/SA/SJ/10/12/28.
8. PA, LGC/2/19.
9. PA, HC/SA/SJ/10/12/15.
10. 'Twenty-eight hours in a hot air shaft', *Votes for Women*, 8 April 1910. Printed in C.P. Collette, *In the Thick of the Fight: The Writing of Emily Wilding Davison, Militant Suffragette* (Ann Arbor, 2013), pp. 62–67.
11. Collette, *In the Thick of the Fight*, pp. 62–67.
12. PA, HC/SA/SJ/10/12/26.
13. PA, HC/SA/SJ/10/12/27.
14. PA, HC/SA/SJ/10/12/27A.
15. PA, HC/SA/SJ/10/12/32.
16. PA, HC/SA/SJ/10/12/35.
17. J. Liddington, *Vanishing for the Vote* (Manchester, 2014).
18. TNA, WORK 11/178, Metropolitan police report, 3 April 1911.
19. 'A night in Guy Fawkes' cupboard', *Votes for Women*, 7 April 1911. Printed in Collette, *In the Thick of the Fight*, pp. 62–67.
20. TNA, WORK 11/178, Metropolitan Police report, 3 April 1911.
21. PA, HC/SA/SJ/10/12/36.
22. 'Suffragist in the House', *Votes for Women*, 30 June 1911. Printed in Collette, *In the Thick of the Fight*, pp. 62–67.
23. For more on Amelia de Laney, see Chapter 6.
24. *Select Committee on the House of Commons (Kitchen and Refreshment Rooms)*, HC 98 (1916).
25. PA, HC/CL/CO/EA/2/8.
26. Ibid.
27. Lettice Fisher went on to found the National Council for the Unmarried Mother and her Child in 1918. C. Moyse, 'Fisher [née Ilbert], Lettice', *Oxford Dictionary of National Biography* online (2004).
28. S. Anderson-Faithful, *Mary Sumner, Mission, Education and Motherhood: Thinking a Life with Bourdieu* (Cambridge, 2018).
29. *Select Committee on the House of Commons (Kitchen and Refreshment Rooms)*, HC 98 (1916).
30. TNA, WORK 11/227; LSE Women's Library, 2LSW/E/03/7.
31. PA, HC/SA/SJ/10/12/66.
32. Tony Benn spoke about his intention to do it in 1988 and referred to it twice afterwards. *HC Debates*, 6th series, vol. 136, c. 1241, 7 July 1988; vol. 191, c. 550, 17 May 1991; vol. 365, c. 510, 22 March 2001.

33. *The Sun*, 7 February 2018.

CHAPTER 9: A WARTIME INNOVATION: THE GIRL PORTERS

1. PA, HC/SA/SJ/9/13/15.
2. Ibid.
3. H. Martindale, *Women Servants of the State: 1870–1938: A History of Women in the Civil Service* (London, 1938).
4. LSE, BOOTH/B/363, p. 193; BOOTH/B/365, p. 59.
5. Children's Homes website (www.childrenshomes.org.uk/TwickenhamPolice/); Metropolitan & City Orphans Fund website (www.met-cityorphans.org.uk).
6. Metropolitan and City Police Orphanage archives, London: Divisional register of widows receiving compassionate allowances, undated; Register of candidates, 1910–1924; annual reports, 1914–1924; correspondence on Australia, *c.* 1922–1924. Jack Clark emigrated to Australia at the age of 14 and died there in 1969, aged 59.
7. *HC Debates*, 5th series, vol. 110, cc. 1461–514, 30 October 1918.
8. Metropolitan and City Police Orphanage archives, annual report, 1918.
9. PA, HC/SA/SJ/9/13/15.

CHAPTER 10: THE MONSTROUS REGIMENT: WOMEN MANAGERS IN THE LORDS

1. *Western Daily Press*, 15 December 1926; *Aberdeen Journal*, 13 December 1926.
2. A.V. John, *Turning the Tide: The Life of Lady Rhondda* (Cardigan, 2013).
3. *HC Debates*, 3rd series, vol. 153, cc. 1587–91, 8 April 1859.
4. TNA, WO 339/14175.
5. TNA, WO 372/5; PA, HL/PO/CO/1/418.
6. *Aberdeen Journal*, 13 December 1926.
7. PA, HL/PO/AC/15/43.
8. J. Berney, *Celebrating 100 Years of Women in Chartered Accountancy* (2019), icaew.com/100years.
9. TNA, T 162/282.
10. *Norwood News*, 15 May 1936.
11. PA, HL/PO/CO/1/574.
12. *Aberdeen Journal*, 28 December 1917.
13. C.E. Hallett, *Veiled Warriors: Allied Nurses of the First World War* (Oxford, 2014), p. 39.
14. Among other achievements of Bowerman was being one of the earliest women barristers in England (and the first woman to appear at the Old Bailey) and being Secretary General and Acting Chief of the United Nations Commission on the Status of Women in 1947.
15. TuckDB Postcards website (tuckdbpostcards.org/items/49317). They may also have connected through other women's organisations; Jane Brown restaurant advertised luncheons and tea during a conference of the National Union of Societies for Equal Citizenship in 1933. *Woman's Leader and Common Cause*, 1 March 1933.
16. *Aberdeen People's Journal*, 2 September 1939.
17. Historic England website (historicengland.org.uk/listing/the-list/list-entry/1043174).
18. Encyclopedia Titanica (www.encyclopedia-titanica.org/elsie-bowerman.html).
19. *Aberdeen People's Journal*, 2 September 1939.
20. Ibid.

21. PA, HL/PO/CO/1/574.
22. *Radio Times*, 16 September 1939.
23. PA, HL/PO/CO/1/574; PA, LGC/10/3/16.
24. *HL Debates*, 5th series, vol. 199, c. 787, 13 September 1956.
25. PA, HL/PO/CO/1/606.

CHAPTER 11: MISS BELL AND HER BELL: THE LATER HOUSEKEEPERS

1. L. Delap, *Knowing Their Place: Domestic Service in Twentieth-Century Britain* (Oxford, 2011), p. 15.
2. TNA, WORK 11/87.
3. PA, HC/SA/SJ/1/4.
4. PA, HC/SA/SJ/1/2.
5. TNA, T 162/550.
6. PA, LGC/2/20.
7. PA, LGC/2/20, letters dated 23 January 1922, 8 August 1922, 1 December 1923, 9 September 1924. TNA, WORK 11/241.
8. PA, LGC/5/21/1.
9. Ibid.
10. PA, LGC/2/20, Butler to the Lord Great Chamberlain, 24 November 1919.
11. Although Elizabeth Gibbons left soon afterwards in 1920, this was after twenty-one years' service, and Caroline Leslie stayed until 1924 by which time she was Head Housemaid.
12. PA, LGC/5/23/2.
13. PA, LGC/5/24/1.
14. Ibid.
15. *House of Lords Offices Committee 1st report*, HL9 (1942); PA, HL/PO/CO/1/574.

CHAPTER 12: EXPERT SHOTS AND DRAGONS: PARLIAMENT AT WAR

1. J. Tanfield, *In Parliament 1939–50: The Effect of War on the Palace of Westminster* (London, 1991).
2. Ibid.
3. PA, HC/SA/SJ/13/10.
4. For more on Ellen Baylis, see Chapter 14.
5. PA, LGC/10/3/7.
6. PA, LGC/10/3/20.
7. Tanfield, *In Parliament 1939–50*, p. 38.
8. PA, LGC/10/3/9, J.D. Waters to F.G. Inch, 18 September 1939.
9. Ibid., Inch to Waters, 22 September 1939.
10. Ibid., 12 December 1939. Elsan Closets were early portable toilets.
11. Ibid., 8 September 1939.
12. Ibid., 22 September 1939.
13. Ibid., H.R. Foyle, Treasury, to Waters, 16 October 1939.
14. TNA, WO 372/23/3072.
15. *Aberdeen Evening Express*, 10 October 1959.
16. Tanfield, *In Parliament 1939–50*, p. 13.
17. TNA, HO 207/69.

18. TNA, MEPO 3/1900. The Commissioner did not blame the Parliamentary officials, writing that it was 'just a real piece of bad luck which might have occurred anywhere, for I lost quite a number of policemen that night'.

19. W. Sansom, *The Blitz: Westminster at War* (1947, reprinted Oxford, 1990).

20. The Firefighters Memorial Trust website (www.firefightersmemorial.org.uk/research/fire-watchers-and-fire-guards/).

21. PA, HL/PO/2/12.

22. PA, HL/PO/2/17.

23. *HC Debates*, 5th series, vol. 385, cc. 735–827, 25 November 1942.

24. M. Takayanagi, '"They Have Made Their Mark Entirely Out of Proportion to Their Numbers": Women and Parliamentary Committees, c.1918–1945', pp. 181–202 in J.V. Gottlieb and R. Toye, eds., *The Aftermath of Suffrage: Women, Gender, and Politics in Britain, 1918–1945* (Basingstoke, 2013).

25. PA, LGC/10/3/20. Among the Fire Watchers were the Home Guard auxiliaries Ward, Bebbington, Shuttleworth and Matthew, of which more anon.

26. PA, HC/CL/CH/3.

27. P. Summerfield and C. Peniston-Bird, *Contesting Home Defence: Men, Women and the Home Guard in the Second World War* (Manchester, 2007).

28. *HC Debates*, 5th series, vol. 365, cc. 1928–1932, 19 November 1940.

29. TNA, WO 32/9423.

30. TNA, CAB 123/205.

31. PA, HC/CL/CH/3/10.

32. Summerfield and Peniston-Bird, *Contesting Home Defence*.

33. M. Roodhouse, 'The politics of business & the business of politics', Parliamentary History seminar, January 2022.

34. 'Vera Heslop and working for MPs', *International Woman Suffrage News*, 4 September 1942, p. 212.

35. Ibid.

36. *The Times*, 12 May 1961.

37. It seems likely that John Ughtred Thornton Shuttleworth was distantly related to his contemporary, Sir Ughtred Kay-Shuttleworth, 1st Baron Shuttleworth (1844–1939), Liberal MP, but the relationship has not been determined.

38. TNA, MEPO 3/3019, Lupton's witness statement.

39. TNA, MEPO 3/3019, Bebbington's witness statement.

40. M.J. Buchanan-Dunne, 'The "Lover's" Death Pact', *Murder Mile UK True-Crime Podcast*, 86, March 2020.

41. TNA, MEPO 3/3019. Symes is known for his role in the conviction of serial killer John Haigh, the 'Acid Bath Murderer', in 1949.

42. TNA, MEPO 3/3019. Sterba had applied for a divorce, but in his will he left everything to his wife including £67,000 and their house in Poland.

43. PA, HC/CL/CH/4/1.

44. Including Ward, Bebbington, Shuttleworth and Matthew, and also Kay Midwinter, first woman clerk. For more on Midwinter see Chapter 13.

45. PA, HC/CL/CH/4/1. The woman quoted is a Miss A. Belfield. She appears to have been a friend of a member of staff in Parliament.

46. M. Christensen, 'The Westminster Munitions Unit', *Archive*, 79 (2013).

47. PA, HC/CL/CH/4/5.

48. PA, HC/CL/CH/4/5. Dorothy Bertha Jeffreys was a violinist, married to Anthony Henry Jeffreys, a Clerk in the House of Lords.

49. PA, WMU/1/1, Lady Sinclair, 'Flying Bombs … & Flowers', *The Star*, 27 June 1944.

50. S.M. Horrocks, 'Pyke, Magnus Alfred (1908–1992), food scientist, author, and broadcaster', *Oxford Dictionary of National Biography* online (2004).
51. J. Berney, *Celebrating 100 Years of Women in Chartered Accountancy* (2019), icaew.com/100years
52. PA, HC/CL/CH/4/4. Hopkinson also praised Mrs Trollope, the cook: 'My experience is that if a man is well fed you can do anything with him, they are susceptible to good food, and Mrs Trollope has done wonders.'
53. PA, LGC/10/3/16.
54. PA, LGC/10/3/19.
55. For more on Davison, see Chapter 13.

CHAPTER 13: 'GIRL CLERK IN COMMONS'!

1. *Evening Standard*, 1 May 1940.
2. For example, Frances Stevenson, Private Secretary to David Lloyd George; Edith M. Watson, Private Secretary to Andrew Bonar Law; Rose Rosenberg, Private Secretary to Ramsay MacDonald.
3. A total of thirty-six women MPs were elected and sat, from Astor in 1919 to Edith Summerskill in 1938. Only a small handful – up to a dozen – sat at any one time, less than 2 per cent of the total 650 MPs.
4. *Yorkshire Evening Post*, 1 May 1940.
5. PA, DRE/A/1/15.
6. The United Nations Office at Geneva website (www.ungeneva.org/en/history/league-of-nations).
7. S. Pedersen, 'Women at work in the League of Nations Secretariat', pp. 181–203 in H. Egginton and Z. Thomas, eds., *Precarious Professionals: Gender, Identities and Social Change in Modern Britain* (London, 2021).
8. *The Times*, 6 August 1937.
9. Bodleian Library, United Nations Career Records Project, MS Eng c.4718, Ms Eng c.4733 (oral history recording, 30 May 1990), Ms Eng c.5778 ff. 111–2.
10. PA, HC/CL/CH/2/2/107.
11. PA, DRE/A/1/16.
12. Bodleian Library, MS Eng c. 4718.
13. PA, HC/CL/CH/2/2/107.
14. Ibid.
15. TNA, T 162/777.
16. TNA, T 221/258, Ward to John Boyd-Carpenter, 6 September 1952.
17. PA, HC/FA/FO/1/171.
18. Bodleian Library. MS Eng c. 4718.
19. Ibid.
20. PA, HC/CL/CH/2/2/107.
21. Ibid.
22. TNA, T 162/777.
23. PA, DRE/A/1/17.
24. *HC Debates*, 5th series, vol. 488, cc. 2676–2686, 14 June 1951.
25. LSE Register; LSE student file, Monica Glory Page/Felton.
26. M. Tippett, *Those Twentieth-Century Blues: An Autobiography* (London, 1991), pp. 46–47.

27. By 1939 they were separated. Berwyn was living with Ann Berkelbach van der
    Sprenkel, a civil servant who was married to university lecturer Otto Pierre Nicholas
    Berkelbach van der Sprenkel, another LSE graduate and lecturer for the WEA. Ann
    changed her name by deed poll to Felton in 1944 and she and Berwyn married
    in 1951.
28. E. Millington, *Was That Really Me?* (Fultus, 2006), p. 8.
29. *International Women's Suffrage News*, 4 April 1941.
30. M. Felton, *That's Why I Went: The Record of a Journey to North Korea* (London 1953),
    p. 75.
31. PA, HC/FA/FO/1/171.
32. M. Clapson, 'The rise and fall of Monica Felton, British town planner and peace
    activist, 1930s to 1950s', pp. 211–29 in *Planning Perspectives*, 30:2 (2014).
33. LSE, DALTON 9/24.
34. TNA, LO/2909.
35. *HC Debates*, 5th series, vol. 539, cc. 1424–1432, 7 April 1955.

CHAPTER 14: HANSARD AND THE BATTLE FOR EQUAL PAY

1. *HC Debates*, 5th series, vol. 491, c. 1710, 2 August 1951.
2. A. Sparrow, *Obscure Scribblers* (London, 2003). PA, HC/SA/SJ/12/5.
3. *Report from House of Commons Select Committee on Publications and Debates*, HC 244 (1919),
   p. 27. MacVeagh was Jeremiah MacVeagh MP.
4. *Report from House of Commons Select Committee on Publications and Debates*, HC 115
   (1931–32), p. 14.
5. British Institute of Verbatim Reporters, 'BIVR's Heritage', 2008 (bivr.org.uk/
   history).
6. PA, PRG/1/4, Press Gallery Committee minutes, 2 December 1919.
7. K. Murphy, *Behind the Wireless: A History of Early Women at the BBC* (London, 2016).
8. PA, PRG/9/1.
9. *The Baron* website (www.thebaron.info/archives/a-pioneer-for-women-who-broke-
   through-barriers).
10. *Liverpool Echo*, 28 April 1960.
11. *Evening Telegraph and Post*, 14 October 1938.
12. *Report of the Royal Commission on West India*, Cmd. 6607 (1944–45), p. 729.
13. *World's Press News*, 11 May 1944.
14. TNA, T 221/258.
15. Ibid.
16. Ibid.
17. *HC Debates*, 5th series, vol. 480, c. 137W, 14 November 1950.
18. *Daily Express*, 3 August 1951.
19. *HC Debates*, 5th series, vol. 500, c. 1774, 16 May 1952.
20. TNA, T 221/258; Bodleian MS Eng 6970.
21. *Liverpool Echo*, 28 April 1960.
22. *The Times*, 9 February 2006.
23. *Liverpool Echo*, 28 April 1960.

CHAPTER 15: THE STRAIN OF CARRYING LADDERS: THE LIBRARY AND ARCHIVES

1. LSE, 6/CCS/3/26/10, 10 March 1955.
2. Ibid., note of meeting by Maton, 6 April 1955.
3. D. Menhennet, *The House of Commons Library: A History* (House of Commons Library Document no. 21 (2nd edition, 2000)), p. 79.
4. J. Symons, 'Thompson, Charles John Samuel (1862–1943)', *Oxford Dictionary of National Biography* online (2004). Fawcett was Caireen Thompson's maternal grandmother Ann's maiden name. She does not appear to be connected to the suffrage leader Millicent Fawcett.
5. *Daily Telegraph*, 25 February 2010; British Library (BL) C1135/09, House of Commons staff oral history collection, Roseanne O'Reilly interviewed by Gloria Tyler (recorded in 2003).
6. BL C1135/09, Roseanne O'Reilly interviewed by Gloria Tyler.
7. BL C1135/02, Mary Frampton interviewed by Gloria Tyler (recorded in 2003).
8. R. O'Reilly, '"The Puppet Show of Memory" Maurice Baring 1922', pp. 5–7 in *House of Commons Library Newsletter*, spring 1986. Courtesy of Isobel White.
9. *HC Debates*, 5th series, vol. 889, c. 579, 26 March 1975.
10. LSE, 6/CCS/3/26/10, 23 November 1955.
11. Ibid., meeting note, 4 April 1955.
12. *Daily Telegraph*, 25 February 2010.
13. BL C1135/09, Roseanne O'Reilly interviewed by Gloria Tyler.
14. 'Library 200: Celebrating 200 years of the House of Commons Library', 2018 (social.shorthand.com/commonslibrary/uC8fiasPiR/library-200).
15. *The Observer*, 22 June 1975.
16. BL C1135/09, Roseanne O'Reilly interviewed by Gloria Tyler.
17. Betty Boothroyd, *Betty Boothroyd: The Autobiography* (London, 2001).
18. *House of Lords Offices Committee 2nd Report*, HL 90 (1949–1950), 25 July 1950.
19. *Newnham College Register 1871–1971,* vol. 2, p. 241 (2nd edition, 1981); Newnham College Archives, AC/5/2/16/Poyser.
20. PA, HL/PO/RO/2/66.
21. PA, HL/PO/RO/2/36.
22. Private communications from Stephen Ellison, May 2022, and Sir John Sainty, June 2022.
23. Private communication from Elizabeth Shepherd, May 2022. A list of archive students at UCL between 1947 and 1955 shows women outnumbering men by a ratio of 3:2.
24. PA, HL/PO/RO/2/161.
25. PA, HL/PO/RO/2/63. One can only hope that Poyser eventually became all things to 'her' archive.
26. PA, HL/PO/RO/2/63.
27. PA, HL/PO/RO/2/36.
28. PA, HL/PO/RO/2/99.
29. PA, HL/PO/RO/2/172.
30. PA, BOND/A/1.
31. PA, ACC/5932, Harry Cobb interviewed by Gloria Tyler (recorded in 2006).
32. E. Poyser, 'Shelagh Bond 1926–1973', pp. 67–69 in *Journal of the Society of Archivists*, 5:1 (1974).

INDEX

Note: illustrations are indicated by *italicised* page references. Entries concerning key women are shown in **bold**.